MAY 0 4 2018

EAST MEADOW PUBLIC LIBRARY

3 1299 00979 0750

East Meadow Public Library
1886 Front Street, East Meadow, NY 11554
(516) 794-2570
www.eastmeadow.info

D1272131

About Island Press

Since 1984, the nonprofit organization Island Press has been stimulating, shaping, and communicating ideas that are essential for solving environmental problems worldwide. With more than 1,000 titles in print and some 30 new releases each year, we are the nation's leading publisher on environmental issues. We identify innovative thinkers and emerging trends in the environmental field. We work with world-renowned experts and authors to develop cross-disciplinary solutions to environmental challenges.

Island Press designs and executes educational campaigns, in conjunction with our authors, to communicate their critical messages in print, in person, and online using the latest technologies, innovative programs, and the media. Our goal is to reach targeted audiences—scientists, policy makers, environmental advocates, urban planners, the media, and concerned citizens—with information that can be used to create the framework for long-term ecological health and human well-being.

Island Press gratefully acknowledges major support from The Bobolink Foundation, Caldera Foundation, The Curtis and Edith Munson Foundation, The Forrest C. and Frances H. Lattner Foundation, The JPB Foundation, The Kresge Foundation, The Summit Charitable Foundation, Inc., and many other generous organizations and individuals.

The opinions expressed in this book are those of the author(s) and do not necessarily reflect the views of our supporters.

Twenty Years of Life

Twenty Years of Life

WHY THE POOR DIE EARLIER

AND HOW TO CHALLENGE INEQUITY

Suzanne Bohan

Washington | Covelo | London

Copyright © 2018 Suzanne Bohan

All rights reserved under International and Pan-American Copyright Conventions. No part of this book may be reproduced in any form or by any means without permission in writing from the publisher: Island Press, 2000 M Street NW, Suite 650, Washington, DC 20036.

ISLAND PRESS is a trademark of the Center for Resource Economics.

Library of Congress Control Number: 2018933658

All Island Press books are printed on environmentally responsible materials.

Manufactured in the United States of America
10 9 8 7 6 5 4 3 2 1

Keywords: California Endowment, community development, health disparities, neighborhood revitalization, philanthropy, public health, Dr. Robert Ross, school reform, trauma-informed schools, violence prevention

For Glenn

Contents

CHAPTER 1
How Neighborhoods Kill

There had never been a rally quite like this one in front of Los Angeles City Hall or, for that matter, at any city hall in the United States. On December 10, 2013, nearly two hundred people assembled, displaying photos of loved ones whose lives were cut short by sickness and holding signs with the words, "Where you live should not determine *how long* you live." They shared stories of their relative's early deaths, a few fighting tears.

Yvette Fuentes, who has lived in poverty-ridden South Central Los Angeles all her life, held a photo of her mother, who died at age fifty-seven, a few years after she was diagnosed with hypertension and diabetes. Every year on her mother's birthday, Yvette takes the day off to visit her mother's grave and to go on outings—a trip to the mall, seeing a movie—that they would have done together had her mother not died prematurely. Fuentes' father had also died prematurely, of lung cancer at age fifty-seven.

Sabrina Coffey-Smith, who lives in the same area as Fuentes, held a sign with a photo of her brother, who suffered a fatal heart attack at fifty-three. He'd left her a voice message shortly before he died, saying, "This is your big bro. I really need to talk to you so call me back. I love you, so call me back." Coffey-Smith didn't get the message until after he died.

Another protester, Liliana Reyes, who lives in another low-income LA community, held a photo of her twin sister, a nonsmoker who died at twenty-four from lung cancer. Reyes's sister remained undiagnosed and untreated for several months after the first symptoms appeared—heavy coughing and back pain—because she was uninsured. Reyes still feels adrift after that loss nine years earlier.

Stories like these abound in poorer areas. Although tragically early deaths occur in all types of neighborhoods, they're far more prevalent in those with high poverty rates and a dearth of the basic resources that support health, like parks, good schools, and grocery stores.

In fact, the 2013 rally was prompted by a first-of-its kind report from Los Angeles's Public Health Department, which revealed a startling twelve-year difference in life expectancy between the wealthier, verdant areas on the city's west side and its far poorer neighborhoods in the inner parts of the vast city.[1]

"There's nothing in the water in Los Angeles that creates that. This is a problem of our own making," Dave Regan, a Service Employees International Union leader, told the crowd. "A walk from the west side to Central LA is really a journey from the First World to the Third World."

Many of the workers Regan's union represents, who labor as hospital technicians and in-home caregivers, among other health care occupations, live in South LA. They showed up to pressure the region's nonprofit hospitals to set aside more money to benefit low-income communities. These nonprofit hospitals are required to do so given their generous tax breaks, but many do not, and there's little enforcement of the requirement. The protesters wanted to see more of that money—tens of millions of dollars annually—actually collected and then spent on neighborhood amenities in their home turf that would make their lives healthier and easier, the same kind of amenities that wealthier areas take for granted.

Consider Pacific Palisades, an affluent enclave on the western edge of Los Angeles in zip code 90272. There, the afternoon sun bathes spacious ocean-facing homes in a golden glow, while beachgoers enjoy the sand and surf of the community's beaches and bikers and hikers travel to the nearby Santa Monica Mountains. Shops, restaurants, and cafes keep the sidewalks busy in its attractive downtown. Most businesses are locally owned, and residents let fast-food restaurants know they're not welcome, beating back an attempt years ago by one burger chain to open one; no fast-food outlet has tried since then. Although it's actually part of the City of Los Angeles, the neighborhood picks an honorary mayor to represent its interests at City Hall. Kevin Nealon, a longtime cast member of the TV show *Saturday Night Live*, currently holds the honorary position; a few of his famous predecessors include Sugar Ray Leonard, Anthony Hopkins, and Chevy Chase.

Pacific Palisades is called the Mayberry of Los Angeles for its small-town, friendly atmosphere, and people living here not only enjoy the good life, they get to do so for longer. Average life expectancy in the Palisades is eighty-five years. It's the highest in Los Angeles, a distinction shared with adjacent Brentwood and Bel Air.

If you travel inland over the LA basin, though, life expectancy steadily declines as you cross into middle-class neighborhoods and then into progressively poorer ones. By the time you reach zip code 90059 in South Los Angeles, where the 1965 Watts riots and the 1992 Los Angeles riots both ignited, life expectancy plunges twelve years to seventy-three, the same as someone born in Samoa.

South LA is no Mayberry, and it has no celebrity honorary mayor. For those who can't afford to live elsewhere or who stay because of their connections to the community, it's a challenging hometown. It has no real downtown, only strip malls along major thoroughfares replete with check cashing outlets, liquor stores, taquerias, and an occasional BBQ joint. In 2010, only a handful of grocery stores served a vast area, and fast-food outlets operated on countless corners, advertising bargain meals. (In South LA, 72 percent of restaurants are fast-food types, compared with 40 percent in wealthier West LA.) Anyone looking for alcohol doesn't have to travel far; nearly nine liquor stores per square mile operate in South LA, compared with two per square mile in West LA. There's only 1 acre of parkland for every 1,000 residents in South LA, versus 70 acres per 1,000 in West LA neighborhoods like Pacific Palisades and Brentwood.[2]

The homes in South LA are typically small and in various states of upkeep, ranging from tidy houses with flower beds to those with peeling paint and unkempt yards storing recliners, car parts, and discarded appliances. Metal fences topped by spikes guard most homes, evidence of the pervasive fear of crime in the area. Residents commonly share stories of the robberies, break-ins, and muggings they or family members experienced; some refuse to venture out at night and do so only cautiously during the day. Young people describe how they have watched friends or neighbors shot or have taken bullets themselves as a target or while caught in crossfire. Even inside homes, distant nighttime gunfire may shatter the quiet.

The paucity of resources for healthful living and the strain of unpaid bills and debt combined with the trauma of living in a high-crime area translate into far higher disease rates for South LA residents—hypertension, heart disease, diabetes, cancer, and depression, to name leading maladies—compared with their nearby neighbors in the verdant, peaceful enclaves of Bel Air or Pacific Palisades.

～

This familiar scenario repeats itself in many cities nationwide, with those living in poorer sections lacking the basics for healthful living—

even a sense of safety—and enduring shorter, sicker lives than wealthier neighbors just a few miles away. In one impoverished Baltimore neighborhood, life expectancy is sixty-five, on par with war-torn Yemen, whereas in the city's wealthy Roland Park enclave, life expectancy soars to eight-four.[3] In the San Francisco Bay Area, residents of an affluent section of Walnut Creek live on average eighty-seven years, while 12 miles away in a tough neighborhood in West Oakland, residents face a life expectancy of seventy-one, about the same as someone in Bangladesh.[4]

Urban dwellers in low-income areas, who are commonly Hispanic and black, aren't the only ones coming up short on the life span yardstick. A 2017 study in the *Journal of the American Medical Association* reported that although the average US life expectancy continued its steady increase over the past century or so, to seventy-nine years at birth in 2014, the disparity between regions began widening in 1980, now reaching more than two decades.[5] And it's poor rural whites in the Mississippi River Basin and in Appalachia, along with Native American populations in North Dakota and South Dakota, who face the shortest life spans—sixty-six years on average. Meanwhile, denizens of central Colorado's affluent ski country enjoy the nation's longest life span, averaging eighty-seven years.[6] In a trend that stunned even experienced researchers, in the United States longevity rates for middle-aged whites are actually declining, a life span loss not shared with any other US racial group or any other rich nation.[7]

~

Dr. Robert Ross knew firsthand the toll of living in the midst of neighborhood poverty, having grown up in a dangerous South Bronx housing project. His family, however, was one of the more fortunate ones, with his African American father and Puerto Rican mother both at home and his father working a steady job. In 1983, with his freshly minted medical degree, the Ivy League graduate arrived at his new job in a public clinic in Camden, New Jersey, full of optimism and ready to expand pediatric services in the impoverished neighborhood. But dismay soon set in as Ross realized how inadequately his medical training prepared him to cope with an onslaught of ill health so deeply intertwined with the sick neighborhoods, physically and psychically, in which his patients lived.

Camden, a small city in the shadow of Philadelphia's gleaming skyscrapers across the Delaware River, was, and still is, among the most violent cities in the United States. Once a thriving industrial town, some sixty thousand jobs were shed as a shipyard, a Campbell Soup factory, the RCA factory, and other businesses moved out in the 1960s and 1970s. Nearly one in five residents is unemployed, and the downtown strip is lined by abandoned, decaying storefronts.[8]

Ross, it turns out, came just in time to watch a community unravel with the advent of crack cocaine. "Before 1984, poor people couldn't buy cocaine. But when some evil genius invented crack, the price point for cocaine went down to five dollars," Ross said. "So now you introduced this very cheap passport out of misery and hopelessness to these distressed communities, and the rest that followed was almost frighteningly predictable and logical. Women in my practice who were previously good and caring and able mothers began to neglect and abuse their kids," he said. "All of a sudden the number of calls I got in the middle of the night to attend deliveries of one-pound babies just blew through the roof. Those became crack babies."

The reality he faced in that clinic dashed his confidence in the established medical system. "It made me somewhat angered and bitter about my training as a physician and as a healer," he said. Ross felt helpless to save his patients, so susceptible to a drug that instantly arouses intense feelings of pleasure and euphoria, a temporary escape from a treadmill of struggle and depression.

"I had this sobering insight that something was just fundamentally wrong with how our medical system engages in the craft of healing," he said. "This whole issue of poverty and housing and hopelessness and unemployment, and the role that it plays in health and wellness, had been completely ignored in my medical training. And to a great extent, although things are a bit better, it continues to be ignored now."

~

A growing body of research backs up Ross's insights. Lack of clinical care actually plays only a small role in the wide differences in health and longevity between zip codes, although that's one of the toughest notions to budge because most people equate good health with visits to doctors' offices. If that were the case, though, why are many US children facing a shorter life expectancy than their parents due to rising rates of obesity and the diseases it brings on—diabetes, heart disease, high blood pressure, cancer, and others—despite these children's access to doctors?[9] No one is diminishing the role of medical care in improving the quality of life: Western medicine excels in emergency and acute care, and new drugs, treatments, and surgeries allow those with chronic conditions to live far longer, and more comfortably, than they would otherwise. But many of these chronic diseases still can shave years off individuals' lives, even with treatment. Nor is everyone diligent about following treatment plans, and some can't even afford it. The best strategy for a long life, of course, is avoiding these diseases altogether, and that's where public health measures shine.

Researchers with the Centers for Disease Control and Prevention (CDC) actually credit public health programs for twenty-five years of the more than thirty-year US life span increase in the twentieth century (the average life expectancy in 1900 was forty-seven[10]). Public health regulations, for example, to ensure clean water and untainted food con-trolled the spread of infectious diseases, as did controls on disease vectors such as mosquitoes and rats. Restrictions on tobacco reduced disease rates linked to smoking, and public education campaigns on sanitation practices such as handwashing further reduced disease spread. Medical advances, including the introduction of vaccines and antibiotics, con-tributed to the rest of that longevity increase.[11]

In another CDC study, researchers concluded that inadequate health care accounts for just 10 percent of premature mortality; the agency as-signed another 20 percent to genetic factors, 20 percent to environmental factors, and 50 percent to lifestyle and behaviors.[12]

It's this last statistic that gets controversial. Some argue that behav-ior and lifestyle choices are entirely an individual's responsibility and thus the health disparities are of people's own making. But most pub-lic health professionals, as well as major organizations such as the CDC, the National Institutes of Health, and the World Health Organization, argue just as strenuously that an individual's choices are constrained by what is accessible, feasible, and affordable. Some use the term *behavioral justice* to push for fairer assessments of the latitude individuals have to make healthy choices when dealing with a very limited menu.[13] In one article, government researchers noted that unhealthy behaviors such sedentary lifestyles, poor eating habits, and drug and alcohol use, "which tend to be blamed on the individual, occur within the context of a social environment." The article then cites high poverty rates, inadequate housing, unemployment, poor education quality, and lack of social support as factors influencing behavioral choices.[14]

Visit some of America's poorest neighborhoods and step inside the homes, and the menu of healthy lifestyle options becomes clearer. Money is so tight that kitchen shelves run bare by the end of the month. Even when the checks come in, the nearest grocery store is often miles away—an inconvenience for those with a car and an hours'-long chore for those without one. That makes $1.99 fast-food meals or a $10 pizza an easy option, especially when the kids are starved and you're just off work, exhausted and strapped for cash.

How about an evening stroll to exercise and relax away the tension of the day? In many areas, that's unthinkable, as you might be walking past a corner where just weeks ago someone shot another dead over a gang rivalry. Broken fragments of a car window litter the sidewalk, the unswept remains of a break-in, and a pack of dogs roams unattended. And you never know when someone might walk up and demand your money. Rarely are there nearby, affordable gyms and recreational facilities— let alone safe parks—to visit. Instead, many people just hunker down inside their houses, some even keeping out of the front rooms to avoid a possible stray bullet.

Even adequate sleep often doesn't come easy in these neighborhoods, in part due to the strain of financial worries, fear of crime, or simply the noise of random gunshots or cars squealing as young men race down roadways, practicing donuts, spins, and other automotive stunts late at night on deserted streets.[15] Residents often mistrust one another and fewer neighborhood groups coalesce, while tensions between racial groups also hinder interactions. This lack of cohesiveness takes a separate toll, as seminal studies show that strong social support from neighbors and local institutions like churches plays a powerful role in fostering long, healthy lives.[16]

As for the environment, commercial truck routes typically run through low-income neighborhoods, steering clear of more affluent areas (where they're often banned due to objections over the exhaust and noise[17]) and exposing residents to fine particulates from diesel exhaust and other pollution, which increases the risk of asthma, cancer, and heart disease. Industrial plants or toxic waste sites sometimes operate nearby, because land is cheaper in these neighborhoods. Older housing stock becomes a haven for mold and mildew, triggering respiratory problems for some, and paint tainted with lead still covers many surfaces, exposing residents to the potent neurotoxin blamed for learning disabilities, lowered IQ, and memory impairment. Children and adults in poorer areas have a sixfold increase in blood lead levels compared with those living in high-income neighborhoods.[18]

~

Ross battled these various ills in the Camden clinic for seven years, but he knew he ultimately wanted to focus on the root cause of poor health, not just run triage. After leaving Camden, he earned a master's degree in public administration and ran public health departments in Philadelphia and San Diego. Then in 2000, Ross took over as president and CEO of the California Endowment, the largest health foundation in California and the fifth-largest health foundation nationwide,[19] with a war chest of $3.5 billion. It distributes some $150 million a year in grants in California.

The Endowment opened its doors in 1996, flush with funding from the conversion of the then-nonprofit insurer Blue Cross of California to a for-profit entity, now part of Anthem. It was among the more than three hundred "health conversion foundations" formed nationwide since the 1970s[20] as many nonprofit health insurers sought to free themselves from the financial shackles of their tax-exempt status and operate as for-profit enterprises. But because these insurers had enjoyed generous tax breaks and subsidies as nonprofit organizations for decades, most state laws require that those converting to for-profit status turn over their accrued assets for the public benefit. That's achieved by transferring those assets to an existing charity or to a new foundation.[21]

Consumer groups got involved in negotiations and demanded fair market valuation of these insurers' assets. In the case of the California Endowment, Blue Cross initially offered $100 million to form a health foundation in exchange for authorization to convert to for-profit status. Advocates including the Consumers Union pushed state regulators to demand far more. In the end, Blue Cross transferred all its assets, more than $2.9 billion, according to a foundation document, which created the California Endowment and a sister foundation called the California Health Care Foundation. As with other health conversion foundations, the California Endowment from the outset ran entirely independent of the insurer; it is regulated by California's attorney general and overseen by a board of directors. In 2017, the racially diverse seventeen-member board, eight of them women, included affordable housing and disability rights advocates, an expert in youth activism, a Native American attorney specializing in tribal interests, the former director of a rural health agency, three physicians, and experts in education and finance. These health insurance conversion foundations must support a health mission, although it's broadly defined, and must spend 5 percent of their endowment annually.

During Ross's early years, the Endowment largely followed the standard, old-school charity model, giving poor people some of the health essentials they couldn't afford, such as neighborhood wellness clinics, vaccinations, HIV prevention, cancer screening, and diabetes management, among other types of medical interventions. The foundation also funded various research efforts, such as examining the health effects of exposures to pesticides and environmental contaminants. It dispersed its grants throughout the state and experimented with a few novel regional initiatives, such as an obesity prevention program targeted at changing environments in eight Central California counties. (Although that project set its sights on broader change and showed promising signs in doing so, at four years it didn't run long enough, researchers concluded.[22]) Ten years after the foundation opened its doors, Endowment leadership took stock of its previous decade of work and came to the frustrating realization that despite hundreds of millions in expenditures, they still hadn't made a dent in slowing the rates of obesity and common killers like hypertension and diabetes, especially among low-income residents suffering the highest rates.

~

The Endowment wasn't the first foundation disillusioned with business as usual. In the early 1990s, after decades of investments in disparate programs did little to change the underlying dysfunctions that kept poor areas poor and their residents far sicker than average, a few large national foundations began looking for more effective strategies for lifting up ailing communities. They turned to a new strategy called *community change initiatives*, which concentrate philanthropic investments in one geographic area and then strive to get the many gears that run a community working more smoothly, just as most middle-class neighborhoods enjoy. That means resources such as well-run schools, pleasant and safe parks, nutritious and affordable food outlets, and decent housing, all of which attract more economic opportunities as well.

Between 1990 and 2010, major organizations such as the Annie E. Casey Foundation, the Robert Wood Johnson Foundation, the Ford Foundation, the Rockefeller Foundation, and the Pew Charitable Trusts spent more than $1 billion collectively on these mega "community change" projects. Although there were some success stories on a smaller scale, none achieved the long-term goal of noticeably changing underlying neighborhood conditions that contribute to shortened life spans. A 2010 analysis from the Aspen Institute on these ambitious initiatives concluded that the primary stumbling block was, not surprisingly, insufficient time and money, or inadequate "dose, scale or duration" by the foundations leading them.[23]

These first community change initiatives usually lasted from three to five years, longer than the one- or two-year projects foundations had typically backed. But given the entrenched social ills in these neighborhoods, and their paucity of political power, it was still not long enough. The Aspen Institute analysis suggested it takes ten years minimum to bring about real change in the machinery that runs a community.

Funding a ten-year project is a big risk for any foundation, especially considering the investment and the price of failure, including fostering cynicism in communities at yet another foundation program that came and went, leaving things largely the same. Nonetheless, these large-scale projects are still considered the best hope for finally healing the country's ailing areas. If changing the fundamentals of a community doesn't work, what will?

Given the limited success of these community change initiatives, many foundations retreated from them. Ross and the California Endowment board, however, decided to invest the right "dosage"—ten years and $1 billion—into a campaign they launched in 2010 called Building Healthy Communities (BHC). It was a serious gamble; the project would consume most of the organization's annual largesse. Moreover, if the project failed, it would fail big, harming the Endowment's reputation while also raising questions about whether the community change model can work on a scale large enough to finally shrink the tragic disparities in life spans around the nation.

Ross was frustrated, though, with cautious approaches and was willing to take the risk, as he was determined to get at root causes. "I just couldn't get it out of my craw. And it ended up being kind of a lifelong pursuit that has translated in large part into this ten-year Building Healthy Communities campaign," he said.

Another major shortcoming in past community efforts was overlooking the greatest strength in these neighborhoods: the latent political power inherent in the residents themselves. When you spend time in these distressed neighborhoods, you see how many of those living there are simply hard-working people, often holding down two or more jobs to pay the bills and create better futures for their children and themselves. Their dreams are just like those of Americans everywhere. It's that passion—to live in a safe, thriving neighborhood, to give your kids a happy childhood and have them enjoy a quality education and start satisfying careers—that the Endowment draws on to drive change.

With its BHC campaign, the Endowment actively engages residents to push for new legislation and funding to build up depleted neighborhoods. It also deploys a statewide team of politically savvy experts to do the same in the state capitol, giving clout in legislative chambers to the concerns of low-income residents. That statewide support is essential because poor communities can't entirely bootstrap their way out of decades of deprivation. In turn, the local communities help win the passage of new state laws with vocal activism, completing this two-way partnership.

That connection between local activism and new state policies, which the California Endowment calls its "grassroots to treetops" strategy, is a critical element of the ten-year campaign. Although the foundation invited fourteen fortunate communities to join this $1 billion experiment, state legislative wins benefit communities throughout California. Given California's policy influence nationwide, these victories often extend beyond state borders.

~

This power-building approach distinguishes the BHC initiative from all that have come before it, at least on this large a scale. A few smaller nonprofit organizations concentrating on community organizing and resident advocacy proved that the model works on a smaller scale. Examples include the twenty-five-year-old Dudley Street Neighborhood Initiative in Roxbury, Massachusetts; Lawrence CommunityWorks in Lawrence, Massachusetts; and the Needmor Fund in Toledo, Ohio. None,

however, has taken on fourteen widely dispersed communities total-
ing some one million residents and then engendered grassroots activism
in those sites to both transform local conditions and forge statewide
policy change.

After the Endowment committed to undertaking this massive endeavor, foundation staff and consultants identified about two hundred
California communities with the familiar deficits in distressed areas: many
families living below the poverty line, a substantial portion of residents
lacking a high school diploma, few if any safe recreational venues or
parks, high rates of obesity and chronic illnesses, widespread drug and
alcohol abuse, limited job opportunities and activities for youth, ample
fast-food restaurants and a paucity of grocery stores, and poor-quality
housing. But they also scrutinized the communities' inherent strengths,
in particular evidence of an established local leadership dedicated to
building a better future for the community. Without that, any change
campaign would almost certainly fail. With those criteria in mind,
they visited twenty communities on the finalist list, whittled it down
to fourteen sites, and then launched the $1 billion, ten-year project in
2010.

Given the diversity of neighborhoods in the campaign, if the project
works in California, it should be able to work anywhere. The fourteen
sites range from a remote, largely white county to mostly Hispanic
farming areas to mixed-race metropolitan neighborhoods. They're located in Sacramento, Oakland, Richmond, Long Beach, Santa Ana,
and San Diego; two in Los Angeles, in South Los Angeles and Boyle
Heights; and six rural or semirural communities in Del Norte County,
Salinas, Coachella Valley, South Kern, Fresno, and Merced.

Although each site is distinctive, a common set of issues binds them.
Whether urban or rural, and regardless of demographics, all these communities sorely need better schools and more academic and social-
emotional supports for students. To achieve lasting change, training for
adults and youth is required so that they can effectively persuade their

school districts, city councils, and sometimes state legislators to enact supportive policies. The same community organizing approach applies to expanding nutritious food options while discouraging new liquor and tobacco stores or more fast-food joints. New parks, soccer fields, bike paths, and sidewalks in areas with none require coalitions of community groups who can mobilize hundreds of people to speak at local meetings to demand funding and government support. To reduce neighborhood violence, several of the BHC communities are testing programs that engage, rather than punish, perpetrators.

It's a vast and complex initiative, one sure to face numerous obstacles. Will enough residents care and leave their homes after a long day's work to attend city meetings? Will community nonprofit organizations set aside their differences to work on shared goals, and will they also work alongside city bureaucrats and politicians they once regarded skeptically or worse? Even if people mobilize, would this effort persuade entrenched powers to change their ways?

A paramount concern for the California Endowment is whether its staff and grantees can harness enough local activism to truly drive statewide policy change, for without that, there is only partial success. The campaign wasn't designed to benefit only fourteen communities; ultimately, it aims to benefit the entire state. Given that it is entering largely uncharted territory, the Endowment staffs a sizable evaluation team to measure progress and spot problems, which Ross and others in the leadership team then use to make course corrections.

In the end, the Endowment will rate its success in large part by the number of local "policy wins" and new state laws enacted as a result of the campaign. It will also tally up how many entrenched systems in the sites, such as public works departments, police agencies, city manager offices, and school districts, changed as a result of citizen advocacy. These victories aren't easy—they are certainly far more difficult than funding a health clinic or disease prevention program—but they are the best hope for shrinking the stunning twenty-year life span gap in the country.

In addition to developing a new philanthropic model that works on a vast scale, a central goal of the campaign for Ross is to change the way we think about the root causes of ill health, namely lack of resources, quality education, opportunity, and chronic stress. Although Ross is a fierce advocate for access to health care, the physician now dedicates his days to advancing a more accurate narrative about well-being, shifting the discussion from doctor visits and personal behavior to healing communities. He is a firm believer that the best healing balm is building community power.

CHAPTER 2

The Stress Effect

To get to the Primate Center at the Wake Forest School of Medicine, 9 miles from the school's main campus in Winston-Salem, North Carolina, you exit a rural road and drive down a long, curving driveway with pastures on the right, backed by stands of tall deciduous trees. A dozen or so buildings then come into view, clustered in the center of the 200-acre satellite campus. It's the site of decades of research into the physiological toll of living in a hierarchical world. The scientists here are studying monkeys, with those lower on the social ladder enduring more stress and paying the price in impaired health. We humans share that vulnerability with our primate cousins, although for us, status is largely determined by income.

Some 400 miles from that serene rural setting, for example, in decaying Baltimore neighborhoods, life expectancy rivals that of Third World countries.[1] In the nearby Appalachian Mountains[2] as well as 2,600 miles away in California's semirural Central Valley[3]—and in numerous communities in between—those living in economically distressed regions face declining or stagnating life expectancies.

During an East Coast trip, I made the trek to the Primate Center to meet with some of the best-known researchers in the field of status, stress, and health—and to witness hierarchy in action in the animal world.

Over the years, the scientists there—Jay Kaplan, Carol Shively, and Matt Jorgensen, to name a few—discovered myriad ways that social rank in the cutthroat primate world either protects or undermines health. Like other highly social species, monkeys organize themselves into clear hierarchies, ranging from the alpha dominants that move with impunity to the subordinates that scramble around avoiding harassment.

The scientists concentrate their attention on the virtually identical stress response system in monkeys and humans, one involving a hormonal rush that primes an individual to fight or flee.[4] This ancient physiological system is common to many animal species—from the tiniest to the huge—which enables a creature under threat to instantly marshal a surge of energy to save its skin. No animal in nature could survive without it.

∼

That hormonal spike, which speeds nutrients to the muscles, sharpens cognition, and mobilizes the immune system, comes with a price: it temporarily upends the body's carefully calibrated equilibrium. That is fine during the occasional emergency, like suddenly facing a snarling predator or fleeing an avalanche, but unluckily for creatures living in hierarchical societies—including monkeys and humans—it typically triggers far more often, especially for those on the lowest rungs of the social ladder, who struggle to control their environment and get second dibs on resources. The result is a life of chronically coping with stress because hierarchy is hard to escape. Among other pursuits, the scientists at Wake Forest Primate Center examine just what this regular activation of powerful stress hormones does to monkeys' organs, blood vessels, and so on, with the aim, of course, of understanding the same in humans.

During my visit on a sunny September day, Matt Jorgensen, PhD, a professor in comparative medicine, gave me a tour of the colony of about 350 African green monkeys, which are divided into sixteen groups. They're the first animals you'll notice when entering the site, playing in outdoor pens with climbing structures and perches and with their indoor shelter accessible through large openings. Jorgensen knows these animals well. He first began working with this colony in 1998 at the University of California, Los Angeles. When the colony moved to Wake Forest in 2008, he moved with it. "Dr. Kaplan may have told you I came in crates with the animals, but that's not true," Jorgensen deadpanned.

Visitors keep their distance by standing behind a yellow line some 15 feet from the pens; from there it's still easy to see the small primates' antics. Two were throwing popcorn at each other, which Jorgensen said were just juveniles playing and testing boundaries. Other monkeys were moving about slowly, while a few raced across the pen and scampered up various structures. Others just sat perched, looking at the observers.

The African green monkeys, characterized by golden-green fur and dark, hairless faces, are matrilineal, so females dominate the groups, Jorgensen said. Most of the green monkeys on campus are in fact females, with a few males introduced on occasion. "The males need to get in the good graces of those females," he added. "They really run the show."

Of course, given the hierarchy, most of the females also need to stay in the good graces of the few dominant ones. These bosses remind others of their lofty status with sideways eye contact, a tilt of the head, or the lifting of an eyebrow that tells another monkey to get back in place. Subordinates, for their part, show their acquiescence by touching their nose or face, rubbing their hands in rocks or dirt, and in general getting out of the way of their higher ups. The few males in each group sort out their own rankings and then do their best to get along with the females by forming alliances.

Although the green monkeys give a sense of hierarchy at work, their familiarity with one another—they've grown up together and are typically related—tends to tone down aggression by the higher-ranking monkeys.

That's not so with the macaques, of which some seven hundred live in buildings nearby. Macaques—an Old World species that originated in Asia—are also matrilineal and establish a top-to-bottom ranking. These larger primates live together in smaller groups of four to five at the center.

Unlike the green monkeys, however, the macaques didn't grow up together and routinely must adjust to strangers in their midst. Under those conditions, the dominant monkey displays aggression more overtly to unfamiliar animals than to the nonstrangers. Bared teeth tell a subordinate to watch out or back off, and sometimes there's physical contact, although usually short of drawing blood. To avoid injuries that are ultimately costly for the entire group, the dominants don't usually inflict wounds; instead, the top monkeys enforce the hierarchy through mere threats of aggression or harassment, which are often arbitrarily meted out and create a sense of unpredictability.[5] The lower-ranking monkeys learn to forestall or prevent trouble by displaying submissive behaviors such as groveling or jumping aside,[6] even without provocation, and remain alert for danger or harassment.

"Dominance is basically being fearless, not attending to the potential consequences," said Jay Kaplan, PhD, director of the Primate Center. "Subordinate animals are always looking around."

$\sim$

Not surprisingly, these subordinates are more stressed than the dominants. That shows up in elevated levels of stress hormones, namely cortisol, epinephrine, and norepinephrine. (In Britain, the last two are also called adrenaline and noradrenalin; this book will use the US terms.) Working in concert, these three hormones almost instantaneously deliver energy throughout the body. That's the chief aim of the stress response: to fuel muscles and a brain that needs to start making fast decisions.

Having spent nearly three decades studying its connection in primates to common diseases, Carol A. Shively, PhD, a professor of pathology and comparative medicine at Wake Forest, knows firsthand the wear and tear of all that stress on monkeys. Arteriosclerosis, obesity, diabetes, hypertension, and substance abuse, among other ailments, show up far more often among the lowest-ranking monkeys than among others, her lab's research shows.

She shared a set of slides from her lab, which had been featured in a documentary series on health disparities called *Unnatural Causes: Is Inequality Making Us Sick?*[7] One slide showed a cross section of a dominant female macaque's healthy artery, which was wide open and let blood flow freely to the heart. The next slide showed an artery lined with plaque, dangerously narrowing the channel and restricting blood flow, which sharply elevates risk for a heart attack. That was the artery of a submissive female macaque. Yet both animals were the same age and fed the same diet.

In addition, Shively's lab found higher rates of depression in subordinate macaques. "Whenever it's present, coronary artery disease is worsened," Shively added.

In stable groups of primates, subordinates generally die younger than the dominants and are more likely to develop various diseases.[8] Researchers have no doubt that these findings with monkeys translate into striking insights on the influence of hierarchy on human health.

Plenty of studies on human populations tell the same startling story. Shively said the best research on humans and social status comes from the Whitehall studies, out of the University of London, which make clear the stunning association between rank and health among workers in the stratified British civil service. The studies found that the lower the worker's employment grade, or "socioeconomic status," the more likely she or he would develop a serious disease and die sooner than those with a higher employment grade. Socioeconomic status reflects not only income and overall wealth, but also education and occupation.

"The reason that is so compelling is because they're all employed. They all have jobs, and they all have access to medical care," Shively said. "And still there's this inverse relationship—for almost every health outcome that they've looked at—with social and economic status, which in this study is measured by job categories," she said. "What we can take away is that there is no question that health is inversely related to socioeconomic status."

The pioneering Whitehall research, led by Sir Michael Marmot, gets its name from the Whitehall thoroughfare in London that is at the center of government in the United Kingdom, with numerous ministries and agencies lining the road.

Marmot, a London-based epidemiologist and a leading light in the world of health disparities research (Queen Elizabeth II knighted him for his work), discovered that with each step down in job grade among these British civil servants, from senior director to midlevel manager to messenger, their risk of heart disease, certain cancers, lung disease, gastrointestinal disease, depression, suicide, sick days, back pain, and feelings of ill health increased, while their life expectancy declined. His influential 1978 study reported that those in the lowest-ranking jobs, such as doorkeepers, were nearly four times more likely to die of coronary heart disease than administrators in the highest grade. Yet all these workers had access to health care and held secure jobs with steady paychecks.[9]

~

The usual assumption has been that bosses bear the most stress because they are the ones making the high-pressure decisions with far-reaching consequences. Their autonomy and power appear to protect them, however; instead it's those lower on ladder, who have to take orders, endure repetitive work, and are told how to perform a task (and easily criticized if it's not done right)—in short, those who have less control over their work environment—who end up with poorer health and shorter lives.[10] And, as with the monkeys at Wake Forest, the lower these workers' status, the more stress hormones researchers found circulating about.[11,12]

All these hormones get into your system after your brain senses a threat to your well-being, which instantly and unconsciously activates the *sympathetic nervous system*, releasing epinephrine and norepinephrine, the first two stress hormones deployed. The sympathetic nervous system starts in the brain and travels through the spinal column before branching out to control virtually every organ and blood vessel in your body, reaching even to the skin (hence goose bumps when you're scared).

Dr. Walter Cannon, a Harvard Medical School physiologist, named that initial reaction the "fight-or-flight" response, introducing the now-familiar term in a seminal 1915 book detailing the biological effects of what he called "emotional excitement." He was the first to elucidate the role of the sympathetic nervous system in arousing a powerful response to a crisis. (In a 1914 article, Cannon was also the first to use the term *stress* in the modern physiological sense, as opposed to its traditional use in engineering.[13]) He had identified an ancient survival mechanism shared by many animal species, from fish and lizards to primates, that delivers energy in a hurry to muscles and the brain.

After an alarmed brain activates the sympathetic nervous system, it triggers a second response, this one in the hypothalamus-pituitary-adrenal, or HPA, axis. The HPA axis is part of the endocrine system—a network of glands that release hormones controlling bodily functions—

and it works at a more deliberate pace. A minute or more after it triggers, the HPA axis delivers into the bloodstream another class of stress hormones called glucocorticoids, of which cortisol is the most familiar.

Endocrinologist Hans Selye, PhD, laboring in his lab at McGill University in Montreal in the 1930s, first identified the HPA axis while studying chronically stressed rats. Along with Cannon's elucidation of the sympathetic nervous system, Selye's discovery laid the foundation for the now-rigorous field of human stress research.

As with the sympathetic nervous system, the HPA axis originates in a small structure in the base of the brain called the hypothalamus. In response to a threat, the hypothalamus starts a hormonal cascade that exits the brain, heads to the pituitary gland, and then makes its way to the adrenal gland, where an intermediary hormone triggers the release of cortisol into the bloodstream. Now cortisol joins epinephrine and norepinephrine in rallying the forces.

～

Through an exceedingly complex array of physiological reactions, these stress hormones—sometimes in concert, other times on their own—start by pumping as much glucose into the bloodstream as possible so as to fuel muscles and the brain. That's done by slowing down insulin secretion because you don't need it to do its usual job of storing energy right now. Cortisol also causes cells to resist the sugar-storing efforts of any insulin left in the bloodstream. In addition, the stress hormones release nutrients stored throughout the body and convert them to glucose, so your blood is now teeming with sugar.

In a crisis, the heart also needs to deliver blood with more force. That's accomplished by the release of the hormone vasopressin, which causes veins to constrict, increasing the blood flow pressure. That higher pressure pumps blood to the heart with more force, which hits the heart walls harder. In response, the walls snap back with corresponding force, and the hard-pumping heart speeds blood flow throughout the body.[14]

To quickly get all this vigorously flowing blood to its destination, arteries relax and open up. But because you only have so much blood to go around, blood flow drops off for nonessential functions such as digestion, growth, and tissue repair, which can wait until this emergency is over.

Because some threats could lead to injury and hence blood loss, you want to conserve as much water as possible during a crisis to ensure adequate flow of glucose- and oxygen-rich blood to muscles. The vasopressin released during the stress response, in addition to constricting certain blood vessels, also serves as an antidiuretic. That stops urine formation and directs the kidneys to release back water they have accumulated. (Once urine enters the bladder, however, it can't go back. That's the reason panicked animals urinate, to lighten the load.)

This physiological crisis mode blocks perception of pain as well through the release of your body's natural painkillers, endorphins and enkephalins. In addition, stress hormones, along with all that extra glucose, act on the brain, where they sharpen cognition and enhance memory to get you out of a similar jam even faster in the future (and why you now distinctly remember a traumatic event from years ago).[15]

The stress response doesn't stop there. It also temporarily—up to about thirty minutes—enhances immune function so as to fight off invaders like bacteria and viruses in the event of an injury. Stress hormones also cause blood to thicken and coagulate more easily, which thwarts infections, slows bleeding from a wound, and increases the capacity of blood to carry oxygen.

Once the crisis has passed, this whole system essentially starts working in reverse. First, the sympathetic nervous system turns off almost as quickly as it turned on, and its corollary, the *parasympathetic nervous system*, switches on. The latter slows down the heart and breathing rates, relaxes constricted blood vessels—lowering blood pressure—and restores building and maintenance functions such as digestion, growth, and tissue repair. In essence, the parasympathetic nervous system brings things back to normal, or what physiologists call homeostasis. Cortisol, a versatile hormone, now starts to play a role in shutting down the physiological commotion it and other stress hormones activated.

In all, the stress response triggers at least fourteen hundred reactions throughout your body, both in turning it on and turning it off.[16] That complexity led Robert Sapolsky, PhD, an acclaimed Stanford University neuroendocrinologist and author of the popular (and often amusing) book on stress *Why Zebras Don't Get Ulcers*, to call it "the miserably confusing system that I study."[17]

~

The sheer number of physiological reactions also makes plain why activating this system too often can wreak physiological havoc. In fact, what led Selye to discover the HPA axis and its foundational role in the stress response were the ulcers, shrunken immune tissues, and enlarged adrenal glands in chronically stressed rats.[18]

Throughout his career, however, Selye also defended stress in the right dose as an essential part of a meaningful existence. "Stress is the spice of life," Selye would say, pointing to both beneficial and harmful stress.[19] He nonetheless was the first to link too much physiological stress to a wide range of diseases, a topic he first raised in a little-noticed half-page article published in 1936 in the journal *Nature*. His research gradually gained renown in subsequent years, and by the time of his death in 1982, he had authored some fifteen hundred articles and thirty-two books on stress and human health, working twelve hours a day during the week, ten on the weekends, one of his researchers recalled.[20] "Stress in health and disease is medically, sociologically, and philosophically the most meaningful subject for humanity that I can think of," Selye once stated.[21]

Since Selye's time, generations of researchers have shared his dedication to understanding the health consequences of frequently turning on and off a powerful hormonal response meant for physical emergencies. It's now clear that psychological stressors, such as untimely traffic jams, financial strain, or an unpredictable boss, stimulate that same stress response, albeit at a smaller scale. They also exact a major health toll, especially for those experiencing them day in and day out.

For starters, psychological stressors are hard on the cardiovascular system. Remember the constricting of blood vessels during an emergency to deliver blood more forcefully throughout the body? That means elevated blood pressure. When that happens too frequently, these vessels develop thicker muscle layers to handle the elevated pressure. That in turn creates a more rigid vessel, which is then more resistant to blood flow, which creates even higher blood pressure, starting a dangerous cycle. It's one way to develop hypertension.

Then this higher pressure begins damaging your blood vessels, especially the points where they split apart, called bifurcation points. Those exposed areas get slammed especially hard with the high-pressure flow, creating lesions and small tears. These tiny injuries draw a crowd of immune cells, which in turn become a sticking point for various molecules passing by in your bloodstream, like fats and cholesterol. This conglomeration begins to create plaque, and now you're on your way to developing arteriosclerosis, which thickens and hardens the lining of your arteries. In addition, elevated blood pressure raises the odds of tearing off a piece of this plaque, sending a clot downstream that can block a vessel and cause a stroke or heart attack.[22]

What about the blood that slams more forcefully against heart walls during an emergency? If that action happens too frequently, the chamber that takes the hardest hit—the left ventricle—may build up muscle mass. That's called *left ventricular hypertrophy*, and it can cause an irregular heartbeat.[23]

The immune system also takes a hit when the stress response gets turned on too often. After that initial thirty-minute bump in function after a stressor, the immune system starts returning to roughly where it started. Scientists believe that it's a protective measure to prevent the finely calibrated system from getting so overstimulated that it actually begins attacking your own, thus triggering an autoimmune reaction. But during a prolonged crisis, stress hormones, and cortisol especially, can depress immune function.[24] (That's why cortisol is a go-to treatment when doctors want to suppress the immune system, such as after an organ transplant.)

For example, chronically high cortisol levels can reduce the size of the thymus, which produces white blood cells that kill infectious agents.[25] Cortisol also inhibits production of natural killer cells, which seek out foreign invaders, as well as production of virus-fighting interferon.[26]

A seminal study from Carnegie Mellon University linked psychological stress and its associated cortisol production with susceptibility to developing the common cold. Psychologist Sheldon Cohen and his colleagues assessed stress levels in about four hundred healthy adults, who were then given nasal drops that contained a small amount of respiratory disease viruses. Those with the highest stress levels had twice the odds of developing a cold.[27] More recently, in a 2016 study, Cohen and his colleagues tested salivary cortisol levels and cold susceptibility and found a direct correlation: the more cortisol, the higher the odds of getting sick.[28]

∼

Chronic stress is also hard on your brain. Too much cortisol inhibits neuron growth in the hippocampus, an area responsible for—among other functions—forming new memories. Chronic stress also increases the size of the amygdala, a part of the brain that controls fear and other emotional responses. An enlarged amygdala can heighten your brain's perception of danger, creating a state of hypervigilance that only increases the frequency of the stress response, resulting in a damaging feedback loop.[29]

Remember how the stress response swiftly floods your bloodstream with glucose, after pulling it from its cellular storage sites? And how it temporarily halts glucose storage by insulin? If that happens too often, cells just remember the insulin-resistant part, even after the stress has passed. You're now at risk of developing diabetes, with sugar building up in your bloodstream, a dangerous condition.[30]

Many other unhealthy conditions arise from chronically activating the stress response, including kidney impairment, depression, chronic fatigue syndrome, skin damage, and a loss of dopamine receptors—and hence higher risk for substance abuse—among other maladies.

On top of that, while recovering from a stressful event, cortisol stimulates a preference for high-fat, high-sugar "comfort" foods,[31] such as ice cream, pizza, or macaroni and cheese. Researchers say that macaques experience similar cravings for rich food after a stressful event. In the wild, that makes evolutionary sense, as it takes huge reserves of energy to stand your ground and fight or to run for your life. When things calm down, you need to replenish those depleted stores, ideally with high-calorie food.

High cortisol levels also throw off appetite regulation, in humans and monkeys, by triggering a resistance to leptin, a hormone that tells you when you've had enough to eat. And on goes the weight.[32]

There's even more. As you recover from the stressor, circulating cortisol, which hangs around for a while, preferentially deposits fat cells in the gut area. (Stressed macaques also develop potbellies.) This visceral fat lodges itself around organs such as the liver and kidney. It behaves differently from other fat cells, actually secreting its own hormones, altering sugar metabolism, and increasing inflammation levels, among other effects.[33]

Too much cortisol reaches deep into the cells as well, ultimately shortening protective casings, called telomeres, at the end of your chromosomes. Excess cortisol depletes the supply of an enzyme called telomerase, which reverses telomere loss, said Elissa Epel, PhD, director of the Aging, Metabolism, and Emotions Lab at the University of California, San Francisco and coauthor of *The Telomere Effect*.[34] When the supply of that enzyme runs low, telomeres shorten, chromosomes begin to deteriorate, and cells die or become inflammatory. "It's not short-term stresses, it's not acute stress. It's repetition over the years," added Epel in a phone interview.[35]

Now guess which groups of people experience repetitive stress more frequently? As with the primates at Wake Forest and the civil servants in the Whitehall studies, it's usually those on the lowest rungs. Unsurprisingly, these groups also have higher rates of chronic diseases.

In the United States, this pattern of poor health shows up in a patchwork of zip codes nationwide. In every region, life expectancy commonly varies by ten to twenty years between wealthy and low-income neighborhoods that are mere miles apart.

∼

Dr. Antony Iton, a senior vice president with the California Endowment who heads the Building Healthy Communities campaign, went to medical school at Johns Hopkins University in Baltimore, a city with one of the worst life-expectancy chasms in the nation between nearby neighbors.[36] He was in fact born in Baltimore, although his West Indian immigrant parents moved his family to Montreal when he was two years old. In a 2016 TEDx presentation in San Francisco,[37] Iton said he loved growing up in Montreal, describing it as a beautiful, cosmopolitan, and diverse city with abundant parks and open spaces, cafes, theaters, a state-of-the-art transportation system, and quality housing. And, of course, being Canada, everyone has access to free health care.

When Iton returned to Baltimore at age twenty-two, the cityscape shocked him. As an upperclassman showed him around, Iton saw a landscape of decaying, boarded-up, or sometimes burned-out row houses, streets devoid of trees, no safe parks, a few children playing on sidewalks in front of homes that were falling apart, trash, and graffiti-scrawled walls.

During his TEDx talk, he recalled how he had asked his classmate, "When was there a war here?" Iton never forgot his classmate's look of disdain or the reply of, "What did you expect? It's the inner city."

He also never forgot his horror at conditions in US cities. "I was supposed to expect this?" he said. "These atrocious and dehumanizing conditions were a norm in an American city? And I was left to wonder, 'Is the US really a First World country?'"

While in Baltimore, Iton worked in a public clinic serving these distressed neighborhoods, and like Dr. Robert Ross, president of the California Endowment, he grew disillusioned with how little medical care could do to heal the ailments he saw in his patients given the chronic stress they endured living in such dysfunctional, dangerous, and deprived neighborhoods. He was especially troubled after looking into the eyes of children. "I noticed the absence of hope, an absence of light. These kids were barraged with messages every single day of their lives that they weren't valued, that they didn't matter," he said.

In medical school, Iton realized that your zip code is a greater predictor than your genetic code in determining your health and life span, an insight he's discussed many times since. "Twenty-five years later that quote was attributed to me by *Forbes* magazine as the number one health care quote in 2013," he said.

After he finished his training in internal medicine at Johns Hopkins, he worked elsewhere in clinical practice as well as in public health.

Along the way he earned a law degree and a master's degree in public health. With the JD and MPH enabling him to more effectively pursue policy changes to benefit low-income communities, he began to tackle the tragedy of such dramatic health disparities in the United States. He subsequently landed at the Alameda County Public Health Department in Northern California, hired as its director and health officer in 2003. There he put his love of data crunching to work and found the same wide difference in life expectancy prevalent elsewhere in the country between the most affluent and the lowest-income neighborhoods in Alameda County.

"So what's happening in these low life expectancy communities?" Iton asked. "Very simply put, these communities are functioning like incubators of chronic stress."

These neighborhoods lack the basic infrastructure to pursue the American dream, he said. "Bad schools, poor housing, inadequate health care, poor transportation, lack of jobs, high crime, neighborhoods that are policed like military zones, a lack of access to parks, grocery stores," he said. "And even, in some cases, no access to fresh, safe drinking water. Any human being placed in such circumstances inevitably develops chronic stress," Iton said. "That's what would happen to you, it would happen to me."

For many in these communities, there's the added stress of feeling largely ignored, added Sapolsky, the Stanford stress expert and 1987 recipient of a MacArthur Foundation "genius" grant, at age thirty. "You have no agency, no impact, you and your existence are irrelevant to the mainstream," he said in an interview.[38]

~

Another factor adds to the stress burden: inequality. In countries with significant disparities between the highest and the lowest income earners, it appears to have a separate corrosive influence on the population's health, and the poor, not surprisingly, bear the brunt of it.[39] As Sapolsky wrote in his book *Why Zebras Don't Get Ulcers,* the flagship for the health/inequality relationship is the United States, with the top 1 percent on the socioeconomic ladder controlling nearly 40 percent of the wealth. He added, "Canada is both markedly more egalitarian and healthier than the United States—despite being a 'poorer' country."[40]

Even the wealthiest in the United States, though, may experience some of the strain of this income inequality. The World Health Organization in 2015 listed the United States as thirty-first in life expectancy worldwide, at 79.3 years, which falls between Costa Rica and Cuba. (The two top-ranked countries were Japan at 83.7 years and Sweden at 83.4 years.)

"That's one of the most subtly interesting, if least important, aspects of the inequality/health relations—that inequality does rotten things to the health of the wealthy as well," Sapolsky said. He attributed part of that to the economic strain associated with "walling oneself off," such as paying for private school for multiple children, the costs of security, and so on. "But the bigger one is the anxiety implicit in having to live a life where you're seceding from society as a whole out of fear," he added.

For more than thirty years, Sapolsky spent summers in Kenya studying wild baboons, assessing sources of stress, measuring cortisol levels in the alpha dominants and the subordinates, and monitoring health outcomes. Despite the rough treatment baboons can dish out to one another, in his book he nonetheless noted how humans have a way of subjugating others like nothing seen in the primate world. When I asked him to elaborate, he said, "Low-ranking monkeys don't feel as if they're less worthwhile because of their rank. They don't think their low rank is their fault, they aren't reminded of the subordination by a fancy sports car that passes them on the highway, by the magazine covers celebrating the rich and famous, by the thousands of consumer items that they see daily that may be out of their reach."

The central goal of the ten-year Building Healthy Communities campaign is in fact turning around that sense of marginalization in low-income neighborhoods by creating stronger community ties and cultivating resident empowerment. That's all done in the interest of bringing more resources into the community, enacting more equitable policies, and what advocates would call restoring the democratic process.

"Rather than asking people to beat the odds, it's time to change the odds," Iton concluded in his TEDx talk. "We are organizing people to come together. And these people are taking control of their environment. And they feel *agency*."

When I described this dimension of the Building Healthy Communities campaign, Sapolsky said that enhanced social cohesion is "good for health insofar as it gets directly at the core psychological building blocks of stress—lack of control, lack of outlets, lack of predictability, lack of social support. Community action like that counters all of those."

CHAPTER 3
Keeping Kids in School

When Cameron Simmons started at an Oakland, California, preschool in 1998 at age four, his mother would give him a packet of Skittles every day to calm his separation anxiety. Then the school principal got wind of the daily candy supply and concluded the young boy was eating the Skittles in class, so the principal took the bag, put it in the lower drawer of his desk, and locked his office. In response, the youngster did what he thought was logical: he climbed through an open window in the office with the aid of a chair and got his candy back. The four-year-old then got suspended for theft.

"It didn't register then that maybe I shouldn't do this. I didn't have the intellect to understand," said Simmons, who was twenty when we met in 2014 for lunch at an Oakland restaurant, where he'd politely ordered a chicken melt sandwich and ice water. "But I don't feel a suspension was the proper response for a four-year-old."

That suspension started a long cycle that proved hard to break. "Once you're known as a disruptive kid, once you have that title on you, that's pretty much it," he said. He's also always been a little portly and teased about it regularly, and he started fighting back. "People who are bullied turn into bullies," he said. In first grade he said that one student relentlessly teased him about his size, and Cameron finally grabbed him and pushed him against the door, saying, "Stop, leave me alone!" He was suspended for three days. "I'm not saying it was right," Simmons said. "I'm just saying no one pays attention until it's boiling over. And then everything goes horribly wrong."

By his junior year in high school he'd been suspended nearly 150 times and expelled four times.[1] Sometimes he resorted to fighting, which he knows wasn't acceptable, although on at least some occasions he felt compelled to protect himself. Other times he said he got into trouble for just being near a fight, although school staff nonetheless charged him with the offense. That happened his sophomore year, and he was up for expulsion. "I had nothing to do with it, I didn't hit nobody. I didn't even see who fought," Simmons said. That time an assistant principal came to his defense, and he was spared the discipline.

Suspensions also followed for small matters, such as wearing a baseball hat to school and asking if he could put it in his backpack rather than relinquish it for the rest of the school year, as policy called for. So he was suspended for defiance. He even ended up in juvenile hall for one month during middle school—a low point—after he threw a carton of milk at a friend while they were roughhousing outside the school cafeteria. Although Simmons and the friend told school officials that it was done in play, the police were summoned. Simmons was charged with assault with a deadly weapon, handcuffed him in front of other students, booked into juvenile hall, and expelled.

For a while his mother homeschooled him, but the isolation chafed, and he missed seeing his friends at school and meeting new people. He also enjoyed the classroom instruction. "I like to learn, because knowledge is everything," he said. He likes many subjects—math, science, and English in particular—and he's always been an avid reader, citing young adult book authors Walter Dean Myers and Ellen Hopkins as favorites and the biography of nineteenth-century social reformer Frederick Douglass as an influential book. So he reenrolled.

He never felt welcomed at school, though. "They obviously didn't want me there. I think they find reasons to not have certain kids around. I felt like I was one of those kids," Simmons said. "You feel they're not for your education, they're against it." He became deeply wary of teachers and administrators. "They made me feel like I wasn't good enough. It breaks the trust, you know," he said.

About 90 miles away, in a Sacramento high school, then-sixteen-year-old Dwayne Powe Jr., a high school junior, described living with a sense of uncertainty, not sure when he'll next get into trouble. He looked embarrassed when we met in a classroom on his campus in October 2014 and I asked how many times he had been suspended. He never did say, but he described his first one, in eighth grade, after he walked to school with some classmates who were smoking marijuana. When they got to school, one girl told a teacher that Powe had pot on him. Powe said he didn't even smoke any of it, and they found no marijuana on him during a search of his backpack, but he was suspended for five days anyway. "How could they accuse me and then not find any?" he asked.

Other school disciplines followed, more recently during his sophomore year when he challenged a teacher's failing grade on an essay and was suspended for "willful defiance," a catchall category of nonviolent misbehavior that includes minor offenses such as ignoring teacher requests to not text or forgetting homework to more serious ones such as swearing at a teacher. It's the most common reason for suspensions, and it's applied to black students far more often than white students.[2]

Powe said he only wrote his name on the first page of the stapled essay, and some of the pages of his assignment were mixed up with other students' work after the teacher removed the staple during grading. But the teacher docked him for the missing content, telling Powe he should have written his name on all the pages. "And then I got mad, and said, 'I did all my work and you still gave me a zero!'" Powe said something angry as he left the class and got a three-day suspension. He got another three-day suspension after someone threw a pencil at another student while the teacher's back was turned to the class. He insisted it wasn't him, that he knew who did it, and that other students could verify it, but the teacher said it was Powe. When he protested his innocence he was not only accused of having disrupted the class but of being defiant to authority. While he fumed at home, watching TV and playing video games during his suspension, he had to miss the final and repeat the class, as he got a D in it.

Another time he was late for his first-period class when his city-run bus ran late. For that he got detention, but he couldn't attend the after-school session without missing baseball practice, so he had to attend a Saturday detention session. "For being late for first period," mused Powe, who wore his hair pulled into a ponytail and spoke with a slightly injured, exasperated tone about his experiences with school discipline. "I always get into trouble for the littlest stuff," he said. A *USA Today* article on school suspensions that profiled Powe described how the teen borrowed a pencil from a classmate at the start of an assignment and was told by the teacher that he was being disruptive; when Powe said that he was only trying to borrow a pencil, he was again suspended for "willful defiance."[3]

These kinds of stories are hardly unique to Simmons and Powe, who are both black. In many communities throughout the United States, students—disproportionately students of color—are getting kicked out of school for minor offenses at alarming rates. In response, rather than continuing to pile on the discipline, some school programs are helping kids get past their anger and confusion and across the finish line of graduation. Both Simmons and Powe got on track after landing in programs funded by the Building Healthy Communities (BHC) campaign, which offered social and emotional support to students with a history of school discipline problems. Neither of the young men—who each completed high school—cares to think about where he'd be without that support. Simmons now works for an organization called

RJOY, for Restorative Justice for Oakland Youth, as a youth advocate for middle-school students, as well as giving presentations and coleading training sessions on restorative justice.

~

School discipline wasn't on the California Endowment's radar when it began its ten-year campaign, but one BHC manager in Fresno realized the gravity of the situation and pushed to make it a priority. Sarah Reyes joined the California Endowment in 2009 as a Central Valley regional program manager in her hometown of Fresno. The city of 500,000 lies in the southern end of the state's vast agricultural heartland, surrounded by vineyards, ranches, and orchards. Reyes was already steeped in policy making: from 1998 to 2004, she had represented the area as a state assembly member, sponsoring legislation that mandated sexual harassment prevention training and established the "do not list" policy for cell phone companies.

Not long after she took the Endowment job, young people in the area began sharing their frustration with what they considered unfair discipline at school. "They were saying 'A lot of my friends are disappearing from school. They're just gone,'" recalled Reyes. She and others in the Fresno office looked into it and found that there were indeed high rates of student suspension and expulsion in the local schools. "And that meant they weren't graduating," she added.

She realized young people in the community felt a deep injustice over the treatment and feared for their futures. So Reyes urged Endowment president Dr. Robert Ross to hear from local students at an upcoming board meeting to be held in Fresno.

The request threw Ross off, and he wasn't sure how to respond, at first saying there wasn't time for the kids to speak. A typical CEO, he told me, "is pretty much a control freak" when it comes to running the board meetings that decide the direction of the organization. When Reyes pressed the issue, Ross asked her, "What are they going to say?" Although the Endowment wanted to hear from young people, the notion of teenagers pitching a new priority to the trustees of a $3.5 billion foundation was unsettling. "We're not really into all that 'youth voice' stuff, are we?" Ross joked. But Reyes insisted that the teenagers had something critical to share, and he finally relented.

The presentation turned into a mind-bender for Ross. More than fifteen impassioned students—mostly Latinos, with some African American and Hmong students (whose families came from Southeast Asia following the Vietnam War)—filled the Fresno conference room, sharing data and stories of harsh school discipline. He was used to hearing about students' need for more health services, improved sports facilities, and better school meals, but not about kids getting kicked out of school for minor matters and how it upended their lives. "I wasn't expecting young people to say that the most pressing wellness issue in their community was zero tolerance and school discipline," said Ross.

Neither he nor any of his senior staff had ever heard that school discipline was a paramount concern, particularly in low-income communities. The Endowment was also spending a small fortune on consultants to determine the most urgent priorities in the fourteen target sites. "We had reams and reams of data and PowerPoint slides about the challenges facing young people in preparing for the BHC plan, and that issue was nowhere," he said. ("They never asked the young people," Reyes added. "What I have learned is if you ask young people, they'll tell you.")

Adding to Ross's bewilderment, his first thought on hearing the term *zero tolerance* during the presentation was, "Aren't zero-tolerance policies good, that they keep bad kids out of the classroom?"

The presentation was the start of a steep learning curve. "They told us, 'We don't have a dropout problem, we have a 'pushout' problem,'"

Ross said. "They said that suspension rates were epidemic, that kids lose hope when they're pushed out of school, or suspended. And that in their view the worst thing you could do to a troubled young person who is acting up at school is to actually release them into the streets, where gang life and violence and drugs are lying in wait.

"That was a wakeup call to hear that," he said. "And when that meeting was over the board was looking at me like, 'Well Bob? Are you going to do anything about this?'" Although the students were initially given a strict thirty-minute limit for their talk, board members kept them there for an additional half hour, asking questions, posing in group photos, and exchanging business cards. "The young people stole the show," Reyes said.

"I really have to credit Sarah for having the guts to insist that these young people be on the agenda, and with their voices unfettered," Ross added.

~

Ross next wondered if it was possibly "just a Fresno thing," but when he asked around, program managers throughout California told him that parents and students in their communities shared the same stories and the same anger. After digging deeper into statewide data, the Endowment staff discovered surprisingly high suspension rates in many districts, with a few outliers suspending as much as one-fourth of their students during the year.

It was the first time state education officials ever heard these stunning statistics, said Daniel Zingale, a senior vice president with the Endowment who heads its statewide team in Sacramento. Zingale started his career as an AIDS activist in Washington, DC, before moving into California politics, where he served as deputy chief of staff to former Governor Gray Davis. In 1999, Zingale was appointed to be the founding director of California's health maintenance organization (HMO) watchdog agency, called the Department of Managed Health Care. There he earned the nickname "HMO Czar" for doggedly pursuing fines against HMOs for what his agency charged were lapses in patient care. He later served as a senior health advisor to former Governor Arnold Schwarzenegger and chief of staff to former California First Lady Maria Shriver.

Zingale maintains close ties to California's top education official, Tom Torlakson, the state Superintendent of Public Instruction, and Zingale said neither he nor Torlakson understood how many kids were getting kicked out of school in California. Nor did other top education officials. "None of us had that on our radars, I'd never heard about it being an issue, and none of the policy experts in Sacramento had it on their radar," said Zingale.

It turns out that zero-tolerance policies had not led to more peaceful campuses with better learning environments; those with more suspensions and expulsions actually had lower rates of schoolwide academic achievement. (Moreover, excessive school discipline funnels many students into the juvenile and criminal justice systems, often called the "school-to-prison pipeline."[4]) In response, an American Psychological Association task force recommended dealing with misbehavior through programs that improve campus climate and "the sense of school community and belongingness."[5]

Before diving too deep into the school reform movement, however, Ross and his senior staff had to get their heads around the idea that discipline was in their bailiwick. After all, their mandate was to improve health, not necessarily to fix schools or promote legal justice. It didn't take them long to make a rock-solid connection between unfair school discipline and health.

∼

There's hardly a stronger influence on health and longevity than education, measured in years of schooling completed. One study linked a five-year life expectancy boost to simply earning a high school degree.[6] In addition, self-ratings of good health follow a stair-step pattern up, ranging from only about 30 percent of those with no high school diploma rating themselves in good health up to college graduates, in which about 70 percent do. The benefits of education also extend to subsequent generations; children of better-educated parents are less likely to die as infants, and they experience better health throughout their lives.[7]

This health boost from education arises from multiple factors, chief among them higher earning power. Those with less than a high school diploma earn about $25,000 annually, compared with $43,000 for high school graduates. Incomes, of course, go up with more education, and the more one climbs the education ladder, the greater one's knowledge of healthy behaviors, the strength of social networks, social status, and a sense of control in life and thus less stress, all of which profoundly influence life span. (High school dropouts also cost public coffers on average $240,000 over a lifetime in terms of lower tax contributions, higher reliance on Medicaid and Medicare, greater criminal activity and hence incarceration, and more reliance on welfare during more frequent than average bouts of unemployment.[8,9])

While Ross and others at the Endowment were considering the issue, they soon learned of a small but growing national backlash against zero-tolerance policies, which started as a solitary effort led by a Washington, DC–based organization called the Advancement Project.

Zero-tolerance policies in the nation's K–12 campuses have their roots in the "tough on crime" trend that took hold in the late 1980s. They were initially part of a Reagan-era crackdown on drug dealing, but also coincided with rising fears about growing ranks of morally bereft, violent adolescents, dubbed "superpredators."[10] (The fears proved unsubstantiated.[11])

In this milieu, Congress in 1994 passed the Guns-Free School Act, which President Bill Clinton signed. The act mandated a one-year expulsion and referral to law enforcement of any student found carrying a weapon to school, with a penalty of loss of federal funding to schools for noncompliance. Then, in the late 1990s, a trend in states to enact mandatory, stringent punishments for serious adult crimes took hold, such as the "three-strikes" laws enacted in various states around the country that require a mandatory life sentence without parole for those convicted of certain felonies. Following that lead, policy makers and school administrators also started urging firmer, unyielding punishment for students who misbehaved, even for minor matters. By 1997, four out of five schools nationwide had adopted zero-tolerance policies not only toward alcohol, drugs, weapons, and assault, but also toward a wide range of common infractions, including dress code violations, minor schoolyard scuffles, truancy, and defiance.

Some schools interpreted the rules so strictly that they deemed toenail clippers and toy swords worn as part of Halloween costumes as weapons and Certs, Midol, and doctor-prescribed asthma medicines as unauthorized drugs. Swearing, pranks, or even innocent mistakes led to exclusion from school. Still, few spoke of relaxing these policies in the wake of horrific incidences of violence, such as the 1997 high school shooting in Pearl, Mississippi, that left two students dead; the school shooting the same year in Paducah, Kentucky, in which a fourteen-year-old opened fire and killed three students; the 1998 Jonesboro, Arkansas, school attack in which an eleven-year-old and fourteen-year-old fatally shot four students and a teacher; and the 1999 Columbine High School massacre in Colorado, which left twelve students and a teacher dead.

During the 1990s, the number of students kicked out of school soared; so too do did anger among parents and young people. Finally, the Advancement Project, which opened in 1999 with offices in Washington, DC, and Los Angeles, picked up on the burgeoning outrage and decided to take on dismantling zero-tolerance policies as its major campaign. It was the first national group to call out zero-tolerance policies as overly harsh and especially punitive toward students of color. Its landmark 2000 report, "Opportunities Suspended," coauthored with the Civil Rights Project at Harvard University, cited federal data showing that 3.1 million American children were suspended in 1998 and 87,000 were expelled, nearly double the rate in 1974.[12] (By 2006, the numbers had risen to more than 3.3 million suspensions, or nearly 7 percent of all US students, and 102,000 expulsions.[13])

African American students fared the worst. Even though they comprised only 17 percent of K–12 public school enrollment nationally, they accounted for 32 percent of suspensions. In comparison, white students, with 63 percent of enrollment, represented 50 percent of suspensions. The 2000 report found that Hispanics were also suspended at higher rates than whites. (A 2013 article from the American Academy of Pediatrics on school discipline practices commented that it was "interesting to note" that the school shootings that bolstered support for zero-tolerance policies had been perpetrated by white boys.[14])

Rather than straightening up wayward youth, these forced absences damage bonds between students and teachers and drive students out of school, where they contend with more than double the unemployment rate of those with a college degree. Prisons, too, are filled with those lacking high school diplomas or equivalency degrees, with especially dire statistics for young African American men: nearly one in four young black male dropouts ends up incarcerated compared with one in fourteen young white, Asian, or Hispanic male dropouts. In contrast, one in thirty-five young male high school graduates finds himself behind bars.[15]

~

In the early days, the battle against harsh school discipline was daunting, said Judith Browne Dianis, a civil rights attorney and cofounder of the Advancement Project. "It was very lonely at first," she said. "Parents and youth groups were out there saying 'This is wrong.' But we were the only national group saying it."

People wondered why the organization was defending "bad kids," Browne Dianis said. "So for a long time, it was just community by community, trying to get some traction on it," she recalled with a slightly weary tone. The Advancement Project pressed on. "We set out to make zero-tolerance a dirty phrase, so it would be abandoned as a phrase and as a practice and philosophy," Browne Dianis said. "We were constantly lifting up all the bad stories."

The "Opportunities Suspended" report included a long list of documented examples of over-the-top responses to incidents that once meant a simple trip to a principal's office for a warning or discussion:[16]

- An African American ninth-grader in Louisiana was expelled for one year from a predominantly white school district and sent to an alternative school because she had sparklers in her book bag. She had used them over the weekend and forgot they were there.
- In Virginia, two ten-year-old Latino boys faced felony charges for putting soap in their teacher's water in what they viewed as a prank.
- On his way to school, a fifth-grade African American boy was shown two razor blades by a classmate who said she planned to use them to hurt two girls who were bullying her. The boy took the blades and hid them in order to prevent a tragedy. Another student notified school officials that the boy had hidden the blades. Although the boy took steps to protect others, he was suspended from school for one year. The district refused a request by attorneys for a due process hearing. He was given no alternative education and had to repeat the fifth grade.
- A ten-year-old African American fourth-grade girl in Mississippi was suspended three times for "defiance of authority": first for failing to

participate in a class assignment, then for humming and tapping on her desk, and finally for "drug-related activity." The "evidence" of that last activity was that she wore one pants leg up. She was referred to an alternative school.

- A tenth-grade female honor student and president of the Black Student Union in Dublin, California, got into an argument with a white student who was regularly taunting her. As she turned to walk away, the white student hit her. In the ensuing scuffle, the black girl accidentally hit a teacher. Despite corroboration that the teacher was not hit deliberately and the student's clean record, she was expelled.
- An African American seventh-grader in San Francisco won a bet on the outcome of a school basketball game. The schoolmate who lost the bet accused the other of threatening him for payment. Without conducting an investigation, the school district notified law enforcement officials, who charged the seventh-grader with felony extortion. He was subsequently expelled.
- An African American honor student in South Carolina who attended a predominantly white school district was suspended indefinitely for fighting. It was her first reprimand.

The *Washington Post* investigated another case cited in the Advancement Project report, a raucous incident on a school bus in Mississippi in 2000. What started with one kid tossing a single peanut erupted into all forty teenage passengers throwing peanuts back and forth. One misfired peanut hit the bus driver, a white woman, who then stopped the vehicle and summoned the police. Although all the students were questioned, the next day only five African American boys were charged with felony assault; they were suspended for two weeks and kicked off the bus for a year, which they needed to reach their rural high school more than 20 miles from home. Four of the boys dropped out of school because their parents had no transportation to get them there. A parent of one of those boys pleaded with the white principal to rescind the bus ban, but he wouldn't yield. The criminal charges were dismissed, however, with the assistance of an attorney and community pressure. One of the boys was later quoted as saying, "I [would have] gone to college. . . . Maybe I could have been a lawyer."[17]

This litany of stories held up by the Advancement Project, which increasingly gained media coverage, began to raise doubts about the wisdom of get-tough practices on K–12 campuses. Then a kindergartener's arrest, which made national news, marked a turning point for the reform movement.

In 2005, five-year-old Ja'eisha Scott was sitting in her St. Petersburg, Florida, classroom and counting jelly beans as part of a math exercise. When the teacher ended the game, the five-year-old became upset and threw a severe temper tantrum. Two teachers tried for more than twenty minutes to calm her down, using techniques they'd learned to end tantrums, and eventually Ja'eisha quieted down and sat still in a school administrator's office. Despite her now-calm demeanor, local police arrested the 40-pound African American girl and placed her in the back of a police cruiser. Video caught the scene, with the girl crying out in anguish as three officers handcuffed her. Police detained her in a vehicle for some two hours as she wailed for her nearby mother; the police finally released the girl after the state attorney's office informed them that a five-year-old would never be prosecuted.[18]

～

The Advancement Project gained a critical ally in 2010 when the Atlantic Philanthropies, a private foundation, took on zero tolerance as a major priority. It was the first large foundation to do so, and it has since given $47 million to support nationwide reform efforts, including substantial funds for the Advancement Project.

Atlantic Philanthropies plans to close its doors in 2020, after giving away $8 billion over thirty-five years. Its founder, Chuck Feeney, chose that shut-down strategy because he wanted the investments to be made "on his watch." Feeney, who made a fortune as coowner of Duty Free Shoppers (the airport stores selling tax-free goods), keeps a low profile, although Warren Buffet and Bill Gates say the eighty-six-year-old is their role model. Even at the height of his wealth, Feeney wore an inexpensive watch and flew economy class, and in 1984 he transferred most of his money into Atlantic Philanthropies.

One investment by Finney's foundation paid big dividends: it funded the most consequential study to date on zero tolerance, the 2011 "Breaking Schools' Rules" report on the Texas public school system prepared by the Council for State Governments Justice Center.[19]

Several state legislators, both Republican and Democrat, had pushed for the analysis, and it's lauded for its bipartisan nature. These lawmakers also helped secure the all-important cooperation of various state agencies. Their data allowed researchers to get a full picture of suspensions and expulsions from public schools in Texas, how they affected students' academic performance, and the connection between school discipline and later involvement in the juvenile justice system.

The study focused on Texas, but given the sheer size of the state's school system—educating one in ten US public school students—it's also nationally relevant. Moreover, Texas mirrors the student demographics of much the United States: 14 percent African American, 40 percent Hispanic, and 43 percent white.

The scope of the study was unprecedented. The researchers tracked outcomes for *all* Texas public school students—not just a sample—who were seventh-graders starting in 2000, 2001, and 2002, nearly one million in all, and examined their data for the next six years, until one year after expected graduation. The study also factored in more than eighty characteristics about each student and his or her school experience, from race and family income to past academic performance. The huge education database also linked to juvenile justice records (a rarity among states) so that researchers could examine connections between school disciplines and later run-ins with the law.

The results were stunning: 60 percent of Texas students of all races—in other words, a majority—were suspended or expelled at least once between seventh and twelfth grades. Another revelation was that of these half million students removed from class, only 3 percent of those removals were mandated because of the severity of the violation, such as weapons possession, assault, and selling drugs. The rest were "discretionary offenses," which, as the name suggests, gives school staff significant latitude to respond. Most of these lesser offenses were "code of conduct" breaches, such as cutting class and dress code violations.

Researchers also noted that for serious violations such as carrying weapons and drug dealing, white, black, and Hispanic students were removed from school at rates proportional to their numbers. (Black boys in ninth grade actually had *lower* rates of mandatory removals compared with ninth-grade white and Hispanic boys.)

For discretionary disciplines, however, the typical disparities held. Among the African American male students, 83 percent had at least one suspension or expulsion for discretionary reasons compared with 74 percent of Hispanic boys and 59 percent of white boys. For female students, 70 percent of African Americans had at least one discretionary action compared with 58 percent of Hispanic girls and 37 percent of white girls. First violations for black and Hispanic students also led to more suspensions.

The Texas study found that suspended students more often failed classes, dropped out, and ended up in the juvenile justice system than students who had not faced suspension. Still, a common question is whether these students, boys especially, just act up more at school. Perhaps it has nothing to do with racial bias? The Texas study researchers also made that inquiry and concluded that for comparable discretionary violations, black students were still 31 percent more likely to be disciplined than white students.

~

Few have devoted more time to examining the role of race in school discipline than Russell Skiba, a psychologist with Indiana University and director of its Equity Project. For years he's probed for reasons behind the disparities in suspensions and expulsions. He saw from discipline records that white students visited the principal more for clearly documented behavior such as smoking, vandalism, leaving without permission, and obscene language than for other offenses. African American students, on the other hand, usually visited the principal for behaviors requiring a more subjective assessment: disrespect, excessive noise, defiance, or loitering.

Skiba also looked into the role of cultural differences between students and teachers. With the teaching force in most districts predominantly white and female, "the possibility of a cultural mismatch or racial stereotyping as a contributing factor in disproportionate office referrals cannot be discounted," he cautiously wrote in a 2011 journal article.[20]

White teachers may interpret the "impassioned or emotive interactions" of some African American boys as "combative or argumentative," Skiba wrote, and thus a threat to class control.[21] Other researchers concluded that teachers judged those using a "stroll" style of walk as aggressive and less academically promising than other students.[22] Another study noted that many school discipline problems arise not from serious disruptions but due to violations of "unspoken and unwritten rules" about the proper way to speak.[23]

When the Endowment staff researched the issue early in the campaign, they were already well aware that high school graduation was a critical step to a healthy, longer life. Then they realized that if harsh school discipline was actually adding to dropout rates, zero-tolerance policies were indeed a health issue and a major priority. "It was the first issue I can say that we took up as a strategic issue for BHC that we had not known a damn thing about," said Ross, the Endowment's president.

The realization also changed the Endowment's approach to the campaign from that point on, said Daniel Zingale, the head of the statewide team. "When we started on this BHC strategy, we came up with what we thought were the ten most important things to change," he said. "Well, guess what wasn't on there? School discipline. Because we didn't know, you don't live it. You know, my kids don't get suspended. So that was a big change for the culture of this place."

Easing heavy-handed approaches also fit with Ross's evolving view of how to tackle the many challenges facing young people of color, men especially, given the high rates of incarceration for black and Hispanic males and their lower rates of employment and hence financial success.

"It's really thorny, vexing, deep and complicated," Ross told me, describing the obstacles facing young men of color who grow up in low-income areas. "It's race, it's poverty, it's violence, it's parenting, it's culture, it's community, it's employment. It's all these issues, and so what happens is the problem just seems so complex and complicated and profound that you don't feel like you get a hook to start.

"But with the school discipline suspension issue, it gave us a hook, right?" Ross continued. "It gave us a hook for how to change the narrative around these young men, how to embrace them rather than push them out. It invoked the issue of race, but it was also a solvable-sized problem. It just felt like we could begin to create some pragmatic level of progress."

Zingale also clearly saw the seeds of a statewide movement. Communities around California were fed up over the issue and ready to speak out, and the solution lay largely in better policies, laws, and outlooks and not so much in huge capital outlays. So the state team took on this relatively obscure issue as its first "grassroots to treetops" campaign. They knew it would test the basic premise of their approach, of driving statewide change, and also that no other nonprofit organization had tried something similar on that scale.

Zingale took heart in his early work as an AIDS activist. "I've lived it to some extent in the HIV/AIDS work I did a long time ago. Where nobody was getting it," he said. "The policy makers, the health care delivery system, you name it. And AIDS activists took it into their own hands and changed America's response to the epidemic. So I know it works, and I see the power of that."

He also recalled how he began community organizing when he was young and how it made him realize that he and his circle of friends weren't alone, in this case fighting the apartheid system in South Africa in the 1980s. He figured that same spirit could animate this new drive to reform school discipline policies in California.

"When you find out you're part of a larger effort, that's a great feeling," Zingale said. And when it actually achieves reform, "it changes the trajectory of your life."

CHAPTER 4
Changing Schools' Rules

Fight Crime: Invest in Kids is a national organization of some five thousand police chiefs, sheriffs, prosecutors, district attorneys, and violence survivors that prides itself on taking "a hard-nosed look at the strategies proven to reduce crime." At first, it might seem like an odd partner to lead up a new school discipline reform campaign taking root in California in 2011. But excessive suspensions and expulsions aren't proven strategies for reducing crime; in fact, data clearly showed they go hand in hand with kids dropping out of school and too often ending up in the juvenile justice system. So when the California Endowment brought that data to Brian Lee, the California state director of Fight Crime, he listened.

Lee remembers those early conversations with Endowment staff, remarking, "It was not their idea. It emerged from the grassroots and they were surprised as anybody." It was also novel for Fight Crime. The organization had long concentrated on reducing crime by lowering high school dropout rates through programs like early childhood education and truancy prevention, but it hadn't yet made the connection to overly zealous school discipline policies. It was news to him, and to many others, that even a single suspension reduces the odds of a student graduating high school, which also lowers lifetime earning potential and increases the risk of chronic health problems.[1]

In the spring of 2011, Fight Crime became a key ally in the Endowment's Building Healthy Communities campaign to reform school disciple policies statewide. Soon joining the effort were veterans in the battle to reform school discipline practices in California: CADRE, the Public Counsel Law Center, and the Labor Community Strategy Center, or LCSC. These organizations had achieved local wins that significantly improved conditions in their communities, but hadn't yet succeeded in igniting a statewide movement, despite efforts to do so.

CADRE, a South Los Angeles nonprofit organization, first challenged the Los Angeles Unified School District in 2001 to stop what it identified as a school "pushout" problem, not a dropout problem.[2] Canvassers for CADRE (which stands for Community Asset Development Redefining Education) had gone door to door in South LA, a high-poverty, high-crime community, asking residents about their most pressing issues. What most aggrieved them was how suspensions, expulsions, and forced transfers were driving students out of school and jeopardizing their chances for future success. In 2005, CADRE teamed with Laura Faer, the statewide education rights director with the Public Counsel Law Center, a public-interest law firm, who had also recently recognized the harm wrought by existing school discipline practices.

The two groups drummed up significant local support from parents and students for changing disciplinary approaches that kept kids out of the classroom. In 2007, they won a David versus Goliath victory after persuading the LA Unified School District to adopt a new discipline policy that would gradually phase out the old, harsher practices. It was no small feat given that LA Unified is the second largest school district in the United States, with 665,000 students.

The new policy focused on cultivating a more positive school climate in which expectations of behavior were communicated clearly and compliance was rewarded in various small ways. As much as possible, staff dealt with misconduct on campus, keeping kids in school and around adults who could guide them in a better direction rather than releasing them to the streets. Called "school-wide positive behavioral support," it was credited with reducing suspensions by 16 percent and expulsions by 57 percent in certain South LA high schools over the next two years.[3] Although it helped students at some schools, however, a 2010 progress report found spotty implementation within the sprawling school district, with its more than one thousand schools. And suspension rates, although better, still remained high.[4]

In 2005, the South Los Angeles nonprofit LCSC launched a separate effort to improve students' school participation by stopping officers from greeting youngsters running late with a truancy ticket, which carried a $240 fine and required the student to miss class to attend hearings. The fines were also a heavy financial blow for their families, and sometimes kids just skipped class rather than arrive late. After a five-year campaign of petitions, protests, and public testimony, LCSC finally won the cooperation of school police, who agreed to stop the "morning sweeps" for tardy students. At one South LA high school where the sweeps had been especially pervasive, attendance soared by 50 percent when they ceased.[5]

～

It was still a district-by-district and school-by-school struggle, though, and outside of those areas with organized advocates, such as South Los Angeles as well as Fresno and Oakland, few were listening. "You felt like you were yelling into the abyss," said Faer, with the Public Counsel Law Center. Echoing Judith Browne Dianis with the Advancement Project in Washington, DC, Faer said that when she started in the work, "school pushout wasn't even a term that was being used, and it was pretty much the consensus that zero tolerance was the way to go and if you didn't kick out the bad kids, then how could you run a school? We were running upstream, trying to change a practice."

Faer, who in 2011 was named an "Attorney of the Year" by the magazine *California Lawyer* for her work in juvenile justice, came to the cause after she began running a free legal clinic focused on education in South LA in the early 2000s. To her surprise, almost all her clients were children who had left school after feeling the heavy hand of school discipline. "They were being involuntarily transferred, suspended, expelled, until they dropped out," Faer said. "And universally, when you looked at their record, you found it started really early and that it should have been apparent to everybody that these were kids who needed help."

Her first client with the free clinic, in fact, was a sixth-grader with special needs. He had been out of school for four months because his previous school hadn't implemented his special education plan and then had involuntarily transferred him after documenting behavior problems such as trouble concentrating and staying still. But the new school wouldn't take him in, so he was languishing at home. After Faer objected to school officials that this situation violated the law, they readmitted him to his former school and implemented his education plan. "Once we got him back in and put a plan in place, he did great," Faer added.

By the time the Endowment started getting involved in 2010, the issue was gradually emerging on the national stage, thanks chiefly to the work of the Advancement Project and several other organizations and with the financial support of a foundation called Atlantic Philanthropies. With the national advocacy groups keeping up the reform drumbeat, the Obama administration grew to support curbing zero-tolerance policies, and in 2011 the US Department of Education and the US Department of Justice launched a joint project called the Supportive School Discipline Initiative to keep students in school as much as possible through supportive programs.

Even with that new federal support, however, the word wasn't spreading fast. With nearly fourteen thousand school districts in the United States, each run with autonomy by district boards, change takes time. In a few places, most notably Colorado and Connecticut, local campaigns had successfully launched state-level school discipline reform efforts. But in California the issue remained largely invisible to state policy makers until the BHC campaign took it on.

~

The first formal effort in the California campaign took place in May 2011, at a convening on school discipline reform at the Endowment headquarters with representatives from several community organizations and eight BHC sites, along with Lee from Fight Crime and Endowment staff. Dr. Robert Ross, the Endowment president, addressed the group, saying, "We are willing to be responsive and supportive, but this issue is new to us. We need your help to get smarter on this issue. It is fundamentally clear to us that it is a compelling moral and strategic obligation that we go down this path."[6]

As the meeting progressed, the participants recognized the seeds of a statewide movement and left excited that day. Over the next few months, Fight Crime, CADRE, and LCSC organized an official coalition named the "Fix School Discipline Policy Coalition." It included the Public Counsel Law Center; large nonprofit organizations with statewide and national reach, including the ACLU, the Youth Law Center, and Children Now; and several community-based nonprofit organizations, which brought years of direct experience with the issue. These community groups could also readily mobilize grassroots support and arrange testimony from young people describing overly harsh discipline practices that undermined their success at school.

To amplify those student stories, someone at the Endowment got the idea to host a "virtual rally" so that young people around the state could share their experiences with school disciplines. Some members of the coalition weren't excited about the idea, preferring instead to concentrate on in-person action. But a few of the members had seen the power of convening like-minded groups from different areas and thought a virtual rally was worth a try. They held it on October 5, 2011, and young people from BHC sites statewide tuned in, watching speakers webcast from the Oakland, South LA, Fresno, and Sacramento BHC campaigns describing the toll of harsh disciplines in their lives.[7]

In fact, the rally transformed the reform effort. Young people around the state realized the breadth of the crisis and now understood that they were far from alone. A number of media outlets covered it as well, providing the first statewide coverage on the issue. "They were able to break away from this just being a local movement to being something larger," said Manuel Criollo, with LCSC, one of the organizations in the coalition.[8]

The virtual rally included memorable testimony from a young Hispanic woman in Southern California, posted on YouTube.[9] "My name is Claudia Gomez," said the dark-haired woman, speaking emphatically at a podium. "When I entered high school I began to witness and experience the school-to-jailhouse track. I began to get truancy tickets for being just a couple of minutes late. I got into a fistfight with a girl and I was automatically suspended instead of being offered anger management classes. I went back a couple of months later and got into a fight with the same girl and was expelled for disturbing the peace and using verbal threats."

Gomez said that no school in the district would take her, so she made long trips on city buses from South LA to a school in an unfamiliar neighborhood. She was often late and dealt with "hood politics"—hostility from other students because she wasn't from the area. "I was eventually kicked out of there for having so many tardies and encounters with other students," she said.

"By the middle of my sophomore year I didn't have a school to go to and I had given up," Gomez continued. "I just didn't want to go to school, even though I really, deeply loved to learn. I was a valedictorian of my eighth-grade class but had a lot of dreams that were taken away. My schools never even knew that my older sister had been murdered by her boyfriend and my other sister shot by him, right in front of me when I was only twelve. I was dealing with all of that pain by myself. And all the time I was struggling with anger management and transportation issues and no one ever asked me what they could do to help." She eventually enrolled in the LA Unified School District's only independent study program. "I'm very proud to say I graduated in 2008," she said to applause and cheers.

~

The newly formed Fix School Discipline Policy Coalition met for the first time in December 2011 and—in a remarkably fast pace—drafted ten proposed statewide school discipline reform laws that month. Several of the coalition members then went to work securing legislative sponsors. By February 2012, various lawmakers agreed to sponsor and introduce the bills.

Now advocates needed to start changing the minds and hearts of lawmakers. The goal was to get the reform laws passed by both chambers and on Governor Jerry Brown's desk by September 2012. Lee, with Fight Crime, started by recruiting prominent sheriffs, police chiefs, district attorneys, and others to make the case for reducing suspension rates as a dropout- and crime-prevention strategy.[10] One police chief told legislators, "Kids who aren't in school are instead likely to be getting 'schooled' out on the streets, with the wrong crowd." They cited research demonstrating "that by increasing graduation rates by 10 percentage points we could prevent 400 murders and over 20,000 aggravated assaults in California each year"[11] (and 3,400 murders and 170,000 aggravated assaults in the United States annually[12]). Lawmakers didn't expect calls to reform school discipline policies from the "tough on crime" crowd, and they had a powerful influence.

In 2012, both chambers in the California legislature were controlled by Democrats, as was the governorship. With that makeup, reform legislation usually has good prospects, said Fight Crime's Lee, but not for this batch of bills. "This issue wasn't as easy as your typical progressive issue," he said. "There wasn't uniform support even among Democrats for it initially. Part of that was because the solutions we were talking about were setting statewide policy that limited discretion of teachers and administrators, who are often close to Democratic legislators," Lee said. In addition, most people assumed that schools suspended kids who deserved it. Eventually, though, Fight Crime won over several initially reluctant Democratic lawmakers.

The rigorous data from the 2011 Texas study, "Breaking Schools' Rules," helped significantly in changing minds. The advocates told California lawmakers that 60 percent of Texas students of all races in a three-year period had been suspended or expelled at least once between seventh and twelfth grades, yet only 3 percent of those disciplines were mandated because of the severity of the violation, such as possessing a weapon or selling drugs. The rest were "discretionary offenses," many related to common behaviors such as truancy, talking back, dress code violations, and schoolyard skirmishes.[13]

To add California-specific data to the talking points, the Endowment searched for the latest statewide statistics on suspensions and expulsions. It turned out that researchers at the Civil Rights Project, which had moved from Harvard to the University of California, Los Angeles, were just then poring over school discipline rates around the country, which the US Department of Education had released a few weeks earlier, and they were drilling down on California statistics.

Typically the group's reports take several months to prepare, but bolstered by an Endowment grant, the UCLA researchers sped up the time line. Six weeks later, in April 2012, they finished it. "We worked day and night. It was crazy," recalled Tia Martinez, an attorney and one of the Civil Rights Project's researchers.

The 2012 UCLA report, called "Suspended Education in California," didn't disappoint. It revealed previously unreported aspects of school discipline practices in the Golden State, including one statistic that shocked everyone: in the 2011 school year, California had suspended more than 400,000 students compared with giving high school diplomas to 382,500.[14] "The sound bite from me being that 'We are suspending more kids than we're graduating in a year.' Amazing," said Daniel Zingale, the head of the BHC statewide team, who works from its Sacramento office in an historic brick building across the street from the state capitol.

The UCLA report also detailed how "nearly 1 out of every 5 African American students, 1 in 9 American Indian students, and 1 in 13 Latino students in California were suspended at least once, compared to 1 in 17 white students and 1 in 35 Asian American students."[15] Ten districts in the state actually suspended one-fourth of the student body every year. Another troubling statistic was that nearly half of the suspensions issued in California the previous two years had been under "willful defiance," the subjective, behavioral category that doesn't involve any crimes.[16]

Like Faer with the Public Counsel Law Center, direct experience inspired UCLA researcher Martinez to embrace school discipline reform. Earlier in her career, she had worked with homeless youth in the San Francisco Bay Area; by age twenty-five, many of those youth were cut off from educational institutions and the labor market. She found that "over and over again, suspension from school mattered," as these homeless kids were repeatedly disciplined and most dropped out. She's also a passionate advocate for ensuring that all students graduate from high school. "It really is our one big, free universal system which is about developing people's strengths," said Martinez.

~

The UCLA report's troubling statistics, especially the disproportionate suspensions by race, along with the sheer number of kids thrown out of school, began to win bipartisan support among more lawmakers. "The fact that these racial disparities were so high was very powerful to people," Fight Crime's Lee said. "And just the general sense of 'Wait, do these suspensions really make sense?'"

The Endowment then funded a major ad campaign, trumpeting that new statistic—more than 400,000 suspended annually versus 382,500 graduating—in newspaper ads, in TV and radio spots, and on billboards and posters, especially in the Sacramento area as legislators were preparing to vote on the bills, either in committee or on the floor. The Endowment also commissioned a statewide poll on views toward school discipline and found that four out of five people polled supported changes. Nine in ten backed a preventative approach such as restorative justice, which focuses on reconciliation and accountability,[17] and "positive behavior intervention support," a school-wide strategy for improving behavior and school climate.[18] Those polling statistics also ended up in ad campaigns, including the tagline, "80 percent of Californians want to fix school discipline. Do you?" Another group in the coalition, Children Now, contacted thousands of children's advocates around the state, urging them to call and write to their representatives in support of the proposed laws.

All this activity led to a new round of media coverage during a critical time in the spring of 2012, when legislative hearings would begin on the proposed bills. For the first time, advocates' demands for school discipline reform and new data on the high rates of suspensions and expulsions made the pages of newspapers and onto broadcast news shows statewide.

With little or no prompting, hundreds of young people in the BHC sites also wrote letters to lawmakers and initiated an online petition, in short order gathering fifteen thousand signatures in support of the discipline reform bills and sending the petition to the governor. As part of a BHC summer training program in youth leadership and community engagement, a couple hundred teenagers arrived by bus in Sacramento and visited numerous lawmakers in their state capitol offices to ask for their support for the proposed laws (visits that often delighted—and influenced—the legislators, several later said).

To their relief, the Fix School Discipline Policy Coalition found little resistance to the bills. They figured that a battle to defeat two ballot propositions on different matters had distracted the California Teachers Association, the most potent source of opposition. After a few modifications, the ten bills actually won the support of the California School Boards Association and the Association of California School Administrators. The bills addressed everything from rules on charter school discipline policies to improving state data collection on school disciplines, restricting suspension or expulsion for willful defiance, adult advocacy for foster youth facing discipline, and opening the door for expelled students or those in the juvenile justice system to return to school.

State legislators held numerous hearings on the topic—most were in Sacramento, but several were in other communities—and each time, students and others came out to urge lawmakers to support the new bills. Young people gave moving, raw testimony at all the hearings, telling of punishments that left them bewildered, hurt, rejected by their schools, and fearful about their futures. The chair of one of the committees, Steven Bradford, a Democrat from Los Angeles, told me after a hearing in Sacramento, "Many times I looked around and there was not a dry eye on the committee listening to these young folks tell their stories."

~

After maintaining a furious pace for months, the coalition members braced themselves for the legislative votes in the summer of 2012, and they rejoiced when their efforts paid off. Of the ten school discipline reform bills, state legislators approved seven. Two of them passed with unanimous Democratic and Republican support; one that gave school districts more discretion in determining their truancy policies and another that ensured that a social worker or an attorney was present when a foster youth was facing expulsion.

Sacramento veterans couldn't recall a package of bills being written and passed by both chambers so quickly and then landing on the governor's desk. "I was not expecting that level of speed," said the Endowment's Ross, reflecting on the campaign two years later when we talked in 2014. "It's a combination of two things," he said. "One is when civic leaders and policy makers actually heard the facts about school pushout and suspension, they were shocked."

Second, Ross said lawmakers understood the economic risk to the state if so many teenagers fail to graduate. Businesses got it, too. "When I laid out the research showing that kids who get suspended even once have a higher risk of dropping out and not attending a four-year college, all of a sudden the civic leaders are saying, 'Wait a minute, that's my workforce!'" Ross said. In California, where six in ten are people of color and nearly three-fourths of those are under eighteen, it's a particularly grave concern. A comparable demographic trend holds true nationwide, according to some estimates.[19]

Now the reform advocates faced the final hurdle as they awaited the governor's decision on whether to sign the seven bills. During that tense interim, Endowment staff came up with another idea: hold a public hearing on the issue featuring national and state civil rights and education leaders to keep elevating the profile of the issue and to get the governor's attention.

The foundation organized and hosted the hearing in Los Angeles on September 10, 2012. The event was cosponsored by the US Department of Education Office of Civil Rights, the California Department of Education, and the State Attorney General's Office. Several prominent officials spoke, although the most powerful testimony came from young advocates.[20] A sophomore named Timothy Walker from a South LA high school shared a story with the crowd. The teen, with close-cropped hair and wearing a blue polo shirt, was now a community organizer with one of the Endowment's major grantees in South LA, the Community Coalition, a longtime nonprofit organization known for running successful community organizing campaigns.

"I'm going to start by sharing with you all an incident that happened just a few weeks ago," Walker said from the podium. "Shawn, a student at a South LA high school, was hanging out in the quad area on campus. He had taken his uniform shirt off because of the heat. The principal approach him and asked him to put the uniform shirt back on. He refused, and in response the principal called the school police. The police officer showed up and grabbed Shawn by the arm. Shawn tried to get him off and the officer accused Shawn of hitting him and then proceeded to call eight other cops for backup. As a result of Shawn's interaction with police he was expelled from school. His mother had to advocate on his behalf to get him readmitted back into school. He just came back last Tuesday after missing two weeks of school."

Cameron Ponn, a young Cambodian man born and raised in Long Beach, spoke next. Overcoming a brief bout of nervousness, he said that more than one-third of Cambodians in the region don't have high school diplomas and that his older brother and sister dropped out and predicted he would, too. He almost did, feeling "unmotivated and unloved" on campus. Two-thirds of Cambodians in the area also suffer from posttraumatic stress disorder from living through a genocide campaign in their homeland, Cameron added, and he also copes with the lasting trauma of watching his cousin get shot during a drive-by shooting and then dying in his arms. Cameron paused to compose himself. He then told the crowd that one day during his senior year he forgot to bring his notebook to his English class, and he was told by his teacher to leave.

"My teacher didn't let me back in the class and dropped me," Cameron said. "It was a week before graduation, and my counselor told me I wouldn't be able to walk at graduation because of this one class. I got an F, and I had to go to summer school and make up the class. I passed the class with a B," he said firmly. "And I picked up my diploma. I felt happy that I graduated but also felt sad because after trying so hard I didn't get the opportunity to walk with my friends. I am the first in my family to graduate and go to college," he continued, as loud applause and cheering broke out. He said a BHC-funded men's leadership program that he attended during high school "helped me build my confidence, helped me build my leadership skills, and most of all treated me like family and helped me get into college," bringing more whoops from the crowd.

In the end, in late September 2012, Brown approved five of the bills, including the two that secured unanimous bipartisan support. It was historic legislation, the first-of-its-kind set of school discipline reform laws in California. Prior to the campaign, Brown, like other Sacramento lawmakers, had been unaware of the high rates of suspensions in California schools, and at first he didn't even believe it. Coalition members, however, showed the governor the reams of data, and he heard the youth testimony. It reached receptive ears, especially because as mayor of Oakland Brown had launched a school for students with discipline problems.

The new laws would require districts to consider suspension and expulsion only after trying other ways to correct students' behavior; to clarify that it's not mandatory to expel students who bring toy weapons, over-the-counter medicines, or their own prescriptions to school; to encourage schools to leave law enforcement out when addressing truancy; to affirm the right of students to return to school after time in the juvenile justice system; and to require the presence of a social worker or an attorney when foster children face expulsion so that they have an advocate willing to speak up on their behalf.

The coalition members were disappointed that the governor vetoed a bill that would have limited school's ability to suspend students for "willful defiance or disruption of school activities." It was the measure that could have most profoundly changed discipline policies, but Brown said he was reluctant to limit the authority of local school leaders.

He also vetoed a bill that would have required training for schools in which 25 percent or more of students had been suspended. After the bill's veto, however, the California Endowment simply funded training programs for the high-suspending districts, which were open to the instruction. "So we won it after all," said Lee.

~

The quest to rein in willful defiance suspensions was only just beginning. The next year, in 2013, the LA Unified School District board made history when it voted five to two to ban suspensions solely for willful defiance, becoming the largest district nationwide to do so. Students at the school board meeting—most from BHC sites in the LA region—erupted into applause after the vote.

Briana Lamb, seventeen at the time, worked on the LA school district campaign with the Community Coalition in South Los Angeles. Briana didn't expect the ban to pass because the votes kept changing, but she and others desperately wanted it to. "It's important because for South LA students, we already have so many things that slow down our progress," said the African American teenager. Although she said she was never suspended, "I've seen a lot of our friends expelled and suspended for no reason, and failing in class." Many times she said it's for infractions like chewing gum in class or students putting their heads down because they don't feel well. "Very often they're depressed, if you take the time and ask them what's going on at home," she added. After the ban on suspensions for willful defiance in Los Angeles schools passed, her confidence soared in the ability of young people to create major change. "I tell my friends, 'You can have power,'" she said.

Alfonso Aguilar, who was sixteen during the campaign and lives across the street from the Community Coalition, said, "When it passed, I jumped up in the boardroom. It was such a beautiful moment. Some lady said we just made history," he said with a broad smile.

That such a large school district passed a willful defiance ban made it easier for reform advocates to keep pressing for a statewide one in subsequent years. Finally, in 2014, they made headway when Brown signed a "watered-down" bill restricting willful defiance disciplines, said Lee with Fight Crime. It was nonetheless a big victory, considering the governor's previous veto. But even the modified version made history, as California became the first state in the United States to limit the discretion of teachers and principals for this offense. It prohibited suspensions for defiance in kindergarten through third grade (although it ended expulsions for this offense for all K–12 students), and its backers estimated that it would keep more than ten thousand students in school each year.[21]

In all, since the BHC coalition in 2011 embarked on its ongoing campaign, eleven new laws reforming school discipline have taken effect. Since then, suspensions and expulsions have plunged in schools throughout the state. From the 2011–2012 school year to 2016–2017, suspensions declined by 46 percent, translating into 327,857 fewer suspensions in 2016–2017 compared with five years earlier, according to the California Department of Education. Similarly, expulsions decreased by 42 percent, dropping from about 9,800 to 5,700.[22] To answer concerns that perhaps this reduction in discipline has compromised academics, research indicates that declining suspension rates are linked to higher academic achievement.[23]

And the BHC school discipline coalition hasn't given up on banning or further restricting suspensions for willful defiance, although the latest version of a bill addressing that was still pending in the legislature when this book went to press.

~

Those involved in the reform work, however, also realize that dismantling zero-tolerance policies is only half the answer. The other half is improving adult guidance and support to students who are indeed acting up, but aren't committing crimes such as carrying weapons and dealing drugs. (The latter still lead to campus exclusion or referrals to the juvenile justice system.)

Fight Crime notes that teachers cite "help in classroom management as one of their top two professional development needs. Teachers clearly need support and a range of responses for dealing with student misbehavior."[24] The group advocates several options, including restorative justice programs, social-emotional skills curriculum, and "positive behavioral interventions and supports," which establish campus-wide expectations for behavior and reward students for following them.

Ross said that after the Endowment embarked on school discipline reform, teacher and education associations began inviting him to speak at their gatherings, a first for him as a pediatrician and a health foundation executive. As he entered this new milieu, he also recognized the divisiveness inherent in education reform politics. During those speeches, he would emphasize to the audience that, in striving to eliminate overly punitive school disciplines, "we were not taking an approach of blaming the teachers. There's enough piling on of teachers."

Instead, Ross would tell them, "'We know the constraints and the strain you're under just doing your day job teaching kids. We know you agree that when these kids act out in school, it is the sign of a deeper problem. But we also know the tools at your disposal to support and manage kids like this are limited. And so let's see what we can do about doing a better job for these supports for not only the kids, but for you.'

"And that conversation," Ross added, "resonated a lot better than, you know, 'bad teachers who don't care about the kids.'"

To transform campuses, the BHC sites are taking advantage of a revolutionary funding system for California public schools approved in 2013 by the governor that diverts billions of dollars to low-income school districts. This "local control funding formula" gives school districts more autonomy over state funds and additional money based on the number of low-income, foster youth, and English language learners. The law also mandates community engagement in deciding on some of the spending. At the BHC sites, teams have organized residents to request more funding for supportive programs, and they're making significant progress. School districts are also increasingly recognizing the value of these changes.

For example, at one San Diego elementary school, Cherokee Point, described in chapter 9, the principal adopted a deeply empathic approach toward student misbehavior. Since he began in 2008, suspensions have plummeted to zero among the nearly six hundred students, and teacher and staff satisfaction has soared. The result so impressed the school board that it is using this new state funding source to implement the same practices district-wide.

"The staff are sold" on the approach, said Godwin Higa, principal of Cherokee Point, "and they wouldn't allow a principal to come in and be punitive."

CHAPTER 5

A Safe Place to Play

When Terry Stanley was seventeen, he joined a campaign to build a skate park in City Heights, a low-income neighborhood in central San Diego. The slender, brown-haired teenager loved skateboarding, but there was nowhere to practice except on sidewalks, streets, parking lots, and alleyways or by sneaking onto school grounds after hours. Visiting the closest skate park 5 miles away took an hour by skateboard, and he couldn't afford bus fare. More importantly, once he and his friends got there, the local kids kept them on edge, and fights broke out a few times. "It was always a hostile kind of environment," Stanley said. "Like a tension or fear. If we wanted to skate and improve our skills, we had to find a place to do that," said Stanley, who was born in City Heights. The sport, which he took up at age twelve, was a prized outlet for him. "Skating to me is like a form of art, to escape reality and just to be creative."

For three decades, parents and youth in City Heights had wanted a local park for skateboarding, a sport that started in the 1940s as a way of "surfing" on land. The city had built more than thirty skate parks elsewhere in San Diego by 2010, so why not City Heights, too? The nearly 7-square-mile City Heights neighborhood—home to 95,000 people—isn't just deficient in skate parks, it's short of any open space.

San Diego as a whole enjoys ample places to relax and recreate, a generous 36 acres of parkland per 1,000 residents, yet in the city's crowded
City Heights neighborhood, a 6-mile drive from downtown San Diego,
that figure plummets to 1.5 acres per 1,000 residents.[1] Still, parks for
City Heights hadn't been a priority for the city council, which had
directed much of its attention to downtown and the wealthier north
San Diego.[2]

At the time he joined the skate park campaign, spearheaded by a newly
formed group called the Youth Council, in 2011, Stanley was also in
trouble: he was on probation for charges related to unauthorized entry
at age fifteen into a middle school to skateboard. Besides joining an
effort to create a local park where skateboarders could legally and safely
practice, he was grateful for the welcome of the group, some fifty kids
and a few adult leaders, who saw him as an asset, not a wayward kid.

"I had a 6 o'clock curfew, I was being drug tested, I was seen as like
a bad student or youth," said Stanley. "And that's why I *loved* the Youth
Council, because at that space I wasn't seen as that. I was seen as useful."
It turns out that his entanglement in the legal system wasn't unique—
many skateboarders report numerous brushes with police for skating in
unsanctioned places[3]—although he got into more trouble than usual
because other kids damaged property while he was on site.

The Youth Council is run by the Mid-City Community Advocacy
Network (Mid-City CAN), Building Healthy Communities' anchor
nonprofit partner in San Diego. Mid-City CAN takes the lead locally
among a collaboration of nonprofit organizations driving the work of
the campaign, most of which are funded by the California Endowment
in the same arrangement as in the other thirteen BHC sites. Mid-City
CAN organizes residents into "momentum teams" to pursue priorities
set by the community. The model has proven so effective that it's now
practiced in all the other sites, although they use different names, most
commonly "action team."

~

City Heights, named for its 400-foot elevation, was a largely white, middle-class neighborhood in the 1950s. Then, in the 1960s and 1970s, city leaders passed policies promoting high-density housing, also called "infill," in City Heights. Apartment buildings replaced single-family homes, and multifamily units now comprise 60 percent of the housing, compared with 9 percent in 1950.[4] Demographics then shifted, starting with an influx of South Vietnamese in 1974 followed by waves of refugees fleeing threats from other countries. More than thirty languages are spoken in City Heights, with a population that's 54 percent Hispanic, 19 percent Asian, 13 percent black, 12 percent white, and 2 percent multiracial.[5]

City leaders backing the higher density hadn't planned on the passage by California voters of Proposition 13, the 1978 property-tax-cutting initiative, however. Prop 13 cut deeply into tax revenue, curtailing city maintenance in the increasingly packed City Heights area, and conditions began deteriorating. In a 1984 article in the *San Diego Union*, Kim Kilkenney, a legislative analyst for the Construction Industry Federation, was quoted as saying, "There was lots of infill on the assumption that the services were there. Well, the services weren't there."[6] Crime also began to spike in the 1970s, and by 1990, it was so bad that the city of San Diego declared a state of emergency in City Heights.

In 2014, the median income in City Heights was $36,000 versus $63,000 for San Diego County.[7] Children in City Heights are heavier and less fit on average than children elsewhere in San Diego County. The toll of diabetes is particularly stark. The diabetes death rate in the City Heights area is 138 per 100,000 deaths versus the countywide rate of 17 per 100,000.[8] In addition, those in San Diego County's top quartile of income can expect to live ten years longer than those in the bottom quartile, where many City Heights residents fall.[9]

The Youth Council skate park campaign started after the skateboarding accident of one of its members, then-sixteen-year-old Marcos

Olascoaga, galvanized the council's determination to open a local facility. The driver of an SUV hadn't seen Olascoaga skateboarding on
the sidewalk, and the driver gunned the gas while exiting an alleyway,
catapulting Olascoaga into the street.[10] Luckily, the stunned and shaken
teen didn't have any broken bones or internal injuries, but he still has
scars on his hip and one arm.

Mark Tran, then the youth organizer on staff with Mid-City CAN,
focused on empowering the young people to run the skate park campaign on their own ingenuity and ideas. He trained them in community organizing and research skills in a conference room off El Cajon
Boulevard, a busy City Heights thoroughfare. The conference room was
designed to fit eighteen people, although sometimes as many as forty
crammed in, along with boxes of pizzas. One lesson that Leslie Renteria, who joined the campaign at age fourteen, distinctly remembers
was called Power Analysis, which helped her understand who had the
authority in the city to make decisions relevant to their campaign.

~

Tran said the best training actually took place inside city chambers,
where team members witnessed civic decision making in action. At first,
a few built up the nerve to approach the podium and ask for support
for a skate park in City Heights. Then others got emboldened. "They
were like, 'Hey, I want to get up next time. I want to talk to our city
council members,'" Tran said. He never gave them a script, and the
young people expressed their own views. He did coach them to stay
persistent. "Demonstrate that you can't ignore us, because we're going to
keep coming back. We're going to keep asking you and pressuring you
until you take us seriously," Tran told them. The teenagers—and most
were teens, with the exception of a few even younger—embraced the
lessons on the mechanics of driving community change.

Tran also built their confidence in speaking to the city's power brokers. "Mark kept telling us, 'Your voices matter, your voices matter. Just speak up,'" said Jose Hernandez, a former Youth Council member.

The Youth Council first zeroed in on city meetings discussing a rare new park in crowded City Heights, this one a "minipark" slated for construction on a 0.65-acre plot of land three blocks off University Avenue, one of the main thoroughfares. Youth Council members argued for features for skateboarders in a small section of the proposed park. City representatives were slow to accept these ideas, but after the youth kept up their attendance and advocacy, the panels involved in the decision changed course: to the team's jubilation, the city announced that it *would* include skate park features in the new Central Avenue Mini Park. Letdown swiftly followed, though: there was no actual funding to build the skate park. Instead, city planners relegated it to "phase 2" of the project, with no completion date specified. "Which we know never gets done," added Stanley.

They weren't going to let this unprecedented opportunity—an actual skateboard-friendly City Heights park on the drawing boards—pass without a fight, however. They also realized that they shouldn't give up on their dream for a full-size skate park. There were more than enough skateboarders to keep two parks busy.

To elevate the issue, they decided on a new tactic. As two candidates competed for the San Diego City Council's new District 9 seat, which includes City Heights, the youth staged a "Candidates Forum" in May 2012. A member of the youth team and the editor of the online *Voice of San Diego* moderated the forum, and the team posted four three-by-five-foot "pledge cards" listing four priorities for the neighborhood's youth, including funding for a new skate park. They asked each candidate to promise to support the priorities if he or she won the seat. Marti Emerald, a tall, outgoing woman who had spent thirty years as a television news reporter in San Diego, won the race and supported them from the start. "I really admired the work they put into their advocacy," she said. The week after the forum, which was covered in the media, another city council member agreed to support their campaign, so now they had at least two San Diego City Council allies. Given that the nine-person city council represents nearly 1.4 million people and faces intense demands for resources, that support was essential.

Emerald was delighted when the youth descended on her office to make sure she kept her pledge. "They came marching on City Hall with their skateboards under their arms and crowded into my office," said Emerald, a two-term council member who retired in 2016. "I loved it, it was wonderful. They knew what they wanted and needed, and they had a very clear and righteous message around it."

What was especially refreshing for Emerald was how the teenagers came in with a specific plan rather than asking the city to solve their problem. And although they were articulate with their requests, they were appreciative. "These kids just came in and said, 'Okay, here are our priorities. Let's get to work. And thank you, *thank you* for listening,'" she said. "So it became a really, really enjoyable and very successful partnership. It's also a blueprint for how government and the community *should* work together." Behind the scenes, Emerald also began advocating for the skate park with city staff and with other elected officials in San Diego.

~

The Youth Council still faced an unspoken deadline: if funding wasn't identified soon, the minipark construction would begin without a skate plaza, and the phase 2 proposal for it shelved as city planners moved on to other projects. So the team members came up with another idea: stage a rally to revive momentum. It took place in December 2012 at Cherokee Point Elementary School in City Heights, where the principal, Godwin Higa, was a big supporter. To the team's surprise, more than three hundred people showed up, and media coverage spread the word that residents in a low-income San Diego community were demanding resources for a skate park. Unexpected support also came from high places: the newly sworn-in mayor came and promised to help, and he introduced the phrase, "¡Skate se puede!," which a few thought a bit corny, but it caught on. Richard Barrera, president of the San Diego Unified School District's Board of Education, told the crowd, "We support you 100 percent."[11] The rally revived the campaign, and Hernandez, the Youth Council member, marveled at the caliber of the support. "We actually had authority figures saying, 'Yes, we support you.' That's all it took to change other people's minds," he said.

After more long nights at city meetings, the Youth Council members got their win. An obviously supportive city department delivered extraordinary news to the young team members. Its leadership had identified a huge pot of unused funds—$847,000—that had been designated for a now defunct project, and they were authorized to transfer it to the minipark project to pay for the skate park features. Brian Schoenfisch, senior planner with the city's Development Services, later said that the funding was a direct result of the Youth Council's work. "The kids were really brilliant in how they brought it to the city's attention," he said.[12] Two months later, council member Emerald organized a media event announcing the funding deal. Stanley, now a leader in the campaign, was the keynote speaker.

The city held a groundbreaking ceremony for the smaller skate plaza, which would occupy just over one-fifth of the 0.65-acre park. News articles featured a smiling Stanley, along with Emerald and six others, all wearing white hard hats and poised with shovels in the ground. At last City Heights would have a park for skating, scheduled for completion in 2015. (In another lesson in patience, however, the project was delayed more than a year due to problems with the contractor. The skate plaza finally opened in June 2016.)

～

Although the Youth Council members celebrated the minipark success, they kept up pressure for a larger park. They continued with the familiar pace of attending long public meetings, usually on school nights, seeking approval and funding. (By the end of the campaign, the teens had attended roughly twenty-five city meetings.) Once again, glorious news came unexpectedly in June 2014, thanks to behind-the-scenes efforts of city officials impressed with the young people's efforts. Council member Emerald, now an enthusiastic champion of the cause, announced that the city had won a $4.5 million state grant it had applied for to build a larger skate park in City Heights as well as one in a nearby community that also needed one.

Yet again a huge hurdle emerged: the Youth Council didn't have approval for the only site that could accommodate the larger skate park (there was no other nearby suitable location), and many neighbors adamantly opposed building it there. Because the $4.5 million grant had an expiration date, that opposition could derail the youth team's dream. To build support among neighbors, Youth Council members started knocking on doors, fanning out for a mile around the proposed site.

Those encounters were the low point in the campaign for Leslie Renteria. "Some people refused to sign the petition, saying 'Why would we want young people here? They're just going to come in and vandalize.' Typical stereotype of what a young skater would be," she said. The young canvassers were trained to listen to neighbors' concerns, share the skateboarders' perspective, and see if a compromise was possible. Some neighbors were worried that the skate park would displace grassy areas used for various activities, and they wanted more trees for shade and more benches. So the Youth Council updated its preferred plan for the park to include those amenities. "That helped bring some residents in, because we have the same goals," Tran said, adding that the young people "wanted a facility that serves everybody."

Other neighbors remained adamantly opposed, however. "I knew they were going to fight it. And they did," Renteria said. In one city meeting, a speaker described skateboarders as "undesirable outsiders who should make better use of their time in a library" and expressed fears of a park overrun with graffiti taggers, pot smokers, and trash. About fifty young people showed up for the critical public meeting for this larger skate park, in December 2014, wearing blue "Mid-City CAN" T-shirts. During the meeting someone also declared, "Skate parks belong in industrial areas!" Others echoed the fear of vandalism and damage to the neighborhood.[13]

Renteria, who was sitting in the back, felt her indignation rising. "Everyone was really against it," Renteria said. But she knew from experience—and from a first-of-its-kind, rigorous study on the health effects of a skate park in City Heights—that these facilities brought numerous benefits to communities and that negative, unfounded stereotypes largely fueled the alarm.

So she spoke up. She calmly told the crowd that there was data to counter the assertions, describing a health impact assessment that was available online. "And if you want it, we can email it to you," she added. Many inquired about the study. Renteria was referring to "A Health Impact Assessment of a Skate Park in City Heights," a study released a few months earlier prepared by Human Impact Partners, a research organization in Oakland, and paid for by the California Endowment.[14]

The study, one of the few to actually look at the health benefits of skateboarding, not just the risk of injury or law enforcement encounters, emphasized that skateboarding is an excellent form of exercise that increases strength, balance, and coordination. Cultivating skateboarding skills also builds self-esteem and confidence, which contribute to stronger cognitive development, goal orientation, and general well-being, the study noted. Nor is skateboarding a big-budget pursuit, as it requires no uniforms or team fees, nor scheduling headaches. It's also a way for young people not drawn to organized sports to develop a sense of camaraderie and social belonging, another powerful long-term health promoter. The assessment did find that the benefits accrue unequally based on gender, with girls often feeling excluded or not treated as serious skaters by male skaters. Female skateboarders said, however, that connecting with other girls doing the same ameliorated that sense of exclusion, and a skate park did make that connection easier.

When the time came for the vote, the youth held their breath and then rejoiced at the outcome: unanimously in favor of approving the skate park location. "There were a lot of smiles, wide, grinning smiles," recalled Tran. "High-fives, hugs. People shed some tears, too. Tears of joy."

Renteria credits the health study in overcoming the final hurdle and giving the youth a powerful tool for responding to critics. "We needed something official to make it concrete," she said. "Here are numbers that will prove our point." Tran agreed. "That changed the tide. Especially for the decision makers," he said.

Earthmovers started tearing into the ground for the new 19,000-square-foot skate park in August 2016, located at Park de la Cruz in City Heights. It opened in January 2018, and the surrounding park also got a new picinic area, walking path upgrades, and a solar canopy.[15]

~

I met with several participants in the campaign at the new smaller skate plaza, which had opened less than a year earlier. Stanley and Renteria were among them, along with Tran, who had left his position as youth organizer at Mid-City CAN to work full time on the BHC campaign in City Heights.

On a breezy spring day in 2017, we sat at a round white picnic table, with skateboarders whizzing behind us on various structures, turning adroitly in the air. Traffic on the I-15 freeway rumbled a few hundred yards away, and we later walked over a pedestrian bridge to view the construction activity under way at the larger skate park on the opposite side of the freeway. There, large machinery and workers in hardhats moved about the long, linear site.

I asked if any of them grew weary of the long public meetings. Jose Hernandez said he found them interesting, and Stanley said they just practiced patience and resolve. "We had to wait, we just had to battle it out. It's not like, 'This isn't going to happen,' but more of, 'When is it going to happen, and how is it going to happen?' And that's what kept pushing us."

They all smiled broadly, looking around at the busy skate plaza, knowing it was the result of their hard work, persistence, and realization that they could actually alter decisions by city leaders, even as teenagers. They credited Tran for cultivating their belief in their own power and agency. "It has made me the person who I am. I can really say that," said Renteria, who is now attending the University of California, Merced, studying public health. "We are who we are because of Mark," said Stanley, who was working full time as the staff youth organizer at Mid-City CAN, in the BHC-funded position Tran once held. Stanley plans to attend college and pursue community work as an organizer or a politician.

Marcos Olascoaga, who left the campaign in its early years to attend college in Chico, California, watched it from afar. Olascoaga graduated in June 2017 with a double major in Latin American studies and Spanish. After earning his teaching credentials, he hopes to move back to City Heights to work.

Daniela Barron, who was sixteen when she joined the skate park campaign, is still on the Youth Council and is studying sociology and Spanish in college. Barron said the Youth Council's latest campaign entailed disrupting the "school-to-prison" pipeline by opening doors for juvenile justice-involved youth to get back to school and graduate. The Youth Council was also working on a campaign to influence the selection of San Diego's chief of police, a process open to public comment.

Hernandez is also in college, studying sociology, and plans to parlay his community organizing experience into a career in state or international level organizing. "Good goals, man," said Tran.

The Tony Hawk Foundation now assists several BHC sites in their skate park quests, which are the most requested amenity in parks in the BHC initiative.[16] After the City Heights victory, the city council of Arvin, a small Kern County town in California's Central Valley, in October 2015 approved $400,000 for a skate park following a campaign organized by the Kern County BHC coalition.[17] In Fresno, a 15,000-square-foot skate park opened in May 2016 after a BHC campaign there, and several other BHC sites led successful drives to open skate parks.

These projects are among nearly six hundred skate parks nationwide that the Tony Hawk Foundation has helped fund, in partnership with government agencies and civic organizations, collectively hosting five million visitors annually. The central and northwest parts of the country host the highest ratio of skate parks compared with the local population, and the southeast has the lowest. More than four hundred skate parks opened in the United States after the Tony Hawk Foundation provided advocacy training and support to local residents, a step that's often essential for winning approval. And, as the foundation stated on its website, the experience can be uplifting for participants. "The process of getting a park teaches kids in the community valuable lessons about perseverance, and that working with their city leaders can be a positive experience."[18]

~

In Fresno, a powerful and sustained city parks campaign yielded far more than a skate park, although it secured one as well. Launching what would become perhaps the most substantial success in expanding park access in the BHC endeavor, in 2011 six nonprofit organizations collaborated to demand parity in parklands in poorer and older neighborhoods in Fresno's south and west sides. These areas had far fewer parks than the wealthier north area, and those they did have weren't as well maintained.

Efrain Botello, a twenty-year-old involved in BHC youth development work in Fresno, a city of 500,000 in California's inland agricultural region, grew up experiencing the discrepancy. Botello said he relishes the opportunity to play in fields in north Fresno. "The maintenance on the grass is wonderful. I wish there was something like that in Southeast Fresno, closer to me, where I don't have to worry about, you know, having an injury because of the bad quality of the field."

"We pay taxes, too" was a key message by the coalition of parks advocates. Moreover, residents' health in these neighborhoods was suffering compared to the rest of the city, and they said a lack of park space was one reason. Nearly 40 percent of residents in that neighborhood are obese, compared with 28 percent statewide in California, and 35 percent consider themselves to be in fair or poor health, compared with 22 percent of resident statewide.[19]

The Fresno coalition's first major success came with a Fresno City Council meeting in 2012, which drew a standing-room-only crowd of three hundred. Most spoke in favor of approving an update to a city plan that would limit sprawl and would concentrate on developing more pedestrian- and bike-friendly neighborhoods. That update would benefit the older neighborhoods in the south and west that are part of the BHC campaigns and that had been neglected for years. One city official commended the preparation of the residents, with little repetition between the roughly eighty who spoke, and one council member lauded the rejuvenation of the "lost art of community organizing." The city council approved the city plan update supported by most of the speakers.[20]

The BHC coalition was pushing for far more, however. Specifically, they wanted an update to the city's Parks Master Plan, which is the blueprint for the city's management of its 1,500 acres of parkland. The master plan hadn't been revised since 1989, despite a legal mandate to do so far more often. So, in 2015, they decided to put pressure on city officials by running an ad using city data to show the city's park disparity and placing it on the sides of city buses running a north–south circuit.[21]

City officials, however, ignited an unintended firestorm by denying approval to run the ad, saying it ran afoul of city law banning political advertising "upon any bus or transit property."[22] The BHC-led coalition, through its lawyer, responded that the ad simply used the city's own recent data on park acreage by zip code in Fresno. But others opposed to the ad argued that even if it cited city-generated data, the stark message and imagery of the ad rendered it political. One city council member accused the BHC campaign of fostering racial divisiveness in Fresno,[23] and Endowment leadership in Los Angeles got more than one call objecting to the campaign's endeavors in Fresno.

The bus ad portrayed how neighborhoods in zip code 93706 in South Fresno had 1.02 acres of park per 1,000 residents—with half of a girl's face shown in black and white—whereas in zip code 93720 in North Fresno, residents enjoyed 4.62 acres of parkland per 1,000—with the other half of the girl's face shown in color. The words, "We need #OneHealthyFresno with better parks for all" ran under the image.

That kind of parkland disparity between low-income neighborhoods and more affluent ones nearby is actually commonplace, noted a study from the National Recreation and Parks Association, and is another aspect of the built environment that makes it harder for those living in some communities to attain levels of exercise essential for good health.[24]

Because of the city's objections, the ad never ran on the buses, but the ban triggered more publicity, and the local newspaper, the *Fresno Bee*, editorialized against the city's position.[25]

Then, in June 2015, the team members got what they wanted. The city council finally approved $450,000 to hire a consultant to develop a new Parks Master Plan, without which no serious citywide park analysis can take place.

Venise Curry, regional director for a nonprofit organization called the CNC Education Fund who led the Fresno parks team, said that toward the end of the campaign, support shifted throughout the city. "The rest of the community seemed to pick up on the idea that, you know, parks actually improve health. They improve your life. And they're really not that political," said Curry, a psychiatrist who regards parks as "preventive psychiatry."

In addition, to immediately fill needs for park space, the parks team opened up 340 acres of recreational land after advocating for a joint-use agreement with the school district. The Fresno City Council approved the $1.2 million deal in June 2016. Today sixteen school grounds throughout the city, including sites in the south and west sides, are open for resident use on weekends.

The parks team prioritizes the expansion of open space and parks and the rehabilitation of existing sites under the premise that no community can truly be healthy without places for safe outdoor recreation. As Adrian Benepe, director of city park development for the Trust for Public Land, a California-based nonprofit organization, wrote, "One of my favorite statistics says that 12 percent of all exercise takes place in a nearby park. But 50 percent of vigorous exercise—that's the heart-healthy, cardiovascular-aiding kind of exercise—takes place in a park. That's a pretty astounding thing."[26]

The Endowment funded a University of California, Los Angeles study on park access and physical activity and, unsurprisingly, confirmed that the closer that teenagers lived to a park, the more physically active they were. The study also reported that in low-income areas, teenagers were more likely to avoid parks—even ones close by—because they feared for their safety, and they were less physically active than those with safe parks easily available.[27]

~

That's just the scenario that one woman, Toody Maher, an entrepreneur turned park activist, decided to change in a city park, called Elm Playlot, in Richmond, California, in a notoriously dangerous neighborhood. It just struck her as wrong that children there should have to stay sequestered inside out of fear.

When Maher first visited Elm Playlot in early 2007, she saw a group of men lounging in the half-acre city park in the Iron Triangle neighborhood in Richmond, a city of 108,000 in the San Francisco Bay Area. This tough neighborhood, named after the railroad tracks that delineate its borders, is part of the BHC campaign there. Because of its reputation for crime and gun violence, outsiders usually avoid it. That year, the homicide rate would earn Richmond notoriety as one of the ten most dangerous cities in the United States.[28] A significant portion of that violence arose in the Iron Triangle, home to about 15,000, many of them families with children. Most of the residents are classified as low income, and 50 percent of children there live in poverty.[29] (In 2017, that meant earning $24,600 or less for a family of four.[30]) Parents rarely let their children outside to play.

As Maher looked more closely at the small park, she noticed the graffiti-covered jungle gym, the ground littered with empty liquor bottles, glass shards, empty gun shells, hypodermic needles, and rough patches of grass. A few dogs roamed off leash. "There were men just loitering, drinking, doing drugs. The swings were all chewed up because they trained these huge pit bulls on the swings, to improve lockjaw strength," Maher said.

Further depressing the scene was that most of the homes facing the park were abandoned, with trash piled in their front yards and auction notices and "Keep Out" signs tacked on plywood-covered windows. Bullet holes punctured a neighborhood stop sign, and fences were tagged with graffiti. One of the still-occupied homes, a brown two-story, was a drug house, she later learned. "So people would buy the drugs and then come hang out in the park," she said.

Maher, a tall, white woman who wears her medium brown hair in two braids, had a few years earlier bought a home on the other side of Richmond. After a successful business career, she had recently embarked on a quest to revitalize a playground in a neighborhood where children had none that were safe to use. She was touring the city's eight "playlots," which are parks smaller than an acre, to target her first park renovation project.

Maher spent her early years in Montreal, with parents who brought her and her brothers almost daily to nearby amenity-filled parks where she experienced the fun and adventure of outdoor activities with other children. Her parents formed friendships with neighbors at the park, and she later realized that people gravitate toward parks not only for enjoyment and relaxation, but also to connect with others. She began viewing parks as "power spots" in neighborhoods. Her father's job at a Brazilian airline meant that the family traveled the world, enjoying activities in numerous countries. But Maher also suffered from severe stuttering as a child, which cultivated her empathy for those outside the mainstream. That childhood challenge, though, was countered by her natural athleticism, and she excelled in various sports like surfing and volleyball, which she took up after her family moved to Los Angeles.

In the first part of her career, Maher launched various business endeavors, most notably at age twenty-three starting a distributorship for Swatch watches in the western United States. She then changed course to pursue her ideal career, that of creating enriched parklands for children and families in distressed neighborhoods. By enriched, she meant creative structures actually designed and built by local residents, all for good wages. In the years since that first visit, she founded and now runs a nonprofit organization in Richmond, called Pogo Park, which has drawn international attention and $16.2 million in grant money to date for Iron Triangle projects, with more than $1 million of it distributed as wages to residents. Her nonprofit organization is also a key member of the BHC coalition in Richmond, where she is lauded for pioneering a unique type of resident engagement that revived a broken local park.

During that first visit to Elm Playlot in 2007, however, Maher was still sizing it up as a candidate. It was a daunting prospect, despite the desperate need for a playground in a neighborhood filled with families. In one poignant moment, a few children leaned out of an upstairs window of one of the few occupied homes across from the park, and one called out, "Why are you taking pictures of the park?"

"I'm thinking of making the park better," Maher called back.

"And they came running out, little black kids, and they were saying, 'Well, you could do this, or you could do that!'" recalled Maher. Their mother briefly joined them and then went back into the house and returned with a bucket filled with broken glass and bottles. "This is the glass I had to pick up from around the picnic table there, just for a birthday cake at the table for my son," she told Maher.

No children were in the park that day; the neighborhood children weren't only scared of the men, but of the loose dogs that chased them. "When I was leaving, the kids leaned out the window and they shouted, 'We hope you pick this park!' And I thought as I drove away, 'That's so sad, but there's just no way. This is too insane. It's too difficult. It just broke my heart, because they're right. But I'm like, nope. This neighborhood has too much going on to overcome,'" said Maher.

Still, even as she considered other park sites in Richmond, something else tugged at her about that half-acre park: the five stately sycamore trees towering over it, casting shade on the benches and picnic tables scattered about. "The key asset of this park is the trees," Maher said.

Trees are few in the neighborhood, and some people call the small seventy-year-old park the "old-growth forest of the Iron Triangle." It was also near an elementary school and was thus easily accessible for hundreds of children.

So she steeled her resolve, pushed her misgivings aside, and against huge odds began plotting Elm Playlot's rejuvenation.

The California Endowment was Maher's principal early supporter, before she had any track record with her newly launched nonprofit organization. She called the organization Pogo Park because it invoked a sense of fun. (Creating some confusion, Elm Playlot is sometimes called Pogo Park, but that's the name of the nonprofit organization managing it, not the park's name.) She said that early funding kept her nascent nonprofit organization viable and provided critical leverage and credibility to secure additional funding. She often says, "No Endowment, no Pogo Park."

Park restorations don't fit the usual criteria for BHC work, but this one wasn't the usual renovation. Diane Aranda, the Endowment's program manager in Richmond for the BHC initiative, said Maher presented a unique vision that promised to create lasting, systemic change. It would test a new way for the city to partner with residents on improving community assets. Maher's plan also heavily invested in residents' capacity to drive the vision, planning, building, and actual implementation of the park renovation, Aranda told me. Moreover, the project, if successful, would create a sorely needed visible victory for the distressed, besieged Iron Triangle neighborhood, as opposed to the policy wins that are the hallmark of BHC success but that can sometimes feel intangible. Maher said that much of the Endowment funding went toward developing residents' skills.

In the early days, when Maher and others first tackled cleaning up the park, she was startled at hearing "the most unhappy sounds" from homes not far from the park. "Of parents just shrieking at their kids, children crying," Maher recalled. "But then once the park was built, the whole sonic thing changed," she said. "It was all these happy sounds, because kids were finally able to get outside and play. And parents have said their kids come home now and they're much calmer."

Her experiences dovetail with what experts say about the necessity of play for children. It's not an optional activity for healthy development in children; it's essential, points out Penny Wilson, a London-based expert in promoting play in low-income communities and a Pogo Park advisor. Play develops coordination, agility, confidence, and problem-solving and social skills, Wilson wrote in *A Playwork Primer* in 2010.[31] And parks that host a wide variety of creative playground amenities—the kind of enriched playground Maher envisioned—support that the best. Play is also crucial for healthy neural development. Children deprived of play, Wilson wrote, experience serious consequences, including learning disabilities, erratic behavior, depression, and difficulty forming bonds.

At the start, Maher, who drives a pickup truck and typically wears jeans and work boots, went knocking door to door in the neighborhood to get residents' input on the park redesign. That itself was a nervy step in a neighborhood where strangers encounter guarded suspicion. Sometimes people wouldn't open the door, so she returned, and many finally cracked the door and talked. That started a planning process that eventually involved five hundred residents.

She was also looking to hire Iron Triangle residents to take part in designing, building, and running the park. Carmen Lee, who lives next door to Elm Playlot and grew up in the Iron Triangle, became the first employee. Her sister Tonie Lee then joined the new team, which now includes nearly a dozen, all original hires. Team members earn living wages, from $16 to $22 per hour, with medical and other benefits; none ever had health insurance before. Pogo Park has also employed nearly 120 people thus far for contract work and another 250 who work two-week stints every year. "People from the community have jobs," Maher said, "and their job is to make neighborhood change." Most important is that those who might disrupt the parks refrain from doing so because they usually know the staff.

Maher's first target was to shut down the drug house. She and her newly assembled resident team worked with the Richmond Police Department, the city attorney, the county sheriff, and the FBI to do so, an effort that took two years. Maher also urged the city to address all those boarded-up homes and trash piles across from the playlot, which sent a depressing message. The city responded by securing a $3.6 million US Housing and Urban Development grant, and within a few years, while the park renovation was under way, all the homes were reoccupied.

Bill Lindsay, Richmond's city manager, became a powerful ally and helped Maher overcome numerous barriers. When they first met, she told Lindsay that American neighborhood parks were often static and unimaginative. She pitched the bespectacled, soft-spoken city manager on the idea of a staffed park, explaining how cities throughout Europe did so to promote creative play and safety.[32] "The staffing was the key," Lindsay said.

The most important step the city took in ensuring the success of the project was authorizing a "sole-source contract" with Pogo Park. That prevented the Elm Playlot project from being awarded to the lowest bidder because the project didn't have to be advertised and bid upon. That scenario would have dashed all Maher's dreams because the design and construction would go to an outside firm, and the same pattern would repeat itself: nonresident professionals designing and doing the work and holding a ribbon-cutting ceremony, and then everyone leaves and nothing has changed. Locals call it putting a mink coat on a skunk. "Transformation needs to be deeper," Maher said.

Instead, because Lindsay supported the sole-source contract, the work went directly to Pogo Park, after city council approval. "This is where we disrupted the system," she said. "When you hire us," Maher added, "not only are you going to get the best park and the best product, you're hiring the whole community!" Lindsay, a rare breed of city manager, largely gave her the reins with the entire project. "Just really kind of getting out of her way," Lindsay said in describing his working approach with Maher. He also said that although sole-source contracting can incite resentment among other contractors, it didn't in this case. "This is a unique set of services that we're getting here, and nobody else would be able to do it," he said.

When Maher learned in 2010 that her nonprofit organization won a $2 million highly competitive grant from the California Department of Parks and Recreation, she knew she had a viable project.

To develop her new labor force, Maher arranged for training in drafting, sculpting, model making, machining, metalwork, welding, construction, and other skills needed to design and build a playground. To her good fortune, just a few blocks from Elm Playlot is Scientific Art Studio, a renowned and innovative playground designer and fabricator. Much of the equipment for Elm Playlot was fabricated inside the huge work spaces at Scientific Art in a partnership between the Pogo Park resident team and the studio staff.

The Pogo Park team also received training in nonviolent communication, both to model it to park visitors and to work out tensions that arise in a diverse team living in a low-income, high-crime neighborhood and whose members may also be coping with past traumas. Every Thursday a counselor named Bruce, whom Maher calls "a really righteous African American man from the Deep South, who has gone through it," meets with staff to work out any conflicts or grievances. "If people have a beef, you save it for Bruce," said Maher.

Without that communication training, and a chance to talk and reflect, Maher said the effort might have imploded. She said many people doubted that her resident-led model would work, predicting that "there's no way these people are going to get along and run this park."

Maher acknowledged that "we had a couple of times that I thought, 'It's over. It's just too explosive, and we don't have the ability to see it through.'" But they worked it out, and the team "is in a really good place now." People need skills, she added, "to know how to process these very complicated emotions."

While the permanent playground structures were in development, she and her team put in temporary play structures and facilities painted in colorful hues and patterns. Then, in June 2014, the newly renovated Elm Playlot officially opened, and a joyous hub has now replaced the once-decrepit and dangerous park. There's a "global village" where children play in miniature versions of homes found around the world. There's a sandbox (with quality Hawaiian sand), disc swings, a tricycle path, a ball wall, a "mountain stream" for a quiet space, and the crowning achievement of the park: a German-manufactured zip line, to Maher's knowledge, the first ever installed in a city park in the United States.

Monday through Friday, staff watches over the Elm Playlot. There's now a permanent bathroom and filtered water fountain, where none were before. The nonprofit Pogo Park also purchased a small building adjacent to the property, with a meeting room and a kitchen, from which staff distributes some nine thousand free lunches during the summer through an agreement with the school district.

An artist comes weekly to teach the children skills with "loose objects" such as rocks, sticks, and fabrics that they can arrange to their fancy. Every Friday a chess expert gives lessons. "We're doing youth development, child development, economic development, public health, public safety. I mean, it's everything in one project," Maher said. Carmen Lee, the first hire on the team, said, "This park changed the neighborhood into a community."[33]

In times of trouble, Elm Playlot also spontaneously serves as a community gathering spot. On the evening of August 6, 2012, when a 1,000-foot plume of emissions shot up from the Chevron refinery in Richmond and then ignited, triggering a fire that spewed black smoke throughout the region, about three hundred anxious neighbors converged on the park, Maher said, seeking information and mutual support. They didn't go to the nearby neighborhood's community center, she noted.

These stronger bonds also strengthen the entire neighborhood—park users and nonusers—as neighbors start banding together for common goals.[34] There's never been an incident of violence at Elm Playlot, and only rarely does graffiti show up on the fence; when it does, staff quickly paints it over.

During one of my visits to Elm Playlot, a little girl stood by a miniature kitchen, stirring sand in a bowl to make cakes, and asked me to help. She lives next to the park and visits almost daily. High-pitched, happy sounds of children filled the air, and a boy smiled shyly as he glided on the zip line. Children climbed on an igloo, other kids played catch, and three teenagers sat at a picnic table talking while parents and caretakers strolled around.

Maher has parlayed her success with Elm Playlot, winning a $5 million state parks grant for a new Pogo Park project called Harbour 8, which opened in November 2015. It's less than a mile from Elm Playlot, built with the same resident-led approach, and includes amenities such as a playground, a community garden, and twenty-one heritage oak trees donated by Apple Computer, with more amenities to come.

In addition, Pogo Park won a remarkable $6.2 million grant from Caltrans, the state transportation agency, to design and build the "Yellow Brick Road," a safe, scenic, pedestrian- and bike-friendly path connecting Elm Playlot and Harbour 8, which also passes near a few schools. Maher said young people in the neighborhood first conceived the idea. It will literally have yellow bricks stenciled in the walkway, and Maher said $1 million goes for lighting. That project is in design phase, with construction expected to start in 2018.[35]

Maher said other organizations regularly inquire about her nonprofit organization's work, but none have tried to replicate the process.

"Pogo Park is really an outlier. We are going places that no other groups we've known about have gone—truly engaging local people to use their own public neighborhood parks to rebuild themselves and their own communities."

In 2016, more than 77,000 children visited Pogo Park's two sites, Elm Playlot and Harbour 8, or more than 200 a day. The California Department of Parks and Recreation profiled Elm Playlot as a "success story" in a 2015 report.[36] Viktor Patino, a manager with the department's grant office, told me that out of thousands of grants administered by his office, Pogo Park's work stands out for "empowering and employing residents to improve their own community" and in particular for engaging them in all three project phases. "Many consider the craftsmanship as a work of art," he added.

As Maher and I sat at a picnic table one busy spring afternoon at Elm Playlot, she looked around and remarked, "This is the middle of the 'hood. A few years ago this was the seventh most violent neighborhood in the *country*. No one would come outside. We would not have been sitting here."

Most of the homes across from Elm Playlot are now well kept up, including the former drug house, and many feature flowering plants. And across the street, neighbors were sitting outside on lawn chairs, talking, smiling, sipping drinks, and enjoying the view of the park.

CHAPTER 6
A Safe Place to Live

"I'm Rohnell Robinson, and I do rebar construction in San Francisco," said the thirty-one-year-old, introducing himself to an audience of about sixty inside a city hall auditorium in Richmond, California. Next to him on stage was LaVon Carter, twenty-nine, wearing a Black Lives Matter T-shirt, who holds a union job as a heavy equipment operator. Both men are new fathers, each proudly told the crowd. Eric Welch, twenty-seven, joined the panel via Skype because he was in Florida, studying for finals and about to earn a four-year degree in political science.

Several years back, these three young black men were considered among the most dangerous people in Richmond, a city of 108,000 about 17 miles northeast of San Francisco. In the Bay Area and beyond, the city is notorious for its gun homicides, many attributed to rivalries in three neighborhoods: the Iron Triangle, North Richmond, and South Richmond.

Robinson, Carter, and Welch once helped stoke the fear that kept so many Richmond residents isolated inside their homes, unable to enjoy normal neighborhood activities, like walking, biking, or playing with their children in the front yard. That changed when each was approached by streetwise, formerly incarcerated men who worked for a new city agency tasked with stopping the bloodshed. These men convinced the younger men to join a nonmandatory fellowship that would support them while they turned away from gun violence and almost certainly early death or incarceration. The fellows were the last speakers at an all-day event held on April 7, 2017, called Preventing Violence and Fostering Hope. It drew leaders of nonprofit organizations, government managers, activists, and others from around the state and nation to learn the inside story of this revolutionary Richmond city agency, which goes by the bland name of the Office of Neighborhood Safety. The agency, often just called the ONS, is also a participant in the Building Healthy Communities coalition in Richmond.

ONS staff single-mindedly pursue one goal: reduce gun violence in besieged Richmond neighborhoods. They do that by eschewing judgment and instead building caring, unconditional relationships with those pulling the trigger, gently but persistently drawing them in a new direction. Although this approach recognizes the humanity of people who have perpetrated violence, helping them become ambassadors for peace, the ultimate aim is to create safer, healthier communities where all residents can feel the same security wealthier areas enjoy every day.

Richmond city leaders took a gamble and opened the maverick agency in October 2007, in the midst of one of the worst homicide spikes in the city's history—forty-seven that year, making Richmond one of the ten most dangerous cities in the United States.[1] It was a better gamble than the drastic step some city leaders and community members had demanded the previous year: declare a state of emergency and call in the National Guard to quell the violence.[2]

Ten years later, nearly ninety young men had completed the program, and death and injury from gun violence in Richmond had plummeted 71 percent. Although it's difficult to say with certainty what is behind the decline, after factoring in other antiviolence efforts like more community policing and a pioneering reentry program in Richmond for the formerly

incarcerated called Safe Return Project (which the ONS helped launch),
many give substantial credit to the Office of Neighborhood Safety.
City leaders laud its unique model for intervening in the lives of those
most likely to shoot or be shot. Tom Butt, mayor since 2015, supports
expanding it, saying that the more funding ONS receives, the more
lives are saved. City coffers cover operating expenses for the agency,
roughly $1.3 million in 2016. Each fellow costs approximately $20,000
per year, which DeVone Boggan, founding director of the ONS, com-
pares to the nearly $400,000 in taxpayer costs alone on average for each
gun homicide, including hospital costs and law enforcement investigations as well as court and prison costs.[3]

The Richmond BHC campaign provided early funding for its
pioneering—and most controversial—program, the Operation Peacemaker Fellowship. This program persuades active offenders to abandon
violence and take up more productive lives through an eighteen-month
intensive support program, and it includes a stipend. (The fellows can
repeat the program if needed.) Once they join, they're called "fellows,"
a status they retain for life. (The Richmond campaign also supports
Operation Ceasefire, another antiviolence program operating in Richmond, which holds night walks through high-crime neighborhoods and
hosts events for at-risk youth.)[4]

Boggan wants young men who join the ONS program to understand
how much power they have to improve their communities. "One of our
key conversations with new fellows is, 'You are clearly directing public
safety policy in the city, and you're not even thinking about it. Can you
imagine what you could do if you begin thinking about it?'"

A Prevention Institute report describes why reducing violence is
so critical for improving the health of residents regularly exposed to
it.[5] Living in fear takes a toll on mental health, provoking stress and
depression,[6] which in turn increase the risk of developing many physical
ailments. A study in inner-city neighborhoods in Pennsylvania found

that community violence increases asthma attacks,[7] and another study of ten rural and urban US sites reported that children living in unsafe neighborhoods are more likely to be overweight than children living elsewhere.[8] One study of mothers in Baltimore found that those living in violent neighborhoods were twice as likely to report poorer health, smoking, never exercising, and poor sleep habits than those living in non-violent neighborhoods.[9] In short, community violence makes it much harder to live healthfully.

~

The April 7 event started in North Richmond, inside the Young Adult Empowerment Center, a one-story beige stucco building. On the surrounding streets, bulging black garbage bags were piled by the curb along with castoff furniture, and a few men gathered on street corners. Although a few homes sported manicured lawns, many others were boarded up and abandoned. The neighborhood is one of the hotspots for violence in the city.

Outside the center, Sam Vaughn, a tall black man with close-shaved hair, warm eyes, and a friendly smile, was greeting visitors. He was one of the original hires by the ONS and now serves as a manager. Vaughn wore a gray two-piece suit, white shirt, and striped tie and shook hands with those arriving for the event. Participants would not only gain in-depth understanding of the increasingly well-known ONS program—which has been covered by media outlets worldwide—but also advice for replicating it in other cities. ONS organized the event, along with the Alliance for Boys and Men of Color, a statewide coalition funded by the California Endowment. The BHC manager for Richmond, Roxanne Carrillo Garza, attended, as did Diane Aranda, the California Endowment's long-time program manager overseeing the BHC work in Richmond.

Inside, folding chairs were arranged in a semicircle, and trays of breakfast foods were kept warm in the back as people mingled and then took their seats. Then DeVone Boggan, director of the ONS, stood up, wearing a sports coat and his signature houndstooth hat shading his piercing blue eyes. Boggan, like many in the room, is African American. He grew up in Michigan and then moved West to attend the University of California, Berkeley, where he later also earned a law degree. He worked in the nonprofit sector for years in the San Francisco Bay Area, including as a consultant to violence prevention programs in Richmond. Tragically, less than a year after he took the helm at the ONS, his younger brother was shot and killed in Lansing, Michigan. He knows well the devastation caused by gun violence.

Boggan asked the group of about sixty people to write down the word *focus*. That word, he said, has been critical to his agency's work. When the ONS opened in October 2007, in a city desperate to stop the gun violence, he and the rest of the staff were going to "build the ship as we sail," he said. (They had a starting annual budget of $611,000; he had asked for $2 million.) But throughout the challenges and course adjustments, he and staff kept firmly in mind one goal: stop the killing. "We had a vision for what we were going to do. Not try, *going* to do," Boggan said. The work is hard, messy, and sometimes traumatic, and he said he wears a hat to cover up the knots on his head. Throughout the daylong event, curse words peppered the talks by various speakers, apropos to the challenging, cutting-edge work, and Boggan joked that his two children put out a pot at home for him to drop in money every time he swears. "I'm really going to do my best to not be a sailor today," he added. "That's why I'm talking slowly."

Between 1986 and 2005, nearly seven hundred people were killed by firearms in Richmond, Boggan told the crowd. "Most of them under thirty, most of them African American, most of them male." And most occurred in the same neighborhoods, he said. Then, in 2007, there were forty-seven fatalities, and an additional three hundred injuries, from firearms. He and others took a hard look at the resources in Richmond set up to help young people and found that most of those involved in gun violence hadn't participated in any of Richmond's service programs. "This population doesn't . . . take . . . services," Boggan said, slowly emphasizing the last few words. About the only organization that had been seeking out this group were the police, he added.

So Boggan decided to seek them out as well, deploying a new category of city employee called neighborhood change agents. The position has one nonnegotiable job criteria: you have to be formerly incarcerated, preferably with a gun charge in your background. "Can you imagine how the human resources department responded to that?" Boggan asked the group. HR staff asked if he could show examples of where this kind of program had been done elsewhere. "No, we can't do that," he had to tell them. Human resources, Boggan said, worried that his office would become "a revolving door of criminality." But with the backing of Bill Lindsay, Richmond's risk-tolerant city manager, Boggan won approval for his unusual job requirements.

(Jason Corburn, PhD, a professor of planning and public health at the University of California, Berkeley, who consults with Richmond on a number of its initiatives, said Lindsay should be recognized for the risks he's taken, with ONS, Pogo Park, and other nontraditional ventures, but that he didn't take blind chances. "He's a supersmart guy, and I think he took really strategic risks. He didn't just adopt ONS without a dynamic leader, proven leader, and a set of strategies.")

Over the following decade, the office hired eleven neighborhood change agents and only lost one to disciplinary action, Boggan said. Moreover, all the first hires for that position, including Sam Vaughn, are still with the ONS. The change agents' own experience with the criminal justice system, combined with their long tenure, "translates into trust on the streets," Boggan said—after they overcame initial suspicions about their motives, because they all now carried a city business card. "All of them had to negotiate the government snitch issue," he said. "The only way they did that successfully was by being who they were, and doing what they said they were going to do, every time. Every time. It's been a blessing to have the kind of quality people that we have had in the Office of Neighborhood Safety facilitating that street outreach."

Another nonnegotiable requirement is that his office would not share any information with law enforcement about the young men joining the program. Many of them haven't been arrested, prosecuted, or incarcerated for gun crimes, Boggan said, but are suspected of such offenses. (Suspects were arrested and charged in fewer than one in three homicides in Richmond from 2011 through 2016.[10]) "So how do we engage him, not asking law enforcement to reduce their engagement in any way? [Police officers are] going to do what they do, and they should. But how do we, from a developmental angle, engage this young man in a way that keeps him from crossing the line again?"

The two city agencies agreed to a communications protocol: a Richmond Police Department liaison would speak to the ONS director, and only the director, on a daily basis, with updates on gun violence in the city, and provide a monthly homicide map. To retain the fellows' trust and continued participation, no information on its fellows is shared by ONS staff with the police department, and Boggan regularly emphasizes that ONS is a "non–law enforcement agency."

~

The ONS evolved rapidly during its first three years and with mixed results. In its first full year in operation, in 2008, ONS concentrated its efforts in North Richmond and the Iron Triangle, also called Central Richmond, focusing on mediating conflicts to prevent retaliation. Homicides dropped to twenty-eight citywide that year, an encouraging improvement. But a higher proportion, compared with previous years, occurred in South Richmond, so some of the gun violence had just moved to a previously quieter area with less oversight, Boggan said. City leaders directed Boggan to deploy his street outreach agents citywide, including South Richmond. Against his better judgment he agreed, but he worried it would dilute the effort. "And what happened in 2009?" Boggan said. "Boom, right back to 45, and 186 nonfatal shootings. That was depressing. And I struggle often with knowing it didn't have to happen."

Then, in 2010, he fortuitously dropped in on a meeting of law enforcement officers discussing the root cause of violence. They concluded that a small number of individuals were responsible for 70 percent of the homicides in Richmond in 2009, and before long, Boggan had a list with twenty-eight names. Suddenly, he had an identifiable and finite group to focus on.

"So I made an executive decision," he said. He would spend his entire 2010 budget, now about $1 million, focused exclusively on those twenty-eight people. "So this broad street outreach work? No more," he said. "I was told by the city manager, 'It better work.'"

He and his staff gave themselves three months to convince the young men on the list of active shooters in Richmond to come to City Hall for a meeting and to consider joining a program designed with them in mind. Three of them were killed before that meeting, but twenty-one out of the remaining twenty-five showed up. To connect with the young men, the street outreach team arranged introductions through friends and relatives, hung out in their neighborhoods, played basketball, and planned other casual but deliberate encounters.

ONS staff divided the twenty-one recruits into three groups and staggered their arrival times to avoid rivals encountering one another. A sit-down lunch awaited each group in the city manager's third-floor conference room, with its scenic view of hills in the distance and with nameplates for each of them. Boggan said they were treated the same as others deemed important to the economic development and health of the city because in fact they were. The violence scared away businesses, depressed housing prices, and harmed residents' health on multiple levels. If the health of these young men could be improved, Boggan believed, so could the health of the city.

~

This perspective treats gun violence as a public health issue, deploying trained "violence interrupters" to hinder the transmission of violence, because it typically spreads within a small circle, like an infectious agent.[11] Then men who complete the ONS fellowship and renounce violence can serve as credible ambassadors in their communities, "inoculating" younger residents against entering a violent lifestyle, to use Sam Vaughn's metaphor from a TED Talk on the ONS program. Vaughn also described growing up in Richmond and his ten years' incarceration, including seven in San Quentin State Prison (during which he earned a degree).[12]

During the time Boggan shifted the ONS focus to this small group of potent individuals, he picked up an in-flight magazine and read about postgraduate school fellowships and how much participants earned. It was another "aha" moment for him, and Boggan decided to do the same for active firearm offenders who agreed to join the new program. Meeting certain milestones would earn the fellow a monthly stipend of up to $1,000. Young people in other social strata routinely earn money in fellowships for advancing their skills, Boggan reasoned, so why not Richmond's young people for doing the same, particularly because developing those skills will quell their desire to turn to gun violence to resolve conflicts and the community as a whole benefits enormously? Thus was born the most innovative, misunderstood, lauded, and derided dimension of ONS's gun violence cessation program.

ONS officially launched the Operation Peacemaker Fellowship program in 2010. Although the ONS street outreach work was initially based on similar work in Boston and Chicago, it has become so distinct—in large part because of the tight focus on a small group of active shooters—that it's now called the Richmond model.[13]

When young men—and they've all been men, typically between age fourteen and twenty-five—sign an agreement to join the fellowship, Boggan and his staff first work with each one to develop a "life map" after undertaking a comprehensive assessment of the new fellow's circumstances. The life map sets out personal, educational, and professional goals he wants to achieve during the fellowship, with short-term goals such as individual counseling, attending substance abuse or parenting classes, or paying off outstanding fines. Longer-term goals include completing a GED or rebuilding family relationships. ONS staff contacts each fellow multiple times daily to check on him and provide a consistent, positive presence in his life.

In another crucial support, the staff works with the fellows to sign up for additional classes and services from other agencies and nonprofit organizations, as navigating the bureaucratic maze would frustrate many. A neighborhood change agent also attends the first few classes to make sure both the fellow and the instructor are comfortable. The most sought-after services include anger management, financial management, and career development.[14]

Six months into the eighteen-month fellowship, if fellows have shown a "true desire" to change their lives as evidenced by participation levels, life map goal achievements, and "peace-building contributions," they're eligible to start receiving a monthly stipend of up to $1,000 for the next nine months. Most receive $300 to $700 monthly, although sometimes fellows aren't provided a stipend, usually based on not yet meeting goals.[15]

∼

Countless headlines have characterized the stipend as a bonus for not engaging in gun violence. That frustrates city leaders, who say it's in fact focused on rewarding positive behavior change.

"My favorite sound bite that everybody latches on to is, 'You're paying people not to shoot people,'" said Bill Lindsay, the Richmond city manager, speaking at the same event featuring the fellows, "which I find to be insulting, and it's a ridiculous characterization of the program." Boggan believes many media outlets can't resist the description because it makes for compelling "click bait." Lindsay pointed out that the stipends aren't funded with taxpayer money; instead, the California Endowment funds them through its Richmond BHC campaign.

Aranda, the program manager overseeing the Richmond BHC work, said the ONS work elevated a group of young men that few—other than law enforcement—were reaching. She funded the stipends and other controversial aspects of the work because she believed "it could expose the humanity of these young men and begin to change the narrative of who they are and to what they aspire." Dr. Robert Ross, president of the California Endowment, described the early backing for ONS as "catalytic funding," both catalyzing a dynamic new program and attracting additional funding from other sources.

The stipend actually reinforces a therapeutic approach practiced in the fellowship, which entails a form of cognitive behavioral therapy. Among other dimensions of the therapy, it helps participants challenge dysfunctional thought patterns and replace them with healthier, pro-social ways of thinking. Other studies have validated this approach for reducing criminal behavior. The stipends initially provide an incentive to join the ONS fellowship, but they then reinforce positive changes and send a message of respect.[16] The eighteen-month fellowship also includes regular meetings with a "council of elders," accomplished men of color who serve as positive role models and mentors.

Boggan wasn't done yet, however, adding another innovation that raised a few eyebrows: excursions around the country and internationally, up to several times a year after the fellows met certain criteria. This part of the program is funded by outside sources, including those from the Richmond BHC campaign, because many taxpayers would balk at that line item on a city budget. Many of these young men rarely leave Richmond or the Bay Area, and travel vastly broadens their horizons to worlds outside the small neighborhoods that they claim so fiercely as their territory, to the point of death.

The fellows have traveled to Washington, DC, New York City, South Africa, London, Paris, Dubai, Mexico City, and other destinations. The trips include service activities, such as feeding the homeless. In South Africa, they visited Robben Island, where former South Africa president Nelson Mandela was once imprisoned. Their tour guide was also imprisoned on the island, but now lives there among the same people who once jailed and beat him, impressing on the fellows the power of forgiveness.[17] They also visit colleges and meet with VIPs such as politicians in Washington, DC.

They also have fun, like a trip to Disneyland that Boggan described at the April event. "I've got some youngsters, big cats, with dreads and Mickey Mouse ears, at the end of the day with tears in their eyes, saying, 'This was one of the funnest things I've ever done in my life,'" said Boggan. "Why is fun important? Because most of these individuals have not had the opportunity to have fun and be kids."

Boggan reminded the group that "the fellowship is for the most lethal young man who is convinced, 'I'm going to shoot somebody again.'" He said he's trying to take that individual from "I don't give a flying f**k," which Boggan called an "urban suicide mission," to a place of "Maybe I do care."

"I'm trying to blow their minds on life, on life, *on life*," Boggan emphasized, slowing his cadence for the last few words. "Because the moment I want to start to live a little bit, that's when I start to make some different kinds of decisions."

The travel comes with a catch, though. Boggan said, "The only caveat is that they have to be willing to travel with someone they're trying to kill. You've got to say yes to traveling with the cat that's on your radar, and you're on his." One man in the audience whistled, another said, "Come on!", while a woman nodded her head and emphatically said, "Uh huh."

"TSA has been a good friend," Boggan added, given the airport security line weapons screening. ONS staff "strategically" place these putative rivals in the same row on airplanes. Most of these young men have never flown, and once they get to a 30,000-foot elevation, both see the mutual fear in each other's eyes, he said. "A few things happen. They realize that they're the same guy," said Boggan. Then they learn they have the same interests, in sports, women, music, movies. "On more than a few occasions, we've heard them come back to this city and say to us, 'I actually like him better than I like the cats that I've been trying to kill him with.'

"Now are we friends and kumbaya?" Boggan continued. "No, but we have a healthy respect and appreciation for each other."

~

Since the opening of ONS in 2007, eighty-four fellows in four cohorts have completed the fellowship. In statistics especially meaningful to that at-risk population of young men, 94 percent are alive, 83 percent have not been injured by a firearm, and 77 percent are not a suspect in new firearm activity. And, in a figure that still marvels many, injuries and death from gun violence dropped 71 percent in Richmond. "I know we've kept a lot of murders from happening because of goodwill," said Sam Vaughn, the longtime ONS staffer.

Lindsay, the city manager who took heat for supporting ONS and its unusual policies, voiced his continuing enthusiasm for the work. "I'm a real fan of the Office of Neighborhood Safety. It's easy to defend, and I don't fear the sound bite anymore. I can certainly articulate why it works so effectively," he said. ONS has also cultivated allies within the police department, with a special investigations commander remarking, "In truth, the ONS is the only agency in this city that targets the 'one percenters' for services. The benefits of the fellowship can be felt everywhere, but nowhere is the impact more visible than in the overall reduction in violent crime in our city."[18]

In an earlier March 2017 interview I had with Boggan, he commented on the criticism they sometimes receive when a fellow does become involved in gun violence. "We're not going to have 100 percent. The fellowship is for *active* firearm offenders," he emphasized. "That's what they do. Every time there's a shooting in Richmond, I suspect that it's one of our fellows. And if a suspected shooter is not in the fellowship," Boggan said, "I'm breathing down Sam's neck, asking him, 'Why isn't that a fellow?!'"

To amplify its work, ONS has formed a partnership with another organization, also in the Richmond BHC coalition, called the RYSE Center. It's the main BHC conduit for youth organizing work in Richmond, and it also supports young people coping with trauma by providing them with a safe, fun environment. In part because of BHC's focus on coalition building, ONS was actually pressured initially to sit in on RYSE board meetings. Boggan, not a fan of time-consuming meetings, attended but wasn't enthusiastic. "I was just really irritated that I had to be there." He said that changed as he began to understand the depth of RYSE's work and how it dovetailed with his own agency's mission. That, in fact, was a rare find; his agency has few tight partnerships in the community, given the nature of the ONS work, and it's an isolation he's striving to end. Before long, Boggan said he became sold on the organization.

RYSE, which (along with an equity-focused organization called Policy Link) helped organize the April 7 event, is now a critical ONS partner, and both organizations express relief and mutual appreciation of each other's support. Located off busy MacDonald Avenue, RYSE offers a colorful, uplifting space for young people to gather, with a music studio, an art lab, video games, hangout areas, a kitchen, classrooms, and a garden and outside area with a basketball hoop. RYSE also recently hired a counselor, who meets with young people to discuss emotional trials, all too often linked to violence they've witnessed or experienced in the streets, at schools, or at home. (The nonprofit organization formed in 2000 in response to a string of homicides among young people near Richmond High School.) RYSE has also hired some of the ONS fellows and has partnered on a program ONS began of hospital bedside visits to gunshot victims in an effort to interrupt any possible plans for retaliation.

~

In the course of their work, Boggan, Vaughn, and other ONS staff also saw that many preteens were getting left behind. ONS outreach workers come across "kids who are babies right now, who *nobody* is engaging," Boggan told me. These aren't kids who walk through the doors of community support programs. Perhaps a twelve-year-old found or stole a gun, said Vaughn, but hasn't used it yet. Now is the time to reach this kid; otherwise, he joins the next generation of fellows, Boggan said.

He identified that gap in community services a few years ago, but turned away because ONS was already stretched thin, especially after staff reductions as part of citywide cutbacks. He hoped some other group would engage, but no one did. A few years later, "Guess who the fellows are?" he asked. "The very people." Now he's finding a way to stretch his resources to reach them, but it's difficult, considering the urgent priority of intervening with active firearm offenders. Both Boggan and Vaughn expressed frustration that other local organizations weren't reaching preteens at risk of taking up gun violence. They acknowledged that it is due in part to the risk-adverse nature of some nonprofit organizations, which might face criticism from a board of directors or funders for serving such a population. That's especially true because results are typically spotty, and when things go wrong, the consequences are far more serious than simply somebody dropping out of a standard youth program, such as an after-school literacy class or soccer clinic.

Considering "all of the resources that are right here, that would change the dynamic," said Vaughn. "I think every organization should have outreach apparatus" to find these kids, Boggan said. "Every last one of them. If they don't know what you do, you go out and knock on doors and let 'em know."

This, of course, isn't Richmond's challenge alone; it's one virtually every community in the nation faces: reaching the preteens who aren't yet actively involved in gun violence, but are highly susceptible to it. Ross agrees with Boggan. "DeVone is absolutely right," Ross said, "and there are actually upstream markers that tell us when these kids are headed for trouble." Ross said chronic absenteeism, truancy in elementary school, suspensions—even one—and not reading at grade level by third grade are all warnings that students are "headed for academic trouble, dropout, and then higher risk for juvenile justice involvement later on."

Diane Aranda pointed to a proposed statute called Richmond Kids First that will appear on the June 2018 ballot in Richmond. The ballot initiative is a direct result of youth-led BHC community organizing work in Richmond under the direction of RYSE; young people developed the idea and then gathered enough signatures by a deadline to qualify it for the ballot. The measure stipulates that up to 3 percent of general revenue funds in Richmond will be directed to youth programs in a city where a significant portion of the budget is allocated to the police department and other law enforcement activities.

If the ballot measure—which is controversial among city leaders—passes, Aranda said it could be a source of new funding to build up outreach services for this often overlooked younger group. "This is a clear gap. This is a population that we need to strengthen support for," she said.

In ONS's quest to expand support services for this group of young men, Vaughn acknowledged it's challenging for other organizations "to accept these young people for who they are." He also knows they can test those who support them, as though attempting to drive them away, a self-fulfilling prophecy of people yet again rejecting them. It's when ONS staff hangs in there and takes the rebuffs and rebellions that trust develops.

"I think we can all honestly say we wish somebody had pushed through a barrier that we put up, to get to the real us and try to help us find who we were supposed to be," Vaughn said. Staff does give stern talks when, to their dismay, they suspect one of the fellows engaged in destructive behavior. "'Like 'You really screwed up, bro,'" Vaughn said he'll tell a fellow. "And that's just unacceptable. But I'm here to help you get through it. And hopefully to help you deal with those emotions in a better way before you feel like this is necessary again."

Although some see this kind of counseling as too soft for dangerous offenders, it's proven effective in steering young men away from violence.

∼

It's that trust that finally won over Rohnell Robinson, and long-timers on the police department have marveled at his transformation. If there was trouble in the Iron Triangle a decade ago, Richmond police officers would figure Robinson had a hand in it, said Lieutenant Arnold Threets, an African American officer and former Marine with more than twenty-five years on the Richmond police force. A June 6, 2016, *Guardian* article by Jason Motlagh on the ONS program quoted Threets on Robinson's transformation:

"He got it, man. Not overnight, but it clicked," Threets said. Robinson's progress visibly moved him. "You've got to realize who Rohnell Robinson was—it's like Al Capone finding Jesus."[19]

In May 2006, Robinson was in a car that rolled up alongside the vehicle of one of his rivals, who was leaving a shopping mall in Richmond. A volley of bullets from Robinson's car missed the intended target, but a seventeen-year-old girl in the other car was seriously injured. The attack launched a retaliatory cycle over the next three months that resulted in as many as a dozen murders. The following year the feud between rivals in Central Richmond and North Richmond led to more than twenty killings.[20]

Robinson was arrested and charged in connection with the shopping mall shooting, but an attempted murder charge was dropped due to lack of evidence. He was, however, convicted on a gun possession charge and sentenced to five years in prison. He was out in two years, in 2009. Before Robinson left prison, ONS staff had been contacting his mother, urging her to get the word to Robinson about their unique program.

He was leery about joining, but they were persistent. Guardedly, he showed up to a meeting in City Hall, suspicious it might be a police setup. "First of all, I thought it was 'Officer' of Neighborhood Safety," he said to some laughter in the auditorium at the event. He did sign on, however.

Still, Robinson hit a crisis point. He had lost his apartment, someone shot at his car, and he was gambling. "Money was gone. No job. And I called Sam [Vaughn], it was like 1 o'clock in the morning," Robinson told the audience. "And he was like 'Man, come down, we're going to get you some food and then we're going to talk, and we're going to make sure everything is all right.'" When Vaughn showed up in the small hours of the night, "that was like a big relief," Robinson said, "because it was close to that point where I was like, you know what, I just need to do what I need to do."

But that commitment by Vaughn kept Robinson from returning to his old lifestyle and cemented his gratitude for the ONS program. "Like, you can't get that from nobody really. I never got that. So that was like a real moment where I was like, 'You know what, all the stuff you been doing, like you got people that really care about you man. How you think they'll feel if you end up back in jail or gone?'" Robinson said. "Like, I really hurt people, so I wouldn't want to hurt nobody who loves me as much as they could. So that keeps me motivated and keeps me going. I'm going to do it so I can make them happy." Later in the talk, he added, "I recently had a daughter, so that just extramotivated me."

Even with the intense support provided by ONS staff, it took Robinson seven years to fully break from the old ways and land a good-paying job. "Seven years?" asked Vaughn, to underscore it to the crowd. "Seven years," said Robinson. He's now a Peacemaker Ambassador.

LaVon Carter got out of prison in 2012 after serving a five-year sentence.[21] "When I first got out, you can only imagine, sitting in prison for five years, what you're thinking about. Thinking about how you got caught, and what I can do to not get caught next time. You learn how to be a better criminal, basically. And I had that mind-set when I first got out," Carter told the audience. "I was straddling the fence, and ONS helped push me in the right direction."

ONS's street outreach workers persuaded him to join the fellowship. The money was an incentive at first, but then the rest of the program began to draw him in. He wearied of his dismal prospects of a short violent life or incarceration and shifted his perspective. "I'm only twenty-nine years old, and half of my class is dead. Or they gone [to prison], and I ain't going to ever see them again."

Soon after Carter got out of jail, he followed up on a job lead from ONS. "I went and saw the union guy, and I got right to work. Once I started making money, I was like, 'Hold on, this is a nice little chunk of change.' It's not illegal, and they can't take it from you," Carter said, although noting with some annoyance, "I still gotta pay the taxes," to which the audience erupted in laughter. "Without this program, ain't no telling where I would be," he continued. He said a powerful influence of the fellowship was spending time with "successful black men," which gave him "hope that I can be that one day."

Carter, now a heavy equipment operator, said he'll be earning $40 an hour soon. He was in the process of getting a loan to buy a home, and he said that one of his chief worries was improving his already solid credit score to get even better terms, to more laughter from the audience. He's also an ambassador to young people and friends, urging them to go down to the union to get a job and to lead healthier, more productive lives. And when he leaves his house early in the morning wearing his work clothes, he's glad to know he's setting a good example for his son.

"You going to work, but they paying good money for hard work," Carter said. With more fellows graduating from the ONS program, Carter said, "It's like a branch now, a generation of people who don't want to see the community like this no more. We want our kids to play outside, just like when our parents grew up.

"My outlook on life is totally different than when I was twenty-four. All the stuff I wanted, everything I thought was important, really ain't nothing," Carter said. "I've got a four-year-old. It makes me want to give him something that I didn't have. Not only do I feel this way about my son, I feel this way about *his* son, and his son, and his son."

When Vaughn introduced Eric Welch, twenty-seven, he said Welch was first shot at age fourteen. Welch was "hanging" with a friend a few blocks from his apartment when a car glided around the corner and AK-47s emerged through the window, spraying him and his friend. Welch remembers fiery pain as a slug struck underneath his left arm, collapsing a lung and breaking his clavicle. His friend was hit in the hip. Welch, bleeding from his mouth and out of his chest, thought he was going to die, but doctors kept him alive. He still has a large scar where the slug exited. After that he felt angry and vengeful, and he bounced around schools. Before he reached twenty-two, he sustained three more bullet wounds, one of them after he joined the ONS fellowship. Vaughn said he was "for sure" headed for prison or a violent death without the fellowship.[22]

ONS staff helped him get through the ordeal of the last bullet wound, Vaughn said, and helped him "not feel like he had to respond."

Welch, speaking on the video monitor, said, "I never had like a father figure, or a grandfather," helping him realize "that I'm going down the wrong road. [ONS is] for me like family." The Skype connection began faltering, so Vaughn finished for him, saying that after graduating from college, Welch is planning to earn a master's degree and then work in public policy "to be involved in the decision-making process, so other folks don't be victims to a policy that doesn't have them in mind. So we applaud Eric," Vaughn said. "I can't wait to get to Tallahassee for his graduation.

"I can look to LaVon, I can look to Rohnell, I can look to Eric, I can look to twenty or thirty other young folks who really got it," Vaughn added. "And it gives me the energy not to fade away. Because it can be difficult. But I get rejuvenated because I see young brothers glad that they got a daughter. We want to acknowledge the hard work that these young men do within themselves, on themselves," he wrapped up, to applause from the crowd.

DeVone Boggan, through a nonprofit organization he founded in 2016 called Advance Peace, now consults with numerous cities interested in adopting the Richmond model. He's working part time at ONS while he advances the model nationwide, consulting with city governments in Oakland, Washington, DC, and Toledo, Ohio, to develop programs similar to the one he designed in Richmond.[23] In December 2017, the Sacramento City Council signed a four-year contract with Advance Peace to replicate the Richmond work in California's capital, although not without intense debate. It's the first expansion of the program outside of Richmond. Soon after, in January 2018, the Stockton City Council also approved a four-year partnership with Advance Peace, following 55 homicides in 2017 in the Central Valley city.[24] Advance Peace is funded by the Draper Richards Kaplan Foundation, with matching funds by the California Endowment. "We're matching support and partnership with DRK to help DeVone try to scale his model," said the Endowment's Ross. "It's been a home run, it's been fabulous."

~

City Heights in San Diego is another neighborhood known for violence. Although conditions are better than in 1990, when the city of San Diego declared a state of emergency in City Heights to cope with the violence, people still often feel unsafe. When the BHC campaign began, residents prioritized reducing violence.

Inside a small, ground-floor office off busy University Avenue, Bridget Lambert, an attorney and development officer with the National Conflict Resolution Center, met with me in March 2017 to describe an effort to reduce juvenile delinquency in the neighborhood.

Soon after the community change campaign began in 2010, the Peace Promotion Momentum Team formed in City Heights, with Lambert's organization leading the effort. This team, which includes residents along with staff from several other area nonprofit organizations, decided to pursue a practice that goes by the ponderous name "restorative community conferencing" and to focus on juvenile offenders.

In short, this approach attempts reconciliation between offenders and victims, asking law enforcement to let the community, with the help of a mediator, take the first crack at finding a resolution. First, though, the offender has to be willing to accept responsibility for repairing the damage he or she has done. If it works, it keeps young offenders out of juvenile court and juvenile hall. But most important for community safety is that studies show that this approach dramatically lowers repeat offenses.[25] The City Heights action team wanted to see if the approach would enhance community safety by persuading young lawbreakers to rethink their actions and to refrain from further illegal activity, while also cultivating in them a stronger bond to their community.

The team first won the essential buy-in from agencies in the San Diego County juvenile justice system, including the probation department, the public defender's office, and the district attorney's office. These agencies refer juvenile offenders who might be open to the process to this program in lieu of regular juvenile justice court proceedings. In another era, it would have been a long shot to even win the agreement of these agencies, noted Lambert. The Peace Promotion Momentum Team members had data showing that the process reduced recidivism, however, and that persuaded the agency staff to try it.

The action team launched a pilot project in May 2014, which started with three San Diego zip codes, including City Heights. It has since expanded to ten zip codes elsewhere in the region.

The reconciliation process is always voluntary and confidential for everyone involved. Team members prepare the juvenile offender and victim for a conference, which is attended by a few family members, social service providers, and a mediator. Goals include holding the offender accountable; discussing the harm done to the victim, to the broader community, and to the offender himself or herself; and then agreeing on a plan for the youth to repair the harm. If they don't reach an agreement, the case goes back to juvenile court.

During the first three years of the pilot program, 109 juvenile offenders were referred to the program. Three-fourths were male, and most ranged in age from thirteen through seventeen, although one was eight years old. The top five charges were battery, vandalism, theft, resisting arrest, and burglary, in that order. Of those cases, seventy-three participated in the community conference, and in each case, all the parties reached an agreement. To top it off, 98 percent of offenders completed their plans.

The recidivism rate among those who underwent the restorative community conferencing process in City Heights is just 5 percent versus 33 percent who did not participate. In addition, 84 percent of the victims found the conferencing process helpful, as did 90 percent of the juvenile offenders. All the victims would recommend the process to others, as would 96 percent of the juvenile offenders.[26]

One woman decided to participate in the project after a seventeen-year-old snatched her purse. Witnesses recovered her bag, so she didn't lose any money, but she was traumatized and angry. During the session, the youth expressed remorse and embarrassment, and the two ended up hugging.[27] As is often the case in these restorative conferences, victims are relieved to understand why they were targeted, which reduces their fear of being hurt again.[28]

This reconciliation model originated in New Zealand in the late 1980s, where it is called family group conferencing. It was started because indigenous Maori kids were being disproportionately affected by the justice system, but it is now used for most juvenile cases in New Zealand.[29] Restorative community conferencing has also been adopted in New South Wales, Australia, for juvenile offenders; in England and Wales for child and social welfare programs; and in Canada for juvenile offenders, family violence cases, and child protection services.[30] It was introduced in the United States in 1995, and programs now run in a few other US municipalities, including Baltimore and Louisville, Kentucky. Although not widespread, programs are actively expanding in California; San Francisco runs one program, and several other BHC sites have launched projects.

One program in Fresno, called the Community Justice Conference, saw a 5 to 10 percent recidivism rate compared with 20 to 30 percent for juveniles with similar charges who didn't participate. The

Fresno program has also been credited with reducing truancy rates and improved scholastic achievement.[31] The Alameda County program processes seventy-five young people annually and and has a recidivism rate of 12%, versus 31% for juveniles facing similar charges but not undergoing the restorative conferencing process.[32]

Although the ONS program and community conferencing focus on accountability and restoring relationships, sometimes residents just push for physical fixes to promote safety.

~

In the central California city of Salinas, physical improvements meant bringing people out of the shadows. After sunset in the city's Acosta Plaza housing development, most of its three thousand residents stayed behind closed doors in the gang-plagued neighborhood. Between 2010 and 2015, seven fatal shootings took place in the high-density housing development,[33] populated now mostly by Hispanic residents and until recently nicknamed "Felony Flats." Salinas, an agricultural city near Monterey, is well known as the home of writer John Steinbeck, and many who live in Acosta Plaza work in the nearby fields.

"We couldn't even come outside because of the cholos (thugs, gang members)," Gabriela Torres, a mother of two and an Acosta Plaza resident, told a reporter with the local newspaper, the *Salinas Californian*.[34] Neighbors scarcely knew one another because they mostly stayed inside, she added. "We hadn't met."

When the BHC campaign came to town in 2010, residents made clear that they badly wanted safer conditions in Acosta Plaza, home to many families. A survey conducted in collaboration with the new campaign found that 98 percent of residents were specifically concerned about the poorly lit streets in Acosta Plaza.

Residents and campaign staff soon formed a Land Use Action Team. Although residents and members from a few local nonprofit organizations make up the bulk of the Salinas land use team, it's led by a BHC staffer who, among other duties, handles much of the organizational work. Andrea Monzo, the BHC manager in Salinas, said they learned that staff presence was essential; a solely volunteer-run team, which they tried first, wasn't as effective.

The land use team began an eighteen-month campaign, including pressuring the Salinas Public Works Department, to install brand-new LED lights throughout Acosta Plaza. The California Endowment gave $100,000 to cover part of the lighting project's costs. The city approved the project, and in October 2015, residents, leaders and members of nonprofit organizations, and city officials gathered to celebrate the new, bright lights. "At night when I walk outside it feels like daytime. I feel safe," said one resident after the installation. "I see more people outside."[35]

The following year, another resident team, this one youth-led and also organized under the BHC umbrella, persuaded the city to set aside $40,000 to build a basketball court in Acosta Plaza, which had virtually no recreational facilities. The same BHC youth team in 2012 also launched an event called Ciclovia Salinas in partnership with the Public Works Department. One day a year, the event shuts off vehicle traffic on a 1.6-mile stretch of Alisal Street in Salinas for a large street celebration, which includes walking, biking, skateboarding, skating, and dancing. It is now an annual event, drawing more than five thousand people in 2016.[36] (The BHC campaign focuses on East Salinas, also called Alisal, which is Spanish for an alder tree.) After the 2016 Ciclovia, the Salinas City Council publicly praised the youth team organizing it.[37]

Ciclovia originated in Bogota, Colombia, in 1976 and is the Spanish term for "bike path." It's been replicated in cities throughout the United States, although the Salinas Ciclovia is the only youth-led one in the country.[38] It's a way of promoting healthful activity as well as taking back areas plagued by violence. The event also shifted the way the broader community, and city leaders, viewed youth from Alisal, who were used to negative stereotypes. As Monzo noted, "The city really started to see BHC as a partner in a lot of the work and started to see youth as assets and local leaders."

~

Meanwhile, the Salinas land use team also set its sights on a community goal with far-reaching effects. After a long and public process, in 2015 it persuaded the city to set aside $250,000 for the Alisal Vibrancy Plan to revitalize the 59,000-population Alisal neighborhood, which the team said that city planners had historically overlooked. This vibrancy plan would not only cultivate economic development in the very low-income area, but it would also improve public safety with more street lighting and sidewalks. The City of Salinas, which has become a strong partner of the BHC work, recently did one better, adding to the revitalization plan a new $49 million public safety building—long needed in Salinas for an expanded base for the police department—which will be located in Alisal. It's touted as the largest public works project in the city's history and is scheduled to open in 2019.[39]

Gary Petersen, the forward-thinking public works director in Salinas, said the effect of the community organizing work by the BHC campaign has transformed the relationship between the Salinas city staff and the residents of Alisal—and by extension residents throughout the city— whom they now view as partners in planning. "The thinking now is, 'Let's look at what the community wants,'" Peterson said. "I have to point to that as being one of the biggest changes in our thinking: for us to stop being the experts, and to start listening to people and giving them actually what they want rather than what we think they need."

CHAPTER 7

Rural Activism

Makenzy Williams smiled shyly as she told me about life in Del Norte County, California. She was sixteen during our interview in 2012 and had just finished her junior year of high school. Makenzy's hometown, Crescent City, is the largest city in the region with a population of 7,500 and is the kind of place kids dream of leaving. The area is as beautiful as you could hope for, with vast old-growth redwood forests, sparkling rivers, and the Pacific Ocean meeting land along rocky coastlines. In fact, it draws adventure tourists from around the world, who spend their days fishing, crabbing, beachcombing, hiking, or sightseeing for birds, elk, and even Bigfoot.

For teenagers, though, Del Norte hasn't promised much of a future. Although tourism brings in much-needed dollars, it's still not enough to offset the devastating loss of jobs in the timber and fishing industries in recent decades. Even the Boys and Girls Club closed in 2010 due to a lack of funding. Jobs had disappeared for many reasons: the depletion of old-growth timber; the conversion of thousands of acres of private land to government ownership, much of it to create parks and protected areas; and new environmental restrictions. Jobs also went overseas. The fishing industry was hit in the 1980s and 1990s with declining fisheries, regulations to control overfishing, and foreign competition. By the mid-1990s, most of the lumber companies had pulled out, with Green Diamond the only one remaining.

Richard Young, a harbormaster in Crescent City who retired in 2014, said the harbor used to host five hundred boats a year during the heyday of recreational fishing; now it's down to about fifty boats, with the annual loss of income from slip fees dropping 80 percent. Two fish processing plants, Sea Products and Eureka Fisheries, went out of business in 2001, he said, and each employed about forty people.

Nowadays, it's tough to make a living in Del Norte County. Makenzy's family was relatively fortunate. She said her father worked in labor relations at Pelican Bay State Prison on the outskirts of Crescent City, one of the good jobs in the town, and her mother stayed home taking care of the family. Aside from jobs at the prison or in government agencies managing public forests or fisheries, Safeway offers one of the best gigs in town, paying union wages. Two-thirds of households are low income, which means they earn 200 percent or less of the federal poverty rate,[1] and unemployment rates consistently remain higher than the state average. More than half of single women with children—and one-fifth of single men with children—live in poverty in the county.[2] On the tribal lands adjacent to Del Norte County, 35 percent of residents live in poverty, although it's even higher in the remote interior areas.[3]

Stress and poverty have taken their toll on residents' health. In a 2011 survey of all California counties, Del Norte scraped near bottom in life expectancy and quality of life, coming in fifty-fifth out of fifty-six counties in California.[4] Men in Del Norte could expect to live to seventy-three, nine years less than those in affluent Marin County 300 miles south.[5] They'll also grapple with more diseases than most Californians, including heart disease, cancer, and respiratory illnesses.[6] And 45 percent of children in 2010 in Del Norte County were overweight or obese compared with 38 percent statewide.[7]

Makenzy told me that because of lack of opportunity and boredom, her peers often drink, do drugs, or leave. She had been echoing the usual Crescent City teen mantra of fleeing after graduation. "I wanted to get out as soon as possible," she said.

Given the major health deficit in the area, Del Norte County might have seemed like a natural fit for the Building Healthy Communities campaign, but it almost didn't make the cut. Dr. Robert Ross, president of the California Endowment, recalled, "When we identified Del Norte as one of the fourteen communities, I have to admit it was a little bit of an afterthought. We had the first list of communities, and then somebody said, 'Boy, you don't have rural in there. Should we have at least one of those?'" Still, the region still gave him pause. "It was just so remote and so different. It's closer to Oregon, for Pete's sake," he told me. (It typically takes a day's journey to get there from most parts of the state, whether driving or flying, given the mountainous roads and sparse schedule of commercial flights into the Crescent City airport.)

As Endowment staff looked closer, however, they saw that the community had a key asset for succeeding in the initiative: a collaborative spirit. Residents, for example, had raised $115,000 for a playground called Kidtown, and four hundred volunteers had showed up to construct it in 2000.[8] Del Norte also stood out for its diverse mix of residents compared to the other BHC sites. In the county of 28,600 people, two-thirds are white, one in ten is Native American, and the rest are largely Hispanic. Ross spoke of "the added demographic benefit of including tribal lands" in the community change initiative. Selecting Del Norte County and the surrounding tribal lands proved a provident choice; the region shares similar challenges to enormous swaths of distressed, rural communities elsewhere in the United States, and the BHC work there is yielding valuable lessons on cultivating community change in struggling rural regions.

It certainly opened new avenues for Makenzy, who started to think differently about Del Norte after BHC showed up. When we met, she had recently begun a summer internship with Youth Network News, a BHC program that trained young people in journalism. Along with fifteen other students, she was learning the art of storytelling and contributing to the BHC-funded media outlet *Redwood Voice*. She had also used a Mac for the first time and was becoming proficient in iMovie and other software for video production. The internship was not only giving her practical skills, but also a new perspective on her hometown. "It's good to meet people who are serious about what they are doing," she said. "It's good to see people wanting to make a difference in their community. I thought they just didn't care."

~

Even before BHC came to town, local leaders were beginning to tackle the question that plagues so many rural communities in the modern US economy: how do you create a thriving place where young people want to stay and raise their own families? The answer, unsurprisingly, started with education, but the devil lay in the details. They knew Del Norte had untapped potential, even as businesses dealt with unmotivated workers and poor performance, which stood in the way of financial recovery. One in five adults older than twenty-five in the county doesn't have a high school diploma, and a significant number of high school graduates aren't academically prepared for college; in fact, many didn't even qualify to apply to the University of California system.

Chris Howard is a business leader who helped spearhead the early economic development work. (He's now a county supervisor, active in the Del Norte BHC work, and general manager of Alexandre Family EcoDairy Farms, an organic operation.) When we talked in 2012, he distinctly recalled the impetus to improve education in the region. Howard used to manage a rancheria run by a local tribe that could rarely retain new employees longer than a few weeks and thus regularly had job openings for its casino and food service operations.

Howard said that the workers would arrive late or simply not show up. Many of those who did clock in were illiterate, couldn't complete orders accurately, or were simply rude to customers, he said. "The work ethic wasn't there, the quality wasn't there," Howard said. "It was a nightmare, an absolute nightmare. We had an almost constantly revolving door, and it was to the point where something needed to change." The community's leaders recognized that change had to begin with the school system. In response, some fifty prominent residents formed an economic development council to focus on preparing students for college and career. The approach included vocational training for jobs in agriculture or machine work, or possibly restoring the aviation program that the high school had once offered. The idea was that an educated workforce, following diverse career tracks, would start local businesses or become productive employees for existing ones, jump-starting the region's economy.

When we talked again in 2017, Howard noted that 80 percent of the land in the region is now publicly owned and that the logging industry workforce will never return to its former size, even though some locals still speak wistfully of its return. "There will never be that opportunity again," Howard said. "We have to reinvent ourselves."

Still, the economic development council began its reform endeavor with limited resources. One member of the group recalled cobbling together grants that would last for a year or two. "Then you'd have to start the scramble all over again, and you lose the momentum," said Lisa Howard, an educator in the area, who is married to Chris Howard. So when the BHC campaign began in 2010, it was a vast relief to secure a steady philanthropic partner. "'If there are rough times, whatever it is, we're here to assist,'" said Lisa Howard, paraphrasing the philosophy behind the ten-year plan. "It's really reassuring to the effort."

That commitment to partner for a full decade differentiated BHC from past efforts focused on geographic areas, called place-based philanthropy. "We were trusted by the sites to stay the course," said Ross, the Endowment president, when we talked seven years into the endeavor. "Were there some nervous about being dropped? Yeah, it was a concern," he added. "The track record of philanthropy has not been stellar in doing place-based, neighborhood-engaged work and sticking with it," he added. "The board was very good about maintaining a strong commitment to 'just stick with those sites, let's stick with them for that ten-year period.'"

Chris Howard also underscored the value of having a few staff members funded by the foundation living in the community. "The paid position is instrumental," he said, emphasizing that community leaders involved in the education reform drive also have full-time jobs. "But when you have somebody talking [about the issue] every day in a paid position, that's huge." The community had previously tried pushing the reforms with volunteer groups, but Howard said it hadn't worked. "We've failed miserably with it," he said.

To tackle the education crisis in Del Norte, the BHC School Systems Implementation Team launched in 2010. Residents led the work, and still do, but with the support of campaign staffers. It turns out that the school systems team would need that commitment by Ross and the board to stay the course.

It's a stable group. Most of the original members are still there today, and the high-caliber nine-person team consists of local VIPs, such as the school district superintendent; directors with child care nonprofit organizations; Chris Howard, who joined at the outset and is now an ally on the County Board of Supervisors; his wife, Lisa Howard; and well-known citizens with strong connections with the school system. From the beginning they all understood the critical link between education and economic vitality, with median incomes almost double for young adults with college degrees compared with those without a high school diploma.[9] Education also confers myriad health benefits. Those without a high school degree, for example, are more likely to have high blood

Plate 1a: Dave Regan, an SEIU leader, at a December 2013 rally that called attention to the large differences in life expectancy between zip codes in Los Angeles.

Plate 1b: Two South LA residents holding photos of loved ones who died prematurely.

Plate 2a: An African green monkey at the Primate Center at Wake Forest School of Medicine in a common dominance display. *Credit: Center for Comparative Medicine Research at the Wake Forest School of Medicine.*

Social Status and Coronary Artery Atherosclerosis in Monkeys

Dominant Monkey   Subordinate Monkey

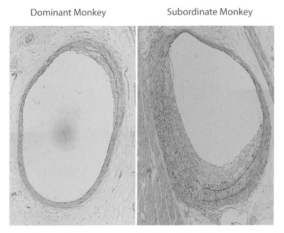

Plate 2b: Cross sections of coronary arteries from female macaques. Compared with dominant macaques, subordinate animals developed more plaque, which restricts blood flow and increases the risk of heart attack. Courtesy of Carol A. Shively, Ph.D., Professor of Pathology and Comparative Medicine at Wake Forest Baptist Medical Center, as adapted for use in the PBS documentary *Unnatural Causes.*

Plate 3a: Dr. Robert Ross, president of the California Endowment, speaking at a convening of the fourteen Building Healthy Communities sites in April 2016. To Ross's left is Bobby Powell, a coordinator with the Sacramento site. Courtesy of the California Endowment.

Plate 3b: Cameron Simmons, in Oakland, in October 2014. The twenty-year-old was suspended nearly 150 times and arrested multiple times before he finally graduated from high school after attending a school that employed restorative justice practices. He now works as a youth advocate.

Plate 4: Youth meeting with Sen. Ed Hernandez, D-Azusa (LA County), in August 2014; a billboard in Sacramento promoting positive school climates; current and former members of a youth council in City Heights, San Diego, in March 2017 at a new skate plaza they championed.

SOUTH FRESNO
93706
1.02
PARK ACRES
Per 1,000 residents

NORTH FRESNO
93720
4.62
PARK ACRES
Per 1,000 residents

 Your **ZIP Code** shouldn't predict **how long you'll live** – but it does. Because where we live, affects how we live. Staying healthy requires much more than diets and doctors. We need **#OneHealthyFresno** with better parks for all. To learn more visit: www.fresnobhc.org

Plate 5: Toody Maher, founder and executive director of Pogo Park in Richmond; ad by the Fresno BHC campaign; mural in Fresno, funded to help foster a sense of community.

Plate 6: Chris and Lisa Howard in Crescent City at the Alexandre Family EcoDairy Farms, which Chris manages; confluence of the Klamath and Trinity rivers in Yurok tribal land; Thomas O'Rourke Sr., chairman of the Yurok Tribe in Northern California, in 2013 in a forest regrowing after a controlled burn: Margo Robbins, a traditional basket weaver who has the chin tattoos common to her Yurok ancestors, in 2013.

Plate 7a: Ray's Food Place in rural Del Norte County closed in 2013 after twenty-one years in business, leaving the closest market 13 miles away.

Plate 7b: The Northgate Gonzalez Market in South Los Angeles, which opened in 2014, boasts an abundant produce section along with an array of healthy foods.

Plate 8a: Sam Vaughn (left), program manager with the City of Richmond's Office of Neighborhood Safety in April 2017 with ONS fellows Rohnell Robinson (center) and LaVon Carter, who are now Peacemaker Ambassadors in the community.

Plate 8b: Rally in August 2014 at the capitol in Sacramento, organized by the Alliance for Boys and Men of Color to urge reform of school discipline policies and health care access.

pressure and cholesterol levels, to smoke, to be less physically active than those with high school degrees, and to gain excess weight,[10] and that's only a partial list of health consequences. One 2012 study linked five-year life expectancy boost to simply earning a high school degree.[11]

To gather data, the BHC campaign early on funded a survey of local high school students, yielding more than 1,100 responses. Many students in the rural county said they didn't feel prepared for life after high school or know what they planned to do for a living. Laura Olson, the first program manager for the BHC work in Del Norte, then funded a study to get a handle on school attendance first. The researchers with Humboldt State University, 90 miles to the south, who analyzed chronic absenteeism—defined as missing 10 percent or more of school days during a year—were in for a stunner. In Del Norte, nearly 30 percent of kindergarteners were chronically absent, a figure no one expected.[12] Nationally, about 10 percent of children are chronically absent in these earliest grades, although one study noted that it ranges widely by the districts it studied, with the best-performing districts showing about 5 percent chronic absenteeism among its youngest students and the worst-performing districts showing about 20 percent—leaving Del Norte's 30 percent still an outlier.[13]

Although on the surface kids missing kindergarten might sound inconsequential (and might explain why many parents frequently skipped it), it in fact mattered greatly. Children of all socioeconomic levels who are chronically absent in kindergarten do worse academically afterward. That's particularly true for poor children whose parents lack the resources to catch them up; for them, chronic absenteeism in kindergarten predicts the lowest levels of academic achievement in fifth grade.[14] Moreover, school districts lose money when children are absent, shortchanging other students.

Despite a few interventions by the schools team to tackle absenteeism, a follow-up study in 2013 discouragingly showed that rates in Del

Norte were about the same. The team analyzed the situation from various perspectives. Were the interventions strong and long enough? Was transportation a problem, given the region's mountainous terrain? Were family problems or other psychosocial issues causing kids to miss school? Or, in the case of kindergarten, did parents simply not appreciate its importance to future success?[15]

Even those who did make it to kindergarten were lagging behind peers elsewhere. Nearly 70 percent of the children were deemed not ready for kindergarten, meaning that they lacked basic skills in language and expression, cognition, math, and social-emotional development, such as being able to listen and sit still.[16] Once again, the Del Norte figure is an outlier, even among poor communities. One study reported that 52 percent of poor children nationally weren't ready for kindergarten, and for children from families of moderate to high income, that figure went down to 25 percent.[17]

Then the worst statistic yet emerged: roughly 50 percent of third-graders in Del Norte County were not reading at grade level, putting them at serious risk for later academic failure. A common adage in educational circles is that children learn to read in the first three grades of elementary school; after that, they read to learn. Beginning in fourth grade, they start reading to gain mastery over subjects such as science and math, to solve problems, and to think critically. Up to half of printed fourth-grade curriculum is incomprehensible to students who read below that grade level.[18]

Those hoping to catch up face slim odds: three-fourths of students who read poorly in third grade remained poor readers in high school. The frustration shows, as students with low literacy achievement tend to develop more behavioral and social problems. Most critically, those who don't read at grade level by third grade are four times more likely to drop out of high school than those who are proficient readers.[19] Education experts now widely view third-grade reading proficiency as the crucial step for breaking cycles of intergenerational poverty.

To lift these alarming figures, the School Systems Implementation Team initiated "professional learning communities" that had teachers, school district leaders, and others come together to figure out what's working and what's not. The team also secured outside funding to support third-grade tutoring.

The numbers didn't budge. "It was a big failure, and it didn't do anything," said Geneva Wiki, the current Endowment program manager for the BHC work. "So they said, 'We don't know what to do.'" Kevin Hartwick, another founding member of the school systems team and a local business leader, said of the lackluster results, "It was really clear that tutoring, although a nice tool, isn't going to solve the issue, especially when you realize that 50 percent of third graders were not reading at grade level. We had to take it on the chin and have a lot of discussion."[20]

Recognizing that there must be deeper obstacles at work, Wiki said BHC staff and the school systems team huddled together, along with a few outside experts, to "design this process to deeply understand what was going on with kids and families." They decided to pursue a route of "empathy-based research" that undertook top-to-bottom assessments of barriers to children's academic success, from home life and transportation to the school setting.

A few members of the school systems team joined two experts in conducting thirty-eight in-depth interviews with parents, teachers, and community members. "We went to their homes," said Wiki. "'What's a day in your life like, what's a week like in your life? What's working for you, what's not working for you? Show me where your kid does his homework, where you eat dinner.'" Sometimes children led the tour.

A common theme was that parents wanted to help their children succeed but didn't know how best to do it, especially because many felt overwhelmed and lived paycheck to paycheck. They worried about keeping their kids away from drugs and alcohol. And no parent fit stereotypes of being indifferent to their child's education. "Guess what, every person cares about their kids and wants them to be successful,"

Wiki said. Wiki is a member and formerly the executive director of the Yurok Tribe and was named, at age thirty, by *Smithsonian* magazine in 2007 to its list of "37 under 36," which recognizes young innovators.

After that intense process, the BHC-led campaign launched its Literacy Initiative in 2015, which also goes by the moniker "3 READ '23".[21] The initiative's goal is for every child in Del Norte County and the adjacent tribal lands to read at third-grade level by 2023. (Children born in 2005 would be graduating from high school then.) Wiki said that the school district superintendent insisted on setting the goal for 100 percent success by 2023 despite the dauntingly high bar. "Teachers were like, 'That's impossible. We can't have 100 percent.' And he said, 'I refuse to say anything less than 100 percent,'" Wiki recounted, because anything less than 100 percent would send a signal that the most challenging students could be left behind; instead, they should dig deeper to understand obstacles for all students.

In analyzing the empathy-based data, the schools team came up with a number of ways to help all segments of the community support literacy in children. One child care provider who had no books, for example, now has a daily reading session, courtesy of a new program called "Wee Read" that offers books to home-based childcare providers. Posters started showing up in various offices, including clinics, the community college, nonprofit organizations, and government agencies, promoting the 3 READ '23 campaign. In 2017, the BHC Youth Training Academy also began certifying young people as in-home childcare specialists; the program's goal is for 100 percent of registered workers to be well qualified by 2023.

BHC paid for a radio ad campaign called "Ready? Set! 'K'" to promote kindergarten readiness and explain what it meant.[22] "No parent could tell you," said Wiki. "And there were 'Kindergarten Ready' guides the school district put out over the summer, with fun things to do." The BHC schools team also ran a media campaign encouraging parents to sign up their kids for school early instead of waiting until the first day of school so that they were more prepared for kindergarten. Talk of literacy began popping up all over the community.

Now, for the first time, the needle in the educational system is starting to move. Although only 33 percent of first-time Del Norte kindergartners were prepared on the first school day in 2015, that figure had risen to 45 percent in 2016. In 2015, only 33 percent of in-home childcare providers met quality standards; by 2017, the number had leapt to 62 percent.[23] Wiki said people are asking her, "What can I do, how can I get on board?"

Chris Howard was clearly excited about progress, saying that the issue regularly surfaces in various forums, including in the local media. He gives progress updates on the literacy campaign at nearly every board of supervisor's meeting, and the city council in Crescent City recently approved $77,000 in federal grant money to support boosting preschool enrollment and book purchases for preschoolers.

Howard referenced "upstream" work under way in Del Norte, a metaphor commonly used to describe the powerful affect of early influences, such as quality preschool education. "As Dr. Ross would say, 'We gotta move upstream, we've got to break the cycle,'" he said. "So we're going to break the cycle with our youth. We give them hope, and we're going to give them a chance. And we're seeing that with kids that come from depressed families, and single mothers, they're learning and they're changing.

"The kids are going to have a chance of a higher education" than their parents, Howard continued. He predicted that many of today's third-graders in the region will exit high school as strong-performing workers, and he sees economic hope for the community in entrepreneurs promoting tourism, agriculture, and small-scale manufacturing. "We're going to have such a beautiful area for people to visit, which everybody wants to see."

~

Formal education is a big part of the plan to revitalize Del Norte, but the community also recognizes the importance of what happens outside school. One thing that happened a lot was underage drinking. Minors in Del Norte drank much more than their peers elsewhere in the state, with 44 percent of Del Norte eleventh-graders reporting that they drank within the last thirty days compared with 36 percent statewide. Del Norte kids were also more likely to binge, meaning knocking back five or more drinks in a short time, compared with peers statewide.[24] Underage drinking doesn't just impair driving skills or land a child in the hospital with alcohol poisoning; it disrupts schooling, promotes aggression and risky sexual behavior, harms normal growth and memory development, increases the odds of abusing drugs, and raises the risk of entanglement in the justice system.

Many young people modeled the alcohol abuse they saw at home, and others got pulled in through peer pressure while stuck inside during the cold, rainy months, when illicit drinking added excitement. Sometimes teens drank alone, self-medicating. Others drank just because it seemed cool.

Then fifteen students chose a BHC-run summer internship in 2013 that concentrated on community organizing. As usual, organizers asked the teens to brainstorm about what issue they wanted to tackle. In a complete surprise to adults, the teens chose prevention of alcohol theft from local grocery stores. A number of young people have died in alcohol-related vehicle accidents in Del Norte over the years, including a seventeen-year-old girl and a woman in her early twenties who had perished just weeks before the internship. The students all knew how easy it was to steal bottles of high-proof alcohol.

With that decision in hand, Melissa Darnell, then the youth community organizer for the Del Norte BHC staff, prepared them for the goal of the internship: a one-hour public "action" to convince community leaders to make changes. She taught them to start with research, such as quality studies, citations, and statistics showing the extent of the problem as well as remedies for it.

Darnell followed the PICO model of community organizing, which was developed by a Jesuit priest in the early 1970s and concentrates on finding shared values and building relationships. As Patrick Cleary with the Humboldt Area Foundation stated, that was the attraction to the model. "PICO has evolved to the point where it's not overtly Christian," Cleary said. "PICO is very much into a win-win, and very much into this idea that you have to build the relationship first. So I'm going to disagree with you on some issues, but if you and I know each other, if we have a relationship, then we're not going let that issue keep us from being able to talk going forward."

The fifteen teens got busy during the eight-week paid internship, studying data on alcohol use, polling their peers to find out how they got alcohol, investigating the consequences of teen drinking, and schooling themselves on industry strategies to prevent store theft.

Then they met with local officials, including the manager at Safeway, health officials, and politicians, to explain the problem and to ask for their support. The students told them how the local Safeway, Walmart, and Shop Smart were easy pickings and that kids would steal several bottles at once, tucking them under bulky sweaters or into deep coat pockets. The revelation jolted adults. Although everyone knew teen drinking was a problem in Del Norte, no one had seriously considered where kids got all this alcohol. "I was amazed," said Gary Blatnick, then director of the county Department of Health and Human Services in Crescent City, who met with the teens. "I didn't realize how in their face it was, how easy it was to steal. None of us did."

Then the youth prepared scripts for the one-hour public action and assigned duties for it, including the all-important timekeeper. Darnell emphasized the importance of starting precisely on time and ending precisely on time. People in power will not expect young people to be so timely, she added, and it will only increase their respect, said Darnell, a white woman of medium height, short brown hair, and a professional and warm demeanor. As she emphasized, "Power respects power." She also teaches the students to speak from a place of equality with the leaders.

The big day came on August 14, 2013. Speaking before a standing-room-only crowd of one hundred, ten young people took turns at the podium, each wearing the same green T-shirt with their group's name, Public Action to Curb Underage Access to Alcohol. They were specifically addressing several audience members: a city council member, managers of three nonprofit service agencies, and the Safeway manager. (Safeway was the sole focus only because the store manager agreed to attend the meeting. Representatives from the other liquor retailers in Crescent City didn't respond to invitations to attend, one event organizer said.)

When Alyssa DeWolf, a fifteen-year-old high school sophomore and mother of an infant daughter, began talking, the dark-haired teen momentarily struggled with tears as she described growing up with an alcoholic mother who sometimes flew into rages. When Alyssa was four, her mom threw her against a wall, sending her to the hospital while her father, a fisherman, was out at sea. "She used to blame me for why she drank, even though she drank before she had me. I never felt good enough," Alyssa told the rapt crowd.

Alyssa started drinking at age twelve, and stealing alcohol was effortless. She'd shoplift a purse at the Walmart, hide a bottle in it, and then walk off with both. "I could easily go back thirty minutes later and do it again," Alyssa told the crowd. She also stole spirits from a small liquor store while a friend distracted the clerk with questions. If teens can easily get alcohol, "of course, they will drink," she said. Alyssa started missing class and got kicked out of school. (When she learned she was pregnant, though, she stopped drinking, and she has since returned to school.)

When sixteen-year-old Sergio Chavez took the microphone, he described how he and his friends had earlier that year walked into Crescent City's Safeway and stole nine "high-priced" bottles for a beach party, including cognac and vodka. They had stashed them under loose-fitting clothing. That night, his older brother, intoxicated, stumbled and struck his head on a rock. An ambulance took the severely injured young man away; he recovered, but the incident shook Sergio. "I've had multiple friends end up with alcohol poisoning or get put on probation or even die from drinking stolen alcohol," he said.

Sixteen-year-old Alberto Gonzales then shared research findings with the crowd. A "startling number of youth" reported that stolen alcohol was their main source, Alberto said, "yet none of the agencies we talked to identified this as a problem." Alberto shared the various minor adjustments stores could make to thwart the theft, such as moving shelves with liquor to more visible locations, installing locking gates or cabinets, improving video surveillance, or placing bulky antitheft plastic caps on bottles.

Then seventeen-year-old Willow Rodgers stood up and asked the five community leaders for specific commitments to reduce teen access to liquor. The Safeway manager, Brian Ridgely, agreed to take steps to thwart alcohol theft, including purchasing and installing the large plastic caps Alberto had mentioned and meeting with the youth and a law enforcement officer in sixty days to discuss progress. Loud applause and whoops filled the room with each of his agreements, and even louder applause broke out when he said he'd gone a step further and asked his remote supervisors to give him more discretion in enacting policies to prevent thefts. The youth were beaming and smiling at the end of the event, reveling in their victory. The city council member and agency managers also agreed to support alcohol theft-prevention policies within their organizations. The *Del Norte Triplicate* ran a front-page article on the event the next day.

Not long after, the Safeway store installed antitheft caps on all liquor bottles. Management also closed the store entrance nearest the alcohol aisle at 10 p.m. and blocked access to it after 2 a.m., refurbished the bathrooms (teens would enter them to better hide their stolen bottles), and worked more closely with local police. The positive publicity so pleased higher-level Safeway executives that they also gave Ridgley something he'd long been asking for: the budget to hire plainclothes security staff. "The word on the street is Safeway is shut down" as a destination for teen liquor theft, Darnell said several months after the action.

After the Safeway success, organizers turned their attention to the local Walmart, and management responded. It took one meeting with a few of the teens and Darnell for the Walmart store manager to agree to use the plastic antitheft caps, reduce liquor inventory, improve video surveillance, and hold more store meetings near the alcohol section where staff could keep an eye on things. When the Del Norte County Board of Supervisors learned of all this activity, they invited the teens to a meeting to describe the results. At the end of their presentation, the students got a standing ovation from the supervisors and the crowd, a rarity in those chambers. In February 2017, a "civic collaboration" was credited with convincing Walmart to further enhance security by putting its liquor supply behind locked glass doors.[25]

In another action soon after that, ninety elementary school students successfully petitioned the city council to put a moratorium on new alcohol and tobacco licenses for retail stores in Crescent City so as to prevent a new tobacco retailer from opening next to the cinema and arcade where young people gather.[26]

~

Substance and alcohol abuse aren't new crises on Native American reservations. Thomas O'Rourke Sr., chairman of the Yurok Tribe, which with nearly five thousand enrolled members is the largest tribe in California and is part of the BHC campaign in the region, emphasizes that drinking and drugs rank among the biggest threats that the tribe faces. A *Los Angeles Times* reporter spent time in Weitchpec (pronounced "Wech-peck") reporting on factors behind the seven suicides in the region, many of them by young people, during an eighteen-month period between 2014 and 2016. In that "upriver" part of the Yurok reservation, unemployment hovers around 80 percent,[27] and 70 percent of the reservation has no access to basic telephone and electrical services, with many relying on generators for power.[28] In addition, the Klamath River, for millennia the lifeblood for the Yurok Tribe and a primary source of its traditional food, is ailing; in recent years catches of fish have been sharply restricted and sometimes banned altogether. The reporter described many residents whiling away their time with video games, drugs, or drinking. A forty-seven-year-old man in Weitchpec told the reporter that everyone he knows in his age group has either survived a bout with substance abuse or was still in the throes of it.[29]

Historic trauma also affects many on reservation lands. The tribes in this region coped with an onslaught of historic horrors, including genocidal campaigns sanctioned in the nineteenth century by the US government[30] and ancestral land taken or swindled away from them; later, their children were forcibly sent to boarding schools, cutting them off from their cultural practices and language. By 2010, there were only a handful of Yurok elders fluent in their language, although the tribe has since launched an extensive fluency program, and it's now part of the school district curriculum. Restoring health entails healing from those historic traumas, said Wiki, program manager for the campaign and herself a Yurok tribal member. "We have to tackle it. It's essential," she said when we first met in 2012. "We won't get to real system change and shifting resources to prevention if we don't get to that."

Critically, that healing begins with healing the tribe's ancestral lands. In surely the most surprising initiative in the entire BHC campaign, community members in the upper part of the reservation decided to embark on that quest. Their goal was to bring back the traditional practice of controlled forest burns, fostering the growth of native plants and reducing the risk of catastrophic fire.

As a result, tribal members have since led controlled burns on more than 500 acres, with many more planned far into the future on the 57,000-acre reservation. They are quickly restoring natural abundance to the region after nearly a century of forest fire suppression by the US government. The project attracted the attention of researchers from Stanford University and the University of California, who are documenting the benefits of the burns, including increased yields from valued plants, dramatic reduction of pests, and improved soil.

The 2012 resident vote to prioritize controlled forest burns over other health initiatives—even youth activities—highlights the importance of cultural and spiritual needs. For the first time in decades, people are spotting elk near Weitchpec along with more deer, bobcats, and black bear. And no longer are Yurok basket weavers running out of material, such as pliable and strong hazel sticks. Acorn crops are healthier, and mushrooms and huckleberries now grow in abundance on sites where the controlled fires cleared overgrowth. Each marks a restoration of traditional ways of life. That's a direct route to better health in all realms, said O'Rourke.

"We're in a very depressed area in one sense because we don't have a lot of money as a people or a community. But that doesn't mean that we're not rich," O'Rourke said when we met in February 2014 outside the first burn site, a steep hillside 5 miles down the highway from Weitchpec that for centuries has been a prime site to gather hazel sticks. Now new sticks were vigorously sprouting after the controlled fire the previous year had cleared off the choking undergrowth. "We are very rich, and that's with the traditional way of life.

"You get up in the morning, and you get out there on the hillside and you start picking hazel sticks. I've thought, 'Man, it feels good to be alive.' And that's what it makes you feel. And you tell me that's not good for your health," O'Rourke said. Job prospects are scarce in that upriver region of the reservation, which is located inland at the confluence of the Klamath and Trinity rivers, and drug and alcohol abuse too common.

Healthy forest burns do in fact foster a form of youth activity. "A day on the hill [gathering plant materials] is a day of prevention. And you have to look at it that way," O'Rourke said, "because ultimately our biggest battle here that deals with health is alcohol and drugs. It leads to abuse, and it leads to basically the breakdown of society. And that comes from a lack of having something to do that is real."

Although fire management is an outlier in the BHC campaign, these burns also perfectly underscore the initiative's main point: that community profoundly shapes well-being, disease rates, and longevity. That argument is obvious to Susan Cameron, PhD, a Navajo/Hispanic scholar who works with the Smithsonian's National Museum of the American Indian in Washington, DC. She said Native Americans' well-being is intrinsically linked to culture and community, as it is for virtually everyone. "Health can only be rooted in your community. There's no other way it can be," Cameron said. And much of what children need to learn to keep the Yurok culture and community strong, she noted, comes from a healthy forest.

A daunting challenge, however, remains healing the Klamath River, the fundamental source of life and sustenance for the Yurok Tribe. The Yurok and Hoopa Valley tribes maintain rights for ceremonial, subsistence, and commercial fisheries on the Klamath River Basin, which includes the Klamath and Trinity rivers. The Klamath was historically the third most productive salmon and steelhead fishery on the West Coast, but since the late 1960s, the fish runs steadily declined because of logging, pollution, and especially four dams upstream that diverted water flows to farmlands.[31]

Due to perilously low populations in 2017, salmon allocations were drastically cut, affecting families' ability to feed themselves and to perform cultural ceremonies. The previous year, at the 2016 Klamath Festival, the cooking pits for salmon were empty for the first time in the festival's fifty-four-year history, following the worst Chinook salmon run on record.[32]

In the midst of the bleak news, however, in April 2016, Governor Jerry Brown, Oregon Governor Kate Brown, former Secretary of the Interior Sally Jewell, Yurok Tribal Chair O'Rourke, and several others gathered at Requa, a historic Yurok village at the mouth of the Klamath, and signed an agreement to remove the dams in 2020. This move marks one of the largest proposed river restoration projects in the country, following decades of activism by native tribes. "Dam removal is a key element of large-scale fish restoration efforts on the Klamath, and we believe it puts the people of the Klamath Basin back on a path toward lasting prosperity," O'Rourke said at the signing event.

~

True North Organizing Network, which launched in 2012, now leads community organizing in the region, where nothing like it has been seen before. The network's early funding came from the Del Norte BHC campaign,[33] but other foundations also now support it. "I think we have a unique story that funders are interested in finding out more about," said Terry Supahan, its executive director and a Native American.

Its region encompasses Del Norte County as well as Humboldt County and tribal lands, areas with a history of divisive organizing campaigns, including those that began in the 1960s and lasted for decades to protect the environment. This activism, of course, arouses intense controversy, pitting jobs and economic well-being against preservation of natural resources.

"We get ourselves in hot water if we don't acknowledge that there's a long tradition and history of people getting involved in our region before us," Supahan said. "We certainly want to honor that, but we also want to say that this organizing is distinctly different from what we have also done in the past.

"The critical distinction is that the kind of single-issue organizing that has taken place in the past was focused on dealing with whatever issue had been prioritized by passionate people, whether preserving redwood forests, old-growth forests, or bringing down the dams on the Klamath River," Supahan continued. "What Building Healthy Communities inspired is for people to think about once you've built the network, how do you sustain it? It's not a single-issue campaign, but building something that has its own legs, and will continue to grow and thrive."

Supahan is from the Karuk Tribe, another federally recognized tribe with lands in Humboldt and Siskiyou counties, both adjacent to Del Norte. Prior to taking over at True North, he spent twenty years working with tribes and rural governments, brokering agreements on community projects.

"As far as we can see, we are the only truly rural-based organization doing community organizing, actively organizing Native Americans in Indian country with Latinos, blacks, whites, Hmong, and others. It is a unique experiment," he said. Recently, two tribal leaders expressed support for his organization and a desire to collaborate, which heartened Supahan. "To have them with their busy schedules, and all the demands of their own people, recognize that community organizing is valuable, because it helps them grow and become more resilient and more confident and more capable, it touched me to hear them speak for True North," he said.

Water resources, immigration, housing, police accountability, and education are the group's current focus. Following the 2016 presidential election, True North representatives began speaking before various groups to ask them to value and protect all people in the community. Supahan said he would remind audiences "that unless you're a full-blooded Indian from this region, everybody's an immigrant. And it shouldn't just be that you got yours, but there's a basis of humanity that you care for all peoples."

As for the nation's political divide, Supahan—who knows from years of experience that rural communities often believe that urban areas ignore their needs—said the 2016 presidential election offers an opportunity. (Donald Trump won by a landslide in Del Norte, with 54 percent voting for the Republican candidate versus 36 percent Democrat and 10 percent Independent. The last time a majority of the county's residents voted Democrat in a presidential race was for Jimmy Carter in 1976.)

"The federal election shined a pretty bright light on our differences in this country, particularly with rural America," Supahan said, "and we have to have ten thousand conversations with people who may not know us, may not like us. We think that we have more in common than people are willing to believe," he continued, speaking for True North. "If they want future generations to be able to raise their families and live here, then more of us should be talking to each other, not less. Our power is coming together, not arguing or skirmishing over the resources that divide us."

True North follows the PICO community organizing model, which relies on relationships. The group adheres to the tenet that there are no permanent allies or permanent enemies because issues change over time. Adversaries could later come together, so it's important to maintain respectful relationships, especially in small towns. Julia Lerma, True North's lead organizer for Humboldt and Del Norte counties, said, "It's all around relationships, one by one, small groups. It takes time. But you're building a foundation that is harder to break or to shake up, that will be here for generations to come. And it's centered around building leadership."

The leadership especially focuses on the area's young people, of all demographics, and True North wants to start running youth organizing year-round in the area, not just during the summer academy. "My objective in working with youth is to give them the self-confidence that comes from finding your voice, telling your story, learning how the process works, and being able to really have some efficacy," Supahan said.

He's keenly interested in recruiting more young Native Americans to join the work and to start sharing stories to heal from trauma as part of the quest to lift up the distressing statistics on reservations. "If we do the hard work of being vulnerable and exposing our heart, our ideas, our thoughts in this constructive way, then it's going to make it easier for my children and my children's children to be healthy. I think the personal storytelling aspect is a key element of addressing historic trauma," Supahan said. "We're not doing ourselves any favor by being mad and angry and dysfunctional. It's there, and it's a part of our history. But the more we start to talk about it, the more we lift the load and share the load."

True North also began hosting nonpartisan candidate forums in 2014, a first for the region, and it has supported the development of young political leaders. One of its notable successes was a True North leader, Alex Fallman, who ran for city council in Crescent City and won the seat in November 2016, when he was twenty years old.

Fallman credits Melissa Darnell with his community organizing training and inspiration to run for office. In a video interview, Fallman described how his mother was addicted to drugs most of his life and had to leave Del Norte County because she couldn't find the services to help her overcome her addiction. He wants to help create a community where residents can stay and thrive. "Her words today that really impacted me are 'I'd be dead if I stayed in Del Norte County.' And I don't want anybody to live like my mom again in my community, in my home."

CHAPTER 8
Good Eats

Chanowk Yisrael, wearing a brown short-sleeved shirt and khakis, with his black dreadlocks dangling past his shoulders, stood grinning outside a Sacramento County office in the spring of 2017, holding his application to open a farm stand. He would be the first urban farmer permitted to sell food on his property in the unincorporated section of the county thanks to a law he worked to pass. Chanowk and his wife, Judith, who stood next to him sporting shorter dreadlocks and a matching smile, had collaborated on the initiative with a coalition of other activists under the Building Healthy Communities campaign in Sacramento.

The coalition wanted to make it easier for urban farmers to sell their own foods in and around Sacramento, the state's capital, which lies in a major agricultural region in California. But laws on the books prohibited that in densely populated areas, even though a number of these neighborhoods are considered food deserts. (The term *food desert* is defined as limited or no access to fresh produce within a 1-mile radius in a city or 10-mile radius in rural areas.) The Oak Park neighborhood where the Yisraels live, a high-crime area known for outbreaks of violence, including four homicides in the first half of 2017,[1] was one of those food deserts.[2]

The permit culminated a decade-long journey for the Yisraels. Chanowk (pronounced "Ka-nowk") began thinking about urban farming in 2007. Although he had a job as a systems engineer with a large telecommunications company, rumblings of an economic downturn left him uneasy, and he disliked feeling vulnerable over something as fundamental as his food supply. In 2008, he and Judith plunged into gardening in their backyard, further motivated by their preference for organic produce for their recently blended family of nine children, which was getting pricey.

"We wanted to break the cycle of poor eating that typically plagues the black community," said Judith Yisrael. "It was very expensive to do. We were shopping at local health food stores, and there were months where our food bill was as high as our mortgage."

It was a rough start, they both recall with a laugh. They first planted vegetables in July 2008, in a region with hot, dry summers. "In a few weeks everything was dead, *everything*. We had a lot to learn about growing food," Judith said. "But there was this paradigm shift that happened within ourselves, that happened within our family, when we started to connect ourselves back to the earth. And here I thought we were just going to get zucchini and tomatoes and cucumbers. We got so much more."

They sought training, they studied, and they plunged back in. Today they have an abundant garden, egg-laying chickens, and an orchard with more than forty trees growing figs, plums, and persimmons. In 2011, they branded their homestead the Yisrael Family Farm. When the house next door went into foreclosure, the Yisraels bought it, expanding their operation into a thriving half-acre farm in an area where gunfire occasionally erupts. During my visit, a police helicopter—which Judith quipped were "ghetto birds"—flew overhead. The Yisraels raise 60 percent of their food supply on their property, she estimates, and growing and preparing it is a family affair that has brought them all close together. The couple got permission to maintain a garden at the closed elementary school across the street, which yields a bountiful cherry harvest that they share with neighbors. In addition, they hold classes in canning, drying herbs, and other food preservation techniques and host a summer youth urban farming program called Project GOOD, for Growing Our Own Destiny. Under a contract with the Sacramento BHC campaign, Chanowk also runs a project building backyard gardens throughout the low-income neighborhood; more than 130 have been planted so far. The Yisrael Family Farm uses the tagline, "Transforming the Hood for Good!"

A few months after the county approved their urban farm stand license, they set up a table in front of their home, piled it with zucchini, tomatoes, eggplant, and squash, and added a sign stating, "Today's Harvest: 110 lbs. of Produce."

Suddenly neighbors have a new supply of highly affordable organic produce and other goods. Although it would take a lot of farm stands to fully supply the neighborhood, the 110 pounds from the Yisraels is a notable start. It also provides a sense of community and teaches residents about healthy eating.[3] The local media regularly feature the Yisraels, and many people enthusiastically support their work, Chanowk said. "I walked by a brother on the street, and he said, 'Hey, you're the guy on TV. We're rooting for you!'"

Studies demonstrate conclusively, but not surprisingly, that making quality, nutritious foods such as fresh produce, lean meats, and whole grains available translates into better health. Research from California and New York found that living in a neighborhood with access to healthy foods—and fewer convenience stores and fast-food restaurants—led to lower rates of obesity and diabetes.

Judith Yisrael's parents kept a garden when she was young, and they regularly ate home-cooked meals prepared by her stay-at-home mother. After her parents split up when she was six, dinners changed to more convenient fare because her mother now worked while taking care of four children. They sometimes brought home extra food from local churches or food banks, Judith said, and she recalls getting bags of pastries, including cream-filled chocolate ones she and her siblings ate regularly. "No limits on it. It was on the table, it was food, and we ate it," Judith said. Her older sister developed diabetes in her twenties, and her mother has hypertension. Her father died of heart disease. Her doctors told her she was headed in the same direction, but she's fighting back against that fate. "I really almost felt like, 'This is your destiny,'" she said.

The Sacramento Urban Agriculture Coalition, a group Chanowk Yisrael helped found in 2013, advanced the ordinance that made his farm stand legal. The roughly fifteen-member coalition of nonprofit organizations is intensely focused on changing the food landscape in that BHC site, located in the southern part of the city and home to a number of low-income suburban enclaves, including Oak Park.

In addition to allowing temporary farm stands, the 2017 county ordinance also legalized beekeeping, raising chickens and ducks on small lots, and selling honey and eggs. It's modeled after a similar law that the Sacramento City Council passed in 2015, also following sustained advocacy by the BHC urban agriculture coalition.

Sacramento City Council member Jay Schenirer, whose district includes much of the BHC site, instantly supported the proposed urban agriculture city ordinance when the coalition pitched it. "We were interested day one because of nutrition issues," Schenirer said. "In the area I represent, especially in Oak Park, we have so many vacant lots. So we were also looking at gardens as a way to get rid of blight." He also likes how urban agriculture stimulates economic development by lowering both food prices and production costs, leaving more money in the pockets of both buyers and sellers. He called the city's urban agriculture ordinance a "three-fer."

In another policy win, the Sacramento BHC coalition secured the passage in 2013 of the Urban Agriculture Incentive Zones Act. This state law authorizes any city or county to let owners of vacant or blighted parcels raise and sell produce or certain animals on the land in exchange for a tax break.

One member of the coalition, Oak Park Sol, took full advantage of the program, convincing a local property owner to let it open a community garden in her large 50-by-250-foot lot on busy Broadway Boulevard. The nonprofit organization's staff and volunteers cleared out piles of debris and planted the parcel with vegetables. Today, Broadway Sol Community Garden is a peaceful oasis and gathering site in the heart of Oak Park for healthy cooking demonstrations led by another group in the coalition called Food Literacy. When I visited, two instructors were teaching children and their parents to make salsa and a watermelon salad with brown rice. Oak Park Sol has taken on a number of vacant lot conversions since the law passed, but it first consults neighbors about what they want—for example, a park or garden—and how it should be designed.

With all the unused urban land nationwide, cities are starting to see possibilities. A 2014 study from Columbia University identified almost 5,000 acres of vacant land suitable for farming in New York City's five boroughs. The study emphasized the economic potential of farming this land, including significant sales of healthy, affordable food in low-income areas and to restaurants looking for local produce.[4]

Urban agriculture is expanding in numerous cities, including New York, Chicago, and Baltimore, at the urging of food policy councils and city governments. As of 2016, the US Department of Agriculture counted 314 urban farms (defined as selling more than $1,000 worth of products a year) in the country, 101 of which were in the Northeast. Nine out of ten of these urban farmers are white, followed by 5 percent African American, and they skew younger than rural farmers. Many work their land with social goals in mind, most commonly improving food security in low-income areas as well as education and community building. Although profitability and labor costs worry city farmers, they also say that regulations are a major hurdle.[5]

Urban bureaucracies are gradually easing up, however, recognizing that growing local produce trumps possible nuisances. Organizations in several other BHC sites, including City Heights and Richmond, are also pushing local governments to support urban agriculture. A Richmond nonprofit organization called Urban Tilth, for example, has been working on the issue since 2005 and now maintains thirteen gardens and farms in the city, including a 3-acre farm that opened in 2016.[6] The group also runs a summer youth apprentice program that offers urban agriculture training along with civic engagement and leadership development.

Shawn Harrison, founder of Soil Born Farms, a Sacramento nonprofit organization that operates two urban farms comprising 55 acres, serves as the lead for BHC's food action team. His is a contracted position, given the time involvement; the team also hired a consultant who helps moderate the monthly meetings and prepares the agenda. This coalition of Sacramento food access advocates formed in 2010 at the inception of the BHC campaign, and in addition to the passage of the urban agriculture ordinances, it has made its mark on the community in several other realms. In an early project, the action team started a gleaning program that has delivered more than 150,000 pounds of unwanted produce from residential trees, including to the food bank. In addition, they've cultivated more than 1,700 community advocates for food access, both youth and adult.

Then, to operate with more sophisticated data, the food team also mapped South Sacramento, identifying the areas with the best and worst access to healthy food. Harrison said that the Harlem Children's Zone in New York City inspired the mapping project. That initiative, launched by education pioneer Geoffrey Canada in 2000, delivers comprehensive services to children in Harlem from before birth to high school graduation. It began with a twenty-four-block section of Central Harlem and now encompasses ninety-seven blocks. The project is renowned for establishing the concept of place-based philanthropy and laid the foundation for the Endowment's BHC campaign, as well as many other community change projects.

Harrison and a few others visited Harlem to gain insight into an intensive neighborhood focus. "That analysis showed me the deep change that happened in a block-by-block fashion," he said. Harrison realized that the team needed to break the Sacramento site into smaller sections, based on the characteristics of each neighborhood, and then work through community leaders to expand healthy food access. "That was huge learning for us," he said. "Huge."

The food team's mapping project revealed that the northern section of the BHC site was doing well, with a robust farmers' market, the Oak Park Sol community garden, and other projects, but the rest of the sections were barren. So they concentrated on finding well-known locals who could begin to make changes.

The team thought it would be simple enough to persuade corner store owners to stock fresh produce, bottled water, and a few other nutritious items, install refrigeration (usually with financial assistance) for these perishables, and then display the healthier fare in the front of the store. But the prodigious effort that followed met with decidedly mixed results, said Davida Douglas, then executive director of Alchemist CDC, the nonprofit organization that led the corner store program for the food team. (Douglas, the organization's first employee, is now its operations director.)

In essence, Douglas found that unless store owners already built fresh food sales into their business plan, they only haphazardly stocked and promoted them, despite repeatedly telling her they thought it was a great idea. "It boils down to they've already got a business model that's keeping the business afloat, it's good enough for them," Douglas said. "And this is just a new thing that maybe sounded like a good idea for the moment, but they hadn't really thought through what that meant for them day to day."

One small store that we visited had earned headlines for joining the BHC-run corner store initiative, but by the fall of 2016, there were only a few sad signs of the effort. A rack of baskets for holding produce was almost empty, with some shriveled and virtually inedible offerings. The store owner told us that he stopped participating because nobody bought the produce, but as Douglas pointed out after we left—walking under a weathered store sign and passing a litter- and cigarette-butt-filled plot of dirt—that of course no one would purchase decaying produce. At another small market, Douglas said her organization, with campaign funding, purchased a small refrigeration unit by the register to stock water. When Douglas returned, the water was gone and the unit restocked with soda. She explained their agreement, and owner agreed to follow it, yet when she came back, it was once again filled with soda. A similar scenario played out at the same store with a basket filled with apples the campaign purchased; soon the owner filled it with pastries. "There's just this inertia going, it's so hard to push against," Douglas said.

It's an assessment shared by Marion Standish, who has long spear-headed the Endowment's healthy food access program. "I have to confess, I have never been a big fan of the corner store conversion. I'm willing to be disabused, but the economic model of the corner store has really been about liquor and cigarettes and canned foods. It's just not been a model for fresh food," Standish said. She did mention some success stories, such as Change Lab Solutions in Oakland, California, which worked with the Southern California city of Baldwin Park to pass a voluntary Healthy Corner Store Policy in 2014. Standish also cited work in Philadelphia, where a nonprofit organization called the Food Trust and the city's public health department convinced a network of six hundred corner stores to sell healthier fare, with 83 percent of the stores meeting basic participation standards.[7] "There are some examples," Standish said. "They may have some unique characteristics."

One of the Sacramento BHC food team's successes does indeed have unique characteristics. Douglas speaks with a mix of enthusiasm and relief at the partnership with the Go Healthy Nutrition Store. It's owned by an African American Seventh-Day Adventist family who refuses to sell tobacco, alcohol, or lottery tickets, despite pressure from sale reps, nor do they stock candy. Douglas and the food team promote the new store through social media, sandwich boards, and flyers, and she purchased equipment for the store, including a produce refrigerator and bike rack, all of which boost the owner's confidence.

"We're getting positive responses from the neighborhood," said owner Ramon Cook. "'Oh, we're so glad you're here,' that type of thing. Especially the ones with the kids," he added, saying that parents appreciate not having to negotiate with pleading children over candy. And he's thrilled to accept the support from the team to help his new store succeed.

~

Getting healthy food into schools is key for children's health. For one thing, it fosters lifelong habits in kids, who also become ambassadors at home. Early on in the campaign, the coalition partnered with the city's school district, putting in salad bars in all seventy-seven of its K–12 schools. The free breakfast program also expanded, reaching fourteen thousand students at thirty-two schools.

Pacific Elementary School, one of the five schools where the BHC food team planted school gardens, changed dramatically as a result of the program. Soil Born Farms runs the school garden project, and the South Sacramento BHC campaign funds it. Fourth-grade teacher Lisa Bettencourt enthusiastically included the garden in her curriculum—the first teacher at Pacific to do so—and now virtually all the teachers in the K–6 school use the garden to varying degrees into their lessons. The day I visited, Bettencourt led her students outside their classroom, asking them to write down words that came to mind as they walked around the garden, through touch, sight, and smell. They then went back to the classroom to write poetry based on the experience. The results were far more inspired, Bettencourt said, than when children used to do the same exercise after looking at photos inside the classroom.

At the end of the school day, Bettencourt asked the students to form a circle and share what they liked about the garden. Echoing many, one girl said, "I like going to the garden because in the classroom we just see pictures of the plants and creatures. And outside we get to see the actual bugs and the plants." Bettencourt weaves the garden into many aspects of the curriculum, such as history, art, and biology and other sciences. It even gave the kids a leg up during a math question on a standardized test, she said. The test asked children to plot dimensions involving a hypothetical garden bed, something they had done in real life. "It was so easy. It was just like we do all the time," the kids reported.

Often the children find that they like something unfamiliar from the garden, such as artichokes and kale, and sometimes learn ways to prepare it. They're also spreading their enthusiasm at home for these foods while occasionally taking home excess harvest. Bettencourt said parents are also now more engaged with the school, with the garden a shared interest. The California Endowment also arranged a visit to Pacific Elementary by television chef Jamie Oliver and the renowned Alice Waters of Chez Panisse. It thrilled the students, who prepared a carrot-and-raisin-citrus salad for the event under Oliver's supervision.

There's now a kindergarten butterfly garden at Pacific Elementary as well as a beautiful sitting area and outdoor classroom near a newly planted school orchard, which replaced one utterly destroyed by vandalism in November 2015.

More than once, vandals have damaged the garden, a heartbreak common to many public gardens. Several times over the years, thieves have cut holes in the fence and stolen equipment, even walking off with the shed, carried piece by piece. The gut-wrenching vandalism of a new orchard at Pacific Elementary left trees stripped of branches and some uprooted entirely. Although the crime shocked the neighborhood and campus, two months later Soil Born Farms hosted a "Vandalism to Victory" event. A few dozen volunteers replanted the orchard, an event covered by local media. Students sent messages to the community, and any future vandals, through their #YouCantStopUsFromGrowing social media campaign.

All the activity prompted the school district to at last put up a long-requested fence to block access to the school from the public park directly next to it, and the school garden hasn't been vandalized since. "The BHC has brought in so many community members. It's like we have these voices now that we didn't have before," said Bettencourt. "That's just made the biggest difference, because suddenly we have these advocates around."

The school, which was once barren except for one tree in the courtyard, is now cheerful and vibrant, with garden-themed murals brightening the walls. The staying power of the food team's work, given the ten-year campaign, made all the difference, Bettencourt added. She remembers an earlier state-funded garden program that never got off the ground because of red tape and its shorter duration. "If the Endowment [campaign] had been a more short-term project, it would have probably failed very quickly," she said. "Because this definitely has taken a lot of time to take root, for lack of a better word."

Tara Lampkins, principal of the seven-hundred-student school, said the garden also helps kids learn communication skills. "We've connected the garden with social-emotional learning," Lampkins said when we talked in the school's cramped front office. "Caring for other living things, helping in the growth of other living things." The time they've spent tending the garden—and interacting with the tiny creatures in it—has sunk in, she pointed out. "I was just in the cafeteria a moment ago, and there was a bug under the table," Lampkins said with a smile. "The students had to notify someone, because they didn't want harm to come to the bug."

~

Sacramento isn't the only place benefiting from healthy food campaigns. A pioneering project comes from Del Norte County and the tribal lands around it, an area where one in three children lives in a household that struggles to put food on the table.[8] The Del Norte BHC campaign secured a $400,000 US Department of Agriculture grant to cultivate four "food forests." These parcels of land are developed on the principles of permaculture and create perennial sources of food, not unlike those found in natural forests. Once established, food forests largely sustain themselves—with the help of basic maintenance—for at least three decades, and in optimal conditions they yield substantial annual quantities of produce.

In Del Norte, the Community Food Council leads this work, and it wrote the successful USDA grant application. Its members include residents, representatives from local agencies, BHC staff, and sometimes hired experts who tackle the pressing need for more locally sourced, affordable, and healthy foods.

Only a few schools had salad bars at the campaign's start; now they are in every K–12 campus, along with more hydration stations delivering chilled water. Consultants taught school cafeteria staff to make affordable "from scratch" meals, now offered daily at the high school. The Del Norte BHC food council expanded a summer lunch program, in coordination with the school district, which in 2016 distributed 23,000 meals during the break. For some of the children, it was the best meal of the day. The group promoted it through media advertisements, flyers, and posters, and the work won a USDA Western regional award for its success in reaching a wide swath of kids.[9] The food council in Del Norte also supported school gardens and provided the initial funding for a now-beloved community garden for the Hmong population living in and around Crescent City, enabling them to grow more of their traditional foods and medicines.

The slogan "Bigfoot Is a Locavore," developed to promote sales of locally grown and produced foods, also came from the food team. A few stores sell baseball hats, T-shirts, and other items with the slogan along with an image of the large, hairy creature some believe lives in the wilds of Del Norte County. The Del Norte BHC campaign also purchased a mobile kitchen for cooking lessons, and the Community Food Council helped the existing seasonal farmers market through advertising and set up the Market Match program, which doubles the value of SNAP (formerly food stamps) benefits at farmers' markets.

Growing food forests, however, is the food council's boldest step. To get the project off the ground, the council teamed up with a federally recognized Native American tribe, the Tolowa Dee-ni' Nation. About half of the tribe's more than 1,600 members live in and around its traditional homeland in Smith River, in the northern part of the county, and it owns some 1,000 acres of land. Erika Partee, the food and garden coordinator for the Tolowa Dee-ni', said the project became even more urgent when the only grocery store in Smith River closed in 2013.

For millennia, the native people in the region lived off its abundant resources, including salmon, steelhead trout, eels, elk, berries, acorns, wild mushrooms, and shellfish. In an area with high unemployment and underemployment and with private and public land ownership limiting hunting and gathering, with dams and water diversions on the

Klamath River reducing salmon and steelhead runs, and with ocean areas under fishing restrictions, however, tribal members now must buy much of their food. Planting food forests is one way to restore at least some of that abundance.

Gardeners will plant apple, peach, cherry, and plum trees, among many other varieties, and tanoaks in one or two sites to grow acorns. They'll also grow herbs and medicinal plants important to the local tribes and plants used to weave baskets, such as bear grass. Huckleberries, blackberries, and other berry plants, along with vines such as grapes and green beans, will grow in the food forests. Groundcover crops will also be planted to nourish the soil while preventing water loss and weed growth.[10]

Food forests require minimal labor once established, which takes four to five years. They're found in scattered cities around the United States, with Seattle boasting the largest food forest on public land in the country, called Beacon Food Forest. Located in the southern part of Seattle, it is now 2 acres, with plans to expand it to 7 acres. The forest contains 420 species of edible plants, and it's free to anyone who comes to pick the harvest. As in Seattle, Del Norte residents will be able to harvest the produce for free, although managers intend to set aside a small portion to process into jams, cider, and other salable products.[11] That kind of offering will be a boon throughout Del Norte County, but especially far inland on tribal lands, where the nearest grocery store is at least an hour's drive away.

The Tolowa Dee-ni' and the food council planned to start the food forests in February 2017, the optimal time for planting bare root trees, but they had to wait because the winter was the wettest on record in California and the ground stayed soggy well into May. Before any plants went in, they also had to put up fences high enough to keep out elk in Smith River, a slightly shorter fence to only keep out deer for the forest site in Crescent City, and another in Weitchpec that needed to keep out not only elk but also hungry black bears. The elementary school in Klamath, site of the Yurok tribal headquarters, hosts the fourth food forest. It's an area surrounded by redwood and conifer forests, but locals decided to forgo any additional fencing beyond the usual school fence and let any animals that enter forage. "They say, "If the elk or the bears come in and take food, then they can,'" said coordinator Partee.

The county's only college—the two-year College of the Redwoods— now hosts one of the food forests. Under that arrangement, the college will run accredited agriculture classes in the food forest, partially in hopes of promoting more local farming for the region. Currently, there is only one full-time vegetable farm near Crescent City, despite demand. The school district would source far more local produce if it could, after the expansion of salad bars and other healthy food efforts, but there's insufficient supply. There's also a local hospital and the 2,500-inmate state prison on the outskirts of Crescent City, so there's an ample local market, said Partee.

In a few years, if all grows according to plan, the food forests won't only fill needs for more fresh food, but will also provide an invaluable learning opportunity, said Partee. The project, she said, intends to "give people in our area the knowledge and the educational power to control their own food supply."

~

Access to healthy food won't come from advocacy alone. Soon after the BHC campaign started in 2010, the Endowment realized that grocery store owners need financial incentives to set up shop in some areas. Many are reluctant to enter low-income neighborhoods, even though advocates will argue that of course poor people still spend money and that it's smart business to keep it local. After conversations with community organizations in South LA that had been trying for years to attract more grocery stores, the Endowment decided that a financing vehicle was needed.

In South LA, one grocery store operates for every 5,957 residents (and many of these stores are value warehouses) versus 3,763 residents per store in West LA. On the west side, the stores are also nicer affairs with more organic food and other healthy offerings.[12] The South LA BHC site includes the South Figueroa Corridor, a busy street lined with pawnshops, cash checking stores, taquerias, auto shops, convenience and liquor stores, and various small businesses, but little in the way of healthy food.

In 2011, the Endowment launched the California FreshWorks Fund, a public-private partnership that started with $273 million. Underpinned by a federal program that provides tax incentives for investments in low-income communities, the fund offers grocers below-market interest rates and various provisions not found in standard loans. Former First Lady Michelle Obama kicked off the project in Southern California, sharing the stage with Endowment president Dr. Robert Ross. Since it began, the fund has supported seventy-eight food businesses, with $70 million invested; similar initiatives have since formed in Colorado, Illinois, Michigan, New Jersey, and New York. (FreshWorks itself was modeled after the successful Pennsylvania Fresh Food Financing Initiative.)

The program had its challenges, and it has recently been restructured for a "FreshWorks 2.0" launch.[13] The new iteration entails a greater focus on assisting small healthy food retailers with outside expertise and grants to scale up such that they can take on the risk of a larger loan and thus spur expansion of access to healthy foods. FreshWorks management made that shift after far fewer food retailers than expected applied for financing from the $125 million designated for such loans given anxiety by small business owners in assuming a large debt. FreshWorks leaders had underestimated that concern, and that program closed in 2015 due to underutilization.

"We really felt we needed to put more emphasis on the technical assistance and support side, and the idea was once we get them ready we think we can package up a loan," said Marion Standish, vice president of enterprise programs with the Endowment. I told Standish that the frank assessments in three independently written 2016 FreshWorks case studies were refreshing given how often organizations only put forward the successes. These reports clearly detailed what worked and what didn't work in this unique venture.[14]

"I appreciate that. It was hard for me personally," Standish said, as she coped with concerns over the funding project's viability, "but in the end I realized that the only way to create a successful program—it had success but it needed to change if it was going to have more success— was to take this hard look."

Still, there are number of unambiguous successes from the financing strategy.

A lot, at the corner of South Central and Slauson avenues, some 2 miles from where the 1992 LA riots broke out following the Rodney King verdict, was once a community eyesore. Today there's a bustling shopping complex here, anchored by the Northgate Gonzalez Market, which received FreshWorks funding and opened in 2014.

As visitors enter, they're greeted by lively Mexican music, a vast produce section, and the scent of fresh bread from a bakery. Meat and seafood counters line the back of the store, and up front, employees bustle around a large prepared-food area, complete with tables for diners. Chef Pablo, a slender man with close-cut dark gray hair and a ready smile, prepared a lunch of grilled wild salmon on a bed of greens, a quinoa roll, and chia seed chocolate pudding, and he served colorful tortillas from a nearby tortilleria. Throughout the store, signs with "Viva La Salud" point out healthy options and good deals. The store also offers healthy living classes, health screenings, and an in-house bank.

Three Northgate Gonzalez stores—the South Los Angeles store as well as one in Inglewood and another in San Diego—have opened in

Southern California with FreshWorks loans, improving food access for approximately 800,000 people. These three stores also created more than 450 jobs with benefits, with 62 percent of the workers hired from the local community.

Trainees from Homeboy Industries, which supports former gang members and the formerly incarcerated, also got jobs in the South LA Northgate Gonzalez store when it opened. One of those Homeboy hires, Tina Sandoval, is still with the store and was promoted from janitor to auditor. When we talked in February 2017, Sandoval had recently placed first for "asset protection" in a chain-wide contest. The store's manager, Alberto Ayala, sat by as Sandoval, a woman with long dark hair, glasses, and a direct gaze, recounted her journey from gangs and prison to landing the job at Northgate Gonzalez, which she had doubted she'd get. With Ayala's support—"He's had a lot of patience with me," Sandoval said—she now regards Northgate Gonzalez staff as family. "I've managed to learn how to control my anger. I no longer walk around with a mask on my face pretending that I'm somebody I'm not. I'm just Tina," Sandoval said. "I'm no longer the person I was when I was growing up." She's getting her gang tattoos erased and meanwhile keeps them covered with long sleeves. She aspires to a management position, a goal Ayala supports. "Most leadership is something that's in your heart, something you just can't teach," Ayala said. "She came with that, she has that."

~

Safe drinking water is perhaps the most basic ingredient in a healthful diet. More than one million residents in California, however, rely on bottled water or, if they're fortunate, an effective filtration system because their tap water contains excessive levels of various chemicals and contaminants. Arsenic is of particular concern because it's linked to bladder, kidney, liver, and skin cancers as well as birth defects and reproductive problems,[15] although the elevated chromium-6 and nitrate levels also alarm many.

Megan Beaman is an attorney and the lead for the BHC Neighborhoods Action Team in the Eastern Coachella Valley, which is working to improve water quality. On a bright October day, she drove me around to show communities with compromised water supplies.

Many people know Coachella Valley, a desert community in Riverside County ringed by mountains, for the lush golf courses of Palm Springs, lavish resorts, and the Coachella Valley Music and Arts Festival. Far fewer, however, visit the eastern side of the valley, home to 88,000. A number of residents here work in the fields, picking dates, grapes, melons, oranges, bell peppers, and many other crops, supporting $626 million in agricultural production in the valley. Others work in service and maintenance jobs in Palm Springs. Many live in trailer parks, which offer a supportive community but substandard conditions, including a lack of safe drinking water—at least until the last few years.

With her blonde hair pulled back and her newborn baby in the backseat of her red pickup truck, Beaman pointed to a metal structure at one trailer park. It was a state-of-the-art reverse osmosis filtration system, which gives the entire park a communal source of safe drinking water. Like most of the trailer parks in Eastern Coachella Valley, it wasn't connected to the municipal water system; instead, it used groundwater wells, which were too often contaminated by high levels of naturally occurring arsenic or contaminants like bacteria from nearby septic systems. Another nonprofit organization, Pueblo Unido, a partner in the BHC work, led the drive to install these systems but, given their novelty, hit a snag because the local water district had no way to approve their installation. Several in the BHC coalition, Beaman included, worked with a local assembly member to expedite approval of state regulations that created a permitting system, overcoming a major hurdle.

Then came the "Agua4All" campaign in 2014, which the California Endowment ran in partnership with Pueblo Unido and the Rural Community Assistance Corporation. With $700,000 from the Endowment and other grants, the partnership installed nearly 190 water stations in BHC sites in Eastern Coachella Valley and South Kern County, which had a similar problem. Placed in schools, community centers, and other high-traffic sites, these stations deliver chilled water and refill bottles. The partnership also installed 127 arsenic remediation filters at homes in South Kern County.

A 2016 evaluation of the Agua4All campaign found that water consumption at one site with the new stations increased by up to 26 percent. That cheered health advocates, who figured that it also meant less soda consumption, a habit linked to diabetes and weight gain.[16] The pilot project captured national attention, and the California state budget in 2016 included $10 million to install many more water stations at schools, reaching an estimated 100,000 students.[17]

Beaman's Neighborhoods Action Team made dramatic headway when it challenged Coachella Valley's all-important water district board. In October 2013, Beaman sent a letter to the board, warning that it was violating the state's Voting Rights Act. Board members were elected from throughout the huge district rather than allowing voters to pick representatives from their geographic area. For Beaman and others, that at-large system explained why the water district board was currently all white, even though most Eastern Coachella Valley residents are Hispanic and even though Hispanics represent 34 percent of all voters in the water district. A month later, the water board announced that it would voluntarily change its elections so that voters could pick representatives by geographic district.[18]

The following year, Cástulo Estrada, a twenty-six-year-old political newcomer, won a seat on the Coachella Valley Water District board for Division 5, where Latinos make up a large majority of the population.

Estrada, a utilities engineer for the City of Coachella, is thought to be the first Latino ever elected to the water district board, and he easily beat an incumbent running for the seat.[19] Estrada made it his quest to push for the construction of water and sewer lines to reach the low-income communities in Eastern Coachella Valley now relying on septic tanks and private wells.

～

The work didn't stop there. The Neighborhoods Action Team decided to push for an advisory committee, which would prioritize the needs of the valley's low-income communities, and approached Estrada with the idea. "He said, 'Funny you should mention that,'" Beaman recalled, as he was thinking the same thing. He recently realized that the water district had citizen advisory committees for golf courses, agriculture, and country clubs, but none for the eastern end of the valley coping with the health crisis of contaminated water supplies. Estrada pushed the idea with fellow board members, as did members of the community and the action team. In February 2017, the water district announced the formation of the Disadvantaged Communities Infrastructure Task Force and appointed various representatives to it from Eastern Coachella Valley.[20]

The new task force is working on short-term fixes like water filter rebates, septic system improvements, and well retrofits. Its long-term vision is to extend the municipal water system into Eastern Coachella Valley, ending the reliance on wells.

The advocacy in Coachella Valley and South Kern County, along with the water crisis in Flint, Michigan, got the attention of California legislators. They are now debating Senate Bill 623, which would create a fund, paid for by a small surcharge on water bills, to get safe drinking water for the nearly one million state residents without it. A recent poll found that 72 percent of Californians said that they would pay up to a dollar a month to fix contaminated water systems.[21]

These rural California communities are hardly alone, however. A 2017 *New York Times* article reported that nearly seventy-seven million Americans live in places where the water systems are in some violation of safety regulations. Water quality, however, isn't a "sexy" issue, as an attorney with the Natural Resources Defense Council noted.[22] Although the notion that every family should have safe water and healthy food doesn't arouse much controversy, attaining those widely accepted goals in the face of entrenched systems still often requires advocacy.

CHAPTER 9

Healing Trauma

Godwin Higa, principal of Cherokee Point Elementary School in the City Heights neighborhood of San Diego, opens the door to his office every day around 5:30 a.m. Classes don't start until 7:45 a.m., but he gets there early to confer with custodial staff, answer email, and do administrative work before the bustle of the day begins. His early morning routine ensures "undivided attention" to students and staff during the school day, Higa said. Parents who work can also drop their kids off as early as 6:15 a.m., and he's available if they want to talk about anything.

Many of the nearly six hundred students in this K–6 school have already dealt with poverty, strife at home, fear of their parents being deported, and neighborhood violence and crime; Higa's benevolent attention calms them. Still, anxious or angry youngsters do sometimes act out, but rather than facing punishment, Higa said he or a teacher will ask, "What happened to you?" not "What's wrong with you?"

"When you ask, 'What's wrong with you?' it's totally negative right away, versus 'What's happening to you, you don't seem right?' As soon as we say that," Higa said, "the kids look at you like 'How did you know that I'm feeling down today?'" When they're done talking, usually the child feels better, returns to class, the disruptive behavior occurs less often and generally fades away after a few more talks, and a trusting bond is formed, he said.

Higa, who has a kindly smile, warm eyes, and close-cut black hair turning gray, said his own difficult childhood animated his compassion for children dealing with adversity. Even though he was just two years old, he still distinctly remembers a dish thrown against a wall in anger the same year his parents divorced. He grew up in Hawaii, on his grandfather's hog farm on Oahu, and money was always scarce. His father left his life after the divorce, and his mother died when he was sixteen.[1]

Higa transformed Cherokee Point into a "trauma-informed community school"—the first in San Diego County, or much of anywhere else in 2015, when he officially made the transition with support from the Building Healthy Communities campaign in City Heights. A culture of respect and support permeates the campus, with adults trained to recognize trauma expressed in misbehavior and students learning strategies for navigating stressful situations without anger.[2] Unknowingly, Higa actually began practicing it after he joined the staff in 2008 as principal.

Stacks of discipline referrals from teachers and other staff awaited Higa when he first started at Cherokee Point. Under the traditional system, those often led to detention, suspension, or even expulsion. That first year, in 2008, he suspended seven students, not too high a number, but he came into the new job with a commitment to treating the "whole child"—meaning understanding students' social and emotional milieus in addition to their academic needs—and kicking kids off school for misbehavior didn't fit that philosophy. He began steering staff toward that mind-set as well, over the objections of some teachers who believed that disruptive behavior should be met with suspensions or even expulsions, not conversation. (Under Higa's approach, students might be asked to sit out recess and contemplate misbehavior. The school also employs a restorative justice approach, in which any child causing harm to another acknowledges it and makes amends.)

For example, a teacher called him to a classroom after a girl began throwing chairs. He surveyed the chaos and then assured the girl that although the classroom was a mess, it could be cleaned up. What was important, he told her, was that he wanted to know what was going on with her. He left the classroom with the agitated student and took a walk with her around the campus while she described what was distressing her. Higa said he told her he understood that people have bad days and asked her to think about it before she did something like that again and contact him if she felt she might. He explained, "If you feel you're going to get angry, just tell the teacher, 'Can I go see Mr. Higa?' And so we worked out a plan. Within a week, she said, 'You know, I'm not going to do that anymore.'" And Higa said she didn't.

Higa realized early in his tenure at Cherokee Point that hunger might account for some student misconduct. He arranged a free breakfast for every child—in a school where 100 percent of the children qualify for free and reduced meals because of their household income. Student behavior quickly improved, staff noticed. He also turned the elementary school into a "community school," developing partnerships between the school and other community organizations and creating an array of new services on campus to benefit not only students and parents, but also the neighborhood. In 2010, for example, a local food bank needed a distribution center, and he offered his school site. "So I have 4,000 pounds of fruits and vegetables come every other week. Parents come and pick up their food, no judgments."

～

In 2011, members of the Peace Promotion Momentum Team, one of the action groups with the BHC campaign in City Heights, contacted Higa. They shared his whole-child philosophy, and suddenly he had a powerful new support team to help make his vision a reality. The team is overseen by a long-time nonprofit organization that partners in the BHC campaign in City Heights, called Mid-City CAN. The peace promotion team's roughly forty members included staff from nonprofit organizations and governmental agencies as well as residents.

The team asked Higa if he was interested in implementing a restorative justice and wellness program on his campus—goals that perfectly fit his own—with grant funding from the BHC campaign. "So I said, 'Of course,'" Higa said. The $684,000 grant launched the Wellness and Restorative Practice Partnership, run in consultation with several San Diego State University professors. Among the partnership's aims: increase on-campus and in-home health care services for students and their parents; develop youth leadership to drive change on campus and in the community; create a positive climate that prevents conflicts; and—critically—train campus staff, from teachers to custodians, as well as parents and students, in restorative practices, which entail repairing harm while building relationships.

Higa also invited professors from San Diego State University to actually teach their university classes—in the elementary school campus classrooms, and during the day and in evenings—on subjects including early childhood development, psychology, and nursing. "It was actually on-the-job type training," Higa said. "For their lab work, they volunteered in the classroom. It was perfect." Every semester, Higa said approximately ten student nurses assist the staff nurse, give classroom presentations, and meet with parents. University interns from the psychology department work on restorative justice, among other projects, at Cherokee Point. The program continues today, with approximately fifty university interns working on campus at various times. When I asked if this kind of program had been done elsewhere, Higa said, "We pretty much pioneered it."

Along with creating a "community school," the university staff involved in the partnership started holding classes at Cherokee Point for parents on topics such as effectively helping with homework and positive parent-child communication. Instructors cultivated parent leaders, who are now integral on the campus. These parent leaders also run workshops for other community members.

With the influx of new resources, in both funding and personnel, a transformation took hold. Medical professionals now give every student a dental, eye, and physical exam, and free counseling is available for any parent or student who requests it. Along with Higa's already compassionate approach, the restorative practices training reinforced a culture of respect between students and staff, creating an all-important sense of safety for students. Higa remembers a few years ago overhearing a kitchen staff worker "screaming and yelling at the kids." He told the staff member, "'You are not going to speak to kids this way. If you continue to do this, I'm going to have to go to the next step. And I want to help you. Do you have issues at home? Whatever is making you this way, I want to help you.'"

Even the school custodian caught the spirit. Instead of scolding children for not cleaning up, he formed a "green team" of students to help keep the school litter-free. Higa said the custodian now comes to him occasionally for a small budget for popsicles and other treats for his team, saying, "I need to take care of my helpers." And children clamor to be on the team, Higa said.

Higa extends his policy of compassion to staff as well. When a staff member needs time off for personal matters, such as bereavement or a serious illness, he tells them to take the time necessary. "I always say take whatever time you need. And I know that they're not going to take advantage," he said.

~

By 2014, suspensions at Cherokee Point fell to zero, and there have been none since then. Given the calm pervading the campus, Higa stopped staffing a campus police officer in 2015. "All he did was stand around," Higa recalled. The officer once told him, "'I have more problems with adults coming in the wrong way in the parking lot than kids.'" The school police chief pulled the officer and told Higa to call if they were needed. "We haven't called them yet," Higa said.

Still, Higa didn't realize that Cherokee Point fit the definition of a "trauma-informed school"—a new class of school with a small but growing number of adherents—that consciously employs practices Higa had implemented based on his own convictions about how to treat children. Administrators in the relatively few schools that explicitly follow trauma-informed practices recognize that these approaches ease the deleterious health effects of trauma on children, which studies now show profoundly affect brain development and harm far more children than anyone realized. The *National Survey of Children's Exposure to Violence* reports that nearly 60 percent of children have been exposed to trauma in the past year, with more than one in ten reporting five or more exposures.[3] Trauma-informed schools counter those experiences with revisions to disciplinary practices, social-emotional instruction, schoolwide training about trauma, parent and caregiver instruction, and intensive individual support as well as developing community partnerships to support these efforts.[4]

Higa began to understand his school's unique status after getting a visit in 2013 from Jane Stevens, a long-time science journalist based in Northern California and founder of the online site *ACES Too High*, which reports on research about adverse childhood experiences. Higa said Stevens contacted him after reading that he didn't believe in school suspensions, considering them ineffective and a path to academic failure. Research does show that students who are suspended are more likely to enter the juvenile justice system than those who are not, and their prospects of graduating from high school drop significantly. Many suspended students are also home alone during the day and end up lured into street life.

Stevens visited the campus and spent a couple of days observing. At the end, she told Higa that he was running a trauma-informed school and asked if he knew what that meant. He didn't. "She said the way the parents feel so safe here, the kids are so wonderful here, the way the custodian treats kids, the way you treat kids and all that," Higa recalled. Stevens asked him how he did it, and he explained, "I believe in understanding the whole child." Stevens then asked if he understood the brain research behind trauma; he said that he didn't. She explained ACE, or adverse childhood experiences. "That's what sold me," Higa said.

This growing focus on childhood trauma emanates from a 1998 landmark study conducted by the Centers for Disease Control and Prevention and Kaiser Permanente. It was one of the largest investigations into the long-term health effects of childhood abuse and neglect.[5] The study found that childhood exposure to neglect, physical and mental maltreatment, poverty, community violence, substance abuse and mental illness in the family, and other domestic dysfunction led to improper brain development. MRIs of study subjects—17,000 adult Kaiser health plan members in Southern California—showed high levels of childhood trauma, in particular impaired brain development in regions involved in processing emotions, memory, decision making, and self-regulation, which also can lead to "hyperarousal," or hyperactivity and hair-trigger responses. Negative experiences also impair a child's cognitive and social-emotional development, not to mention the harm of actual physical abuse, including head trauma.[6] Later in life, the cumulative total of adverse childhood experiences proportionally increases the risk of developing heart, lung, and liver diseases, obesity, cancer, hypertension, anxiety, depression, and other mental and physical maladies as well as the likelihood of smoking or abusing drugs and alcohol. Early traumas also shorten lives. A 2009 study reported that adults with six or more adverse childhood experiences died nearly twenty years earlier than those with none.[7]

Thus Higa began calling Cherokee Point a "trauma-informed community school," and word began to spread of his novel approach to keeping peace on campus. One principal contacted Higa, pleading with him to enroll a disruptive fourth-grade student who had been suspended multiple times. Higa agreed and scheduled a meeting with the student and his father, who arrived fifteen minutes early for their 7:30 a.m. appointment. The father explained that he was on the verge of losing his job because he had to leave work to retrieve his son from school too often, and the boy said that his long discipline record was unfair. Higa listened and gave the boy's story some credence by noting that the other school administrators had been trying to expel him but couldn't find enough evidence to do so. As the boy sat there quietly, Higa looked at him and his father and then tore up his discipline record. "I said, 'Okay, I'm going to give you a chance to come here. All I ask you to do is *try*. Try your best,'" Higa said.

Several months later Higa met with the father, who was amazed at the changes in his son. Higa said that the boy struggled a bit but worked hard, and Higa put him on the student patrol, a prestigious position. "He's doing so well," Higa said. "He's a fifth-grader now, and he always checks in with me. If he has a bad day, he'll come in and talk to me."

~

School administrators from around the United States now visit the Cherokee Point campus, which exudes serenity. Sometimes parent leaders conduct the tours, and several have been invited to speak at conferences around the country. Higa is an in-demand speaker and serves on a statewide committee called the California Campaign to Counter Childhood Adversity, or 4CA, funded largely by Kaiser Permanente and the California Endowment. The group educates the public on the extent of childhood adversity and advocates for policies to prevent and mitigate it. Because teachers and staff now embrace his compassionate whole-child approach as well as the calmer school environment, Higa also has little anxiety that the approach will fade out after his tenure.

To varying degrees, schools in most of the BHC sites now use practices that consider trauma. In Crescent City in Del Norte County, for example, schools integrate many of the same approaches, which may go by different names, such as positive behavior interventions and support. Geneva Wiki, program manager for the BHC work in Del Norte, remembers how anxious she was about enrolling her children in an elementary school in Crescent City after returning from New Zealand and what she called some of the best schools anywhere.

"Honestly, we had a lot of anxiety moving home," Wiki said. "We got Joe Hamilton, which is the lowest-income school in Crescent City. And I was terrified." That changed soon after they entered the school, however. Wiki realized that while she was gone, parents and residents working with the BHC campaign had made advances. "I could see BHC fingerprints all over the school. They have positive behavior interventions and support fully implemented. It is everywhere. The kids are doing it, the teachers are doing it." All students now had breakfast every day, and for students running late, the front desk offered breakfasts to go. "And then you walk into the classroom, and the first ten minutes or whatever, the lights are kind of low, there's soft music, the kids have a quiet activity to do, they can eat their breakfast if they need to. Kids have salad bars and other healthy food," she added. "And I just know my kids are having a fundamentally different experience in Del Norte County schools than they would have pre-BHC. Amazing."

Slowly, more schools have taken on the mantle of trauma-informed schools, including ones in San Francisco, Spokane, Seattle, and Walla Walla at Lincoln High School. Lincoln High was profiled in the documentary *Paper Tigers*, highlighting the 85 percent reduction in suspensions after adopting a trauma-informed approach.[8] The State of

Washington has implemented its Compassionate Schools Initiative and Massachusetts its Flexible Framework Helping Traumatized Students Learn program. Several state departments of education now provide resources to address trauma, including Illinois, Wisconsin, and Massachusetts. In Idaho, 75 percent of school districts have sent staff to attend Idaho State University's mental health training program, which includes trauma education, while the Menominee Indian School District in Wisconsin has embraced trauma-informed schools and practices throughout its community.[9] In Washington, DC, where one in four children lives in poverty—and half in some neighborhoods—the DC Children's Law Center has successfully advocated for additional trauma training for several hundred school district educators, although a *Washington Post* article noted that there is no system-wide coordination of such services.[10] Given the resounding success at Cherokee Point, however, the San Diego Unified School District has implemented such system-wide coordination. It now deems itself a trauma-informed school district, and its website includes a tool kit to support teachers, parents, and community groups who wish to practice the approach.[11]

~

Although Higa points out that it doesn't cost anything to treat students and staff with compassion, it does take funding to run school-wide trainings, to reach parents and caregivers, and to provide extra support to students. The San Diego school district is paying for its expansion of programs through a California school funding strategy enacted in 2013.[12] This law goes by the moniker "Local Control Funding Formula," but the unwieldy name conceals its revolutionary nature. In short, it replaces a forty-year-old school finance system and sends significantly more money into school districts with a high proportion of low-income children, foster youth, and English language learners. By 2017, the law had swung $31 billion extra into these districts.[13] (California public education budgets certainly need infusions. The state ranked forty-first in the United States in 2015–2016 for per student spending. Still, that's an improvement over 2012–2013, when California ranked fiftieth among states.[14])

As its name implies, the new funding law gives districts far more control over how money is spent, with the proviso that citizens must also vigorously participate in those decisions, called participatory budgeting. School districts also have to demonstrate that they have sought this community engagement.

As soon as the local control funding law passed, BHC campaign leaders around the state urged parents and students to get involved. BHC coalitions in all the sites concentrated on cultivating local advocates for expanding trauma-informed practices and other school reforms. The BHC campaigns ran radio, newspaper, billboard, and social media campaigns and hosted town hall meetings with free dinners and childcare, sometimes offering rides there on a large yellow school bus emblazoned with "School Success Express," which traveled around the state, even navigating the mountainous roads into Del Norte County.

The new funding law also requires school districts to measure success beyond grades, including school climate, rates of suspensions and expulsions, and assessments by students and parents. In 2017, the state education department launched an online "dashboard" to display these various measurements, making it easy to find the results.[15] A state task force, which included members of the BHC school discipline policy coalition, helped develop the dashboard.

∼

Reducing trauma is now front and center of the BHC campaign. Like school disciple, the issue wasn't always a priority, however. "It really was pretty much a BHC discovery for us," said Endowment president Dr. Robert Ross. He credits two nonprofit organization leaders in particular for bringing it to their attention: Jerry Tello, founder of the National Compadres Network, headquartered in San Jose; and Nane Alejandrez, executive director of Santa Cruz Barrios Unidos, located in the beach town of Santa Cruz.

Tello recalls trying to persuade Endowment leadership to take a closer look at the nexus between trauma and health and well-being, but initially the message wasn't getting through. "To be honest with you, in the beginning of the [BHC] initiative they didn't even have it on their radar, and in fact they pushed back against it, the whole aspect of trauma and healing," Tello said. "That was not something they were interested in pursuing. And what has happened is now they realize that it's at the core of a lot of things."

"We now have more or less officially become trauma-informed as an organization," Ross agreed, "and it's become much more systematically integrated into our work." Grant requests addressing trauma now rise to the top for consideration.

When I asked Ross about his organization's willingness to acknowledge oversights, he responded, "Every organization tries to position itself as a learning organization. I try to really mean it. I think [Endowment staff] brings a lot to the table because we're smart and educated and we have a lot of experiences. But my goodness, there's a whole world out there of experiences and wisdom that we haven't tapped into yet."

In March 2017, Ross spoke at the Society of Behavioral Medicine conference in San Diego. "This issue of trauma is more profound than we like to admit," he told the audience. "I would say hands down that this exposure to childhood trauma is number one, and then everything else—cancer, heart disease, diabetes, and everything else—is secondary. If we follow the breadcrumbs upstream from those particular diseases, you find this more often than not—children who are exposed to trauma."

Ross described the ACE study that shows a "direct dose-response relationship between exposure to trauma and how bad your health is twenty to fifty years later. No surprise right?," he said, speaking to a few hundred in a hotel ballroom. "The one that says time heals all wounds? That's bullsh**," he said. "That one's wrong."

~

In 1988, Jerry Tello gathered a group of Latino men to discuss the many challenges they faced, from family problems to community dysfunction, and ways to cope. As they began to tell stories, something shifted: men started to open up, sharing more deeply held fears. Tello realized the healing power of authentically sharing one's stories, including the painful, hurtful, and shameful ones, and how futile it was to try to heal a family or community without first healing oneself.[16]

From that gathering, seven men went on to form the National Compadres Network, which has since held thousands of healing circles, following an ancient practice. The group had already worked with the California Endowment prior to the BHC campaign and now holds healing circles in many of the BHC communities, including in Santa Ana, Oakland, and Fresno and with the school district in Eastern Coachella Valley. Every summer, Tello leads a daily practice at the weeklong Sierra camp the Endowment runs for boys and young men from the BHC sites. Even Ross joined a circle one year as a large group sat under towering trees around a campfire. Tello, with his signature black fedora, which he wears in honor of his hard-working father, who wore a hat every day to his job, is a beloved figure.

A healing circle in Fresno that he convened to talk about tensions between law enforcement and community members, especially young men—a common theme—stood out in his memory, Tello told me. The group included a judge, a probation officer, and the Fresno police chief, along with the young members of an endeavor called the Alliance for Boys and Men of Color, which the California Endowment formed in partnership with other nonprofit organizations.

That healing circle moved the participants, leading to more conversations. Afterward, Fresno Police Chief Jerry Dyer announced the formation of a Police Chief Youth Advisory Council for youth from sixteen to twenty-four years old. Given the national crisis over police relations with people of color, the council made local news, and Dyer, who's been with the Fresno police force since 1979, with sixteen years as chief, told me he now looks forward to the youth council meetings. "They almost always have an idea or suggestion as to how [a problem] can be solved," Dyer said. "It's refreshing, to the point where the youth want to end the meeting before I do, quite frankly. I like spending more time with them, but they got other things going on."

For Efrain Botello, a member of the Fresno Boys and Men of Color group, the meetings were a chance to be heard. "It was really satisfying. First of all, it just made us feel good because, like, the chief of the police, he's so busy and he's having time to meet with us young people. He's actually paying attention to us," said Botello, a fit twenty-year-old with short black hair, a trim beard, and studs in both ears. Among many topics, youth discussed feeling unfairly judged by police, and Botello prized the opportunity to directly share their experiences. "He can hear from other people, but it's more impactful when he's in the same room and he's hearing our stories," Botello said of Dyer. Botello attends a community college and plans to major in sociology, pursue a master's degree in counseling, and may one day run for city council, a far cry from his parents' path. One summer, his parents, who both worked in the fields, pressured him to join them picking grapes, a tactic to nudge him toward different endeavors. "It definitely worked. I was dying out there in the heat," Botello said.

$\sim$

Jerry Tello also brought his healing circles to East Salinas, a BHC site heavily populated by people working low-wage jobs, including in the surrounding farm fields, and largely Hispanic. That section of Salinas has long been called the Alisal district, and many migrant farm workers who fled their Great Plains farms during the Dust Bowl settled there. Salinas's most famous native son, John Steinbeck, born there in 1902, memorialized their plight in his novel *The Grapes of Wrath*. Salinas, population 155,000, is 8 miles inland from the central California coast.

Tello worked in partnership with a Salinas nonprofit organization involved in the BHC campaign called MILPA, for Motivating Individual Leadership for Public Advancement, training more than 140 in holding healing circles. The reach of that training proved invaluable, he believes, given the tragedy about to hit East Salinas.

Between March and July 2014, Salinas police officers shot and killed four men, all Latino. One man was brandishing pruning shears and ignored multiple commands to drop the shears and stop walking as he approached a busy intersection; the scene was caught on video. It was the second killing in less than two weeks by Salinas police officers, and it triggered days of protests. (A melee broke out in one area; one bystander was fatally shot by an unknown person, and an officer trying to help him was injured by being hit in the head with a bottle.[17]) Within months, two more Latino men were killed in officer-involved shootings, further traumatizing and enraging residents.

Although many affiliated with MILPA had uneasy relationships with the police, one of its founders, Raul Tapia, urged calm following each shooting. He and others also held healing circles for the community. In one protest, hundreds walked past the police station and City Hall in a nighttime march, but no violence or vandalism broke out. Tello is certain that the community's experience with the healing circles before the shootings, and in the midst of them, kept the community from erupting.

"It's important to understand that when the shootings happened, we had people on the ground trained," Tello said. They "sat down with community folks and really allowed them to vent, allowed them to share the anger, and say 'How do we channel this so we're not just burning down buildings?'" he said. "Because of the healing process that had gone on before, there wasn't the same level of reaction."

Then the California Endowment's program manager for the BHC work in Salinas, Lauren Padilla-Valverde, realized that Tello's skills could ease the crisis between the police department and the East Salinas community.

~

Padilla-Valverde first pushed for city leadership to attend trainings on a practice called "governing for racial equity," an in-depth examination of how government policies may affect various ethnic groups. Padilla-Valverde, who was raised in Monterey County, understood well how the shootings had escalated racial tensions, and government agencies in the United Kingdom had successfully adopted a similar racial equity governing approach years ago. Early US adopters of that approach include agencies in King County, Washington, and Multnomah County, Oregon.[18]

She had gotten to know Gary Petersen, the public works director in Salinas, after he'd approved permits and hammered out logistics for the Ciclovia festival and a 5K run BHC put on in East Salinas. They had a track record of collaboration.

"She and I had a very fierce conversation," Petersen said. "She said, 'You need to do this [training]. You need to get your chief of police and your city manager.' I didn't even know what racial equity was," he added. "I said, 'Nice, but I don't tell them what to do. You got this hierarchy thing mixed up.'"

Petersen nonetheless persuaded the city manager, Ray Corpuz, to drive with him 100 miles north to Oakland, through stretches of congested Bay Area freeways, to attend the training. I met with Corpuz in his office inside the Salinas City Hall near the historic downtown district, and he recalled how Petersen had urged him to attend, noting that BHC was heavily investing in building up their community. "I said, 'Well, if you really think I need to go, I'll go,'" he told me.

The police chief, Kelly McMillin, also agreed to attend, "although it might have had something to do with me saying he had to go," Corpuz said with a smile. "But he was open to it," he added. It was a major time investment for the city leaders. "These are three bodies that are just always in motion," Corpuz said. "And a day of life of my little world is like . . . there are about fifty things I could accomplish."

He hoped the training could yield something he'd been seeking, however: a constructive way to respond to the rage, protests, and unrest of the past few months. "There were some meetings we had which were very helpful, but sometimes they got out of control. Emotions outran everything else," Corpuz said. And the talks weren't leading to meaningful outcomes, he said. "OK, now what? You've screamed at me, now what?"

Corpuz, a Filipino, was sensitive to racial issues. "I have my own history of being discriminated against," he said. Still, he wasn't equipped for the community crisis. "I felt like 'I don't have a tool here, I don't have a pathway.'" He did know communication was key. "We cannot shut the door, as painful as it may be to hear some things about the city and our officers, and who we are," Corpuz said. "We have to keep the door open, we have to be willing to step into the light, get out of the shadow and talk about it."

On July 15, 2014, the three city leaders drove to Oakland and attended the eight-hour racial equity training, run by Rinku Sen, executive director of the Oakland-based Race Forward organization. The day didn't finish with the training, though; a dinner meeting followed, one that ended up altering the course of city-community relations. Several community leaders—a few reluctant—were also persuaded to drive up from Salinas, including Raul Tapia and two others with MILPA. They joined the dinner, hosted by Padilla-Valverde and a Salinas BHC manager, inside the California Endowment's Oakland office, with its view of downtown Oakland. It was neutral territory—hence the decision to hold the meeting outside of Salinas.

During the dinner, "we got into a frank discussion," said Corpuz, letting their job titles recede and speaking authentically. "I had to be Ray Corpuz, and I had to tell them my feelings about race and what I think we ought to do, and why this could be important for us. So it was an interesting and somewhat tense conversation." But it was the start, Corpuz said, of "really thinking about how we could take advantage of governing for racial equity and how that might help our community."

After the dinner, city staffers and members of community organizations, who once regarded each other warily, met to organize what became a weeklong training on governing for racial equity. Key city staff members as well as local community leaders were invited.

Padilla-Valverde wanted to dig deeper, however; she understood that buried psychic wounds could prevent the community from coming together. So she introduced Jerry Tello to Rinku Sen and asked them to plan the training together. They had never met, but they went on to develop the powerful program, which they led in November 2014.

∼

Ray Corpuz eloquently described the experience in a blog post titled "Governing for Racial Equity and Healing Week Reflections," dated December 18, 2014:[19]

After decades in local government, and three years as the City of Salinas City Manager, I have learned that it is essential that City Government find a means for connecting with its Citizens, meeting them where they are, rather than where we would like them to be. I have seen many efforts to accomplish this, often with mixed results. However, one of the most successful I have ever experienced was on November 21st, the culminating day of the City of Salinas' weeklong Governing for Racial Equity Training & Launch.

Despite all of its assets, Salinas has many challenges, including racial issues that have deep roots in our City and span many generations. Similar to other cities, Salinas has experienced police involved shootings that have disrupted the fabric of our community. What is different in Salinas is that we are willing to recognize that the issues of race are much more complex than the recent police officer shootings, and more challenging as well. We have understood that to address the root causes of inequity it is essential for our organization to acknowledge racism as an issue and to respond with specific steps for change.

Unlike the community responses we are seeing in Ferguson and Staten Island, and largely due to the leadership of skilled and wise community leader from all sectors, the anger and outrage of police shootings was met with opportunities to build upon existing work to develop culturally rooted healing, so that community members could approach the city from a place of strength and leadership rather than hurt and fear. But without City action to address some of the underlying causes contributing to the inequities facing communities like East Salinas, we would not have succeeded in meeting our citizens in productive and useful ways.

So in July, when The California Endowment offered, we took the opportunity to attend training on tools to address systemic racism, led by Race Forward. Attending were myself, the Public Works Director, and the Police Chief. At this training we explored the multiple levels of *systemic racism and began to understand how racial bias is pervasive in many of our systems, regardless of individual intentions. Following the training, we were ready to engage our community at a deeper level and met with a small group of Salinas's residents where we shared what we had learned at the training and what we planned to do with our knowledge.*

Through a series of conversations among partners including The California Endowment and Building Healthy Communities, the idea for a week of healing and governing for racial equity training was born. The week was led by national leaders in racial justice (RACE Forward) and healing (National Compadres Network) who integrated both perspectives into healing-informed racial equity training. Just before Thanksgiving, a very appropriate time for this work, 49 Salinas community members and non-City institutional leaders spent two days going through workshops on racial equity and tools to promote racial equity, as well as healing from the trauma that the racist structures impose on all of us, white and people of color. Then 51 City staff—including all division heads—went through the same two-day training. On the fifth day, the community and city groups joined to begin charting a course towards integration of a racial equity approach across the entire City. Out of this week concrete next steps were agreed upon including the formation of a 10-member City of Salinas-BHC Governing for Racial Equity workgroup.

It is hard to describe how powerful and moving this experience was for me. Over the course of my career, there are very few times when we've been able to move from an "us vs. them" mentality, both on the city and community sides. On the fifth day of learning, healing, and planning together, I saw the walls start to come down. Community members holding on to so much pain because of the loss and neglect they've endured expressed hope for true partnership moving forward. City staff, often defensive of their hard work, understood the critiques at the systemic level, and yet also took responsibility for changing the system. I heard City staff apologize for the harm they've done, however unintentional, as they've carried out their tasks without attention to the disparate racial impacts—the impacts on real community members who they now call allies—and the overall commitment from everyone present to finding ways to promote health and safety without harming those most vulnerable.

The transformation occurring in Salinas would not be possible without a deep attention to healing. The healing work provides a space to see and hear each other's struggle and triumph, allowing each person the opportunity to begin to move forward, and allowing the group to build the trust necessary for tackling issues of racism, together. And without the tools to put our understanding into practice—tools like Racial Equity Impact Assessments—there is nothing to help us move from healing into action. We are just beginning our Governing for Racial Equity work. But as nascent as our work is, it is clear that the Governing for Racial Equity approach is not only powerful, but timely as we all struggle to figure out how to prevent the next unnecessary death, whether it be from a police shooting or chronic stress or diabetes or any one of the epidemics ravaging our most vulnerable communities. We are proud to take this important step forward together as a united community to realize equity in the Salinas Valley and Monterey County for generations to come.

After the training, a MILPA representative—who was once uncomfortable even being around police officers—met with Police Chief McMillin to discuss developing a community-based policing orientation. Ultimately, the city committed to train the entire police force in "fair and impartial policing" and revised hiring criteria to attract more people of color.

Corpuz is close to his goal of 100 percent of city staff attending training sessions on the topic, typically daylong events. I attended an all-day session run by Tello and Sen in August 2016; the audience that day represented various departments, including public works, the fire department, the city attorney's office, and library services. As the two speakers emphasized to the crowd, the training entails identifying implicit, unconscious bias. "This exercise is not about finding the racist and punishing that person," Sen told the group of about fifty people gathered in a large second-floor conference room. "This training is about all of us figuring out how our system, and including our own participation in it, is causing racial inequity."

Among many topics, Tello talked about "rooted teachings" in various cultures, which emphasize that "you are wanted, welcomed. You are valued. You have a valued purpose." Those attitudes, he emphasized, extend to interactions in daily life and on the job. He used the example of schools with staff welcoming students with a handshake as they enter the campus, which he said dramatically improved relationships and student behavior.

Andrea Manzo, the "hub" manager for the Salinas BHC campaign who works alongside Padilla-Valverde, acknowledged that the racial equity training won't resonate for all city staff or even residents. "Not everybody buys into it. It's a reality, even with community members," Manzo said. "But you will have more allies in the works to try to change the policies and practices that are really hindering our community from having an inclusive democracy. If it clicks for a few people, and they continue to build allies within the system, that's when we're going to start seeing the change."

CHAPTER 10

Red and Blue Visions of Health

As the shock of Donald Trump's 2016 presidential upset spread across the United States, it landed hard in the offices of the California Endowment. The foundation's ten-year Building Healthy Communities campaign was premised on just about everything the incoming Trump administration would challenge.

For starters, the BHC campaign led efforts to enroll Californians in "Obamacare," with four million new enrollees statewide. Under its #Health4All campaign, the Endowment also spread the word of the economic contribution of undocumented residents and publicized the passage a state law providing health coverage for undocumented children. It ran an energetic #Vota! campaign to encourage voter participation, which Alex Padilla, California's secretary of state, credited with better turnout.

After the 2016 election, #Vota! morphed into the #StayLoud campaign, which encourages residents to speak up about issues that matter to them. Daniel Zingale, who heads the foundation's state team, was questioned about the campaign in an interview with a Sacramento TV station. The reporter was covering a controversy over a billboard featuring the #StayLoud hashtag, along with the word "Resist" in multiple languages, and an image of the state flag's grizzly bear. "This campaign is about encouraging all Californians to make sure their voice is heard," Zingale told the reporter. "That our voice is heard in Washington, that our voice is heard here in the capital in Sacramento." Some Republicans cried foul at the billboard's message, saying that the foundation was inserting itself into politics and that federal tax rules prohibited private foundations from lobbying for legislation or supporting any political candidate. But Zingale said the message is meant to encourage civic engagement, regardless of political affiliation, and the foundation planned to expand the campaign.[1]

On January 18, 2017, members of the state team met in the foundation's Sacramento office, two days before the president-elect took the oath of office, to discuss the way forward. The group of about twenty people sat in a circle in the conference room of a historic brick building walking distance from the state capitol. A large poster on a brick wall showed a clenched fist holding an American flag; nearby hung a sign from the #Vota! campaign, not far from an American flag on a pole. Rain gently hit skylights overhead.

Dr. Robert Ross, the Endowment's president, flew up from Los Angeles for the meeting. Ross, still evincing a sense of shock, pulled up a chair to join the circle and spoke about the dramatically changed landscape.

"I've been in the work of the public sector, public policy for maybe thirty years now," Ross said, "and I have to say, from an old hand like me, this election was, has been, and continues to be unsettling."

Ross, who favors sports metaphors, talked about the relative predictability of fastballs and curveballs compared to the uncertainty of knuckleballs. "And this is a knuckleball, even for a grizzled veteran," he said. He described the potential for a $20 billion loss in California's revenue for health care if the new president followed through on his campaign pledge to repeal the Affordable Care Act.

But the new president "isn't the enemy," Ross emphasized, as he has in many subsequent speeches. "The enemy is really the narrative that his campaign represented, right? And our narrative is in substantial contradiction to that campaign. What we're seeing taking over now in the White House is virtually, point by point, a narrative that is counter to everything we believe in and stand for."

Ross noted that the national election was decided by some 70,000 people in three states. "You could not fill [UC Berkeley's] football stadium with 70,000 people," he pointed out. "If that's not a reminder of the importance of what that sign says in the corner, #Vota!, of civic participation and advocacy and voice, I don't know what better cup of coffee you use to wake up."

∼

Two months later, delivering a keynote speech in San Diego, Ross struck a determined tone in responding to the changes taking hold in the country. "There is certain language at the Endowment that is now center stage, that was virtually absent pre-BHC," Ross said. "One of them is trauma—trauma-informed, restorative justice. The second one is the power of the narrative development and narrative change—that you can't solve something in an enduring and authentic way unless it's framed with a narrative that's accessible to people."

Although creating a different narrative about the sources of good health—deemphasizing medical intervention and concentrating on cultivating healthy neighborhoods and schools—was a priority early in the BHC campaign, it has taken on new urgency following the election.

Ross often speaks about how "health happens in schools" or how "health happens in neighborhoods." In other words, where you live and spend your time profoundly affects your well-being. In academic circles, that's known as "social determinants of health," meaning that factors such as stress, subpar living conditions, and low social status get under your skin and make you ill. It's not a phrase that goes over well with the general public, however.

"People didn't have any idea what it meant, and didn't like it," said Drew Westen, an Emory University professor who describes himself as a clinical psychologist, neuroscientist, and pollster. He's also the author of *The Political Brain*.[2] Westen consulted for the Robert Wood Johnson Foundation on how to talk about health disparities.[3] The foundation, based in New Jersey, also works to broaden discussions about what shapes health and wanted better language to explain why neighborhood conditions matter for human well-being.

That foundation's 2010 report, "A New Way to Talk about the Social Determinants of Health," struck a nerve, and nearly two thousand people nationwide participated in a webinar on the findings.[4] Joining Westen on the webinar was Elizabeth Carger, then a senior project manager with Olson Zaltman Associates in Pittsburgh and an expert on how unconscious metaphors shape our worldviews, or what her firm calls "deep metaphors." The New Jersey foundation hired Carger and her colleagues to explore how Republicans and Democrats viewed the reasons why life expectancies sometimes varied by up to twenty years between nearby neighborhoods.

In the summer of 2007, she and James Forr, Olson Zaltman's director, reached out to Republican and Democratic congressional staffers (the Congress members were too busy to meet) as well as health policy experts linked to either conservative or progressive institutions. She and Forr first asked the thirty-one interview subjects who agreed to participate "to collect images that represent their thoughts and feelings, in this case about health differences across populations across the United States." Then a week later they started conducting interviews.

The Olson Zaltman firm pioneered a unique method for understanding the fundamental frames through which people view the world and how they process new information. The founder, Gerald Zaltman, an emeritus professor at the Harvard Business School with a doctorate in sociology, developed this method after a 1990 trip to Nepal. During that trip, he gave a number of locals cameras and asked them to take photos of images that represent their lives. Zaltman realized that the images they took, along with their accompanying stories, let people to fully express their views on various topics and how they arrived at them. With that realization, he codeveloped a method using images and stories to draw out the unconscious metaphors by which people live. Numerous corporations hire the firm to understand audiences so that they can design more effective advertising campaigns.

The researchers spent up to two hours asking each participant to share the stories behind the images and how they related to the issue of health disparities between US populations. The researchers then analyzed transcribed interviews for metaphorical language. They found striking and consistent differences between Democrats and Republicans.

~

The metaphor of "system" underpinned Democrats' view on the social determinants of health, Carger said. "The system is the concept that all of the parts work together to create a greater whole. That it's difficult to separate one piece out," she said during the webinar. She quoted one Democrat as saying, "It's all tied together—housing, health care, energy, food." Democrats see poor health through the lens of "a system that has broken down." Changing one piece of it, such as increasing access to insurance, isn't going to fix it entirely, although it's a start. Democrats can find talking about these health disparities frustrating because the conversations get complex. Not surprisingly, these conversations also frustrate Republicans.

Another metaphor commonly used by Democrats is that of a "container," keeping low-income communities cut off from the mainstream.

"For the Democrats, first of all, low-income communities are isolated and contained, never able to leave the culture of poverty," Carger said. "They also frame poverty as a hole that traps individuals in unhealthy lifestyles." This container metaphor shows up in language such as "rigid barriers that prevent their entrance" to the mainstream or the concept of "lifting people" out of poverty.

In a phone interview, Forr said that metaphors may also frame how people within low-income communities view their situation. For many, he said, these health disparities have been generational. "They've seen their parents and their grandparents before them suffer from the same inequities and the same problems. So when you see that over and over again, your own situation can seem kind of hopeless. It can feel like you're in a container and you're not able to move forward," Forr said.

The metaphor of "balance" also strongly emerges for Democrats. An interconnected world that tolerates pockets of isolated, impoverished citizens leaves Democrats with a profound sense of imbalance. Big gaps in wealth and health between the haves and have-nots sometimes angered those being interviewed. Democrats also spoke of "equality," of assuring a fair and equitable distribution of resources. That word is almost toxic to Republicans, though, as Carger explained later.

~

"Journey" is the dominant metaphor for Republicans. "Republicans see individuals traveling on journeys of health," Carger said, "and poor health arises from choosing bad paths. And the inability to overcome obstacles on that path.

"Republicans talk about getting back on the right track, 'We need to get people a road map,'" she said, paraphrasing a common perspective. They also see society as a whole on a journey and thus view the nation's health status more optimistically, often pointing out how much longer people are living compared with a century ago or even thirty years ago and how much healthier Americans are compared with many other countries. A collage of images from one Republican interviewee actually showed a highway, superimposed with the image of a child holding healthy food, connected with an image of an expensive car presumably owned later in that child's life. And below that image was a child holding a McDonald's meal, which was connected to an image of a taxi running low on gas.

In addition, the researchers noted that because things change during a journey, Republicans are often reluctant to institutionalize programs, believing that conditions may change but government bureaucracies often don't.

"Resources" was another frequent metaphor for Republicans, who believed that "we need to be realistic, that we cannot provide everything to everyone," Carger said, paraphrasing the perspective. "So there's a great emphasis on the fact that we can't just be pie in the sky, give everyone everything, because we have a limited amount of resources." In addition, how we distribute those resources during the journey so that they actually help people make better choices becomes a critical issue for Republicans.

"Balance also came up with Republicans, but it was dangerous territory," Carger continued, because they associated the concept with equality. "Republicans understand equality as an undesirable lowering of some individual's health status in order to raise the status of others to create one uniform level." Given their view of the strong role of choice along one's life path, that strikes them as unfair, she said.

Carger and Forr's research found that Republicans believe in supporting a basic level of health and making sure people have the opportunity to make healthy choices. But, Carger added, "it's very important to Republicans that public policy does balance how much aid you provide with how much individual responsibility is expected."

Forr added that interviewees on both sides of the political spectrum saw the health gaps around the country as relevant and important to address. "They may have disagreed on exactly how to address it, but all of the people we interviewed were definitely engaged and passionate and really had heart for trying to make this situation better," he said.

~

To translate this new knowledge into an effective communication strategy about the nations' tragic schism in health, the Robert Wood Johnson Foundation turned to Drew Westen, the Emory University professor. Westen talks about the "neurological ambivalence" of some Americans, particularly swing voters, when it comes to people of other races. The word "immigrant," for example, might initially bring up grumblings of them taking jobs or not paying taxes, but then move into expressions of admiration for their hard work ethic in pursuit of a better life, even when documentation status wasn't mentioned.

Westen said that when he tried to explain to swing voters that even roughly two-thirds of undocumented immigrants pay some form of payroll tax, they simply didn't believe him. He said that "if you argue with a swing voter about that, you get absolutely nowhere. They say it's not true." He said the same often happens when he tells conservatives that one out of three African American children is born into poverty. "They'll say, 'No, they're not.' And the discussion ends there," Westen said. "So the question is how do you persuade people, how do you reach their better angels, on social determinants without engaging in these fruitless arguments that get you nowhere, because their brains won't go there?"

The same dilemma comes up with health care. "The 'uninsured' is a great example of exactly the kind of word that gets bandied around all the time, and it's phenomenally counterproductive to people who actually want to see people who are uninsured be insured," Westen said. For many, that word almost unconsciously activates the "just world" hypothesis, he said. "Which is, at least in the West, a tendency unconsciously to want to believe that the world is just, and that people deserve what they get. Because imagine the opposite; if it's not just . . . what does it mean might happen to you tomorrow?"

"Universal health care" is another phrase that can fall flat. The ability to see a doctor when you're sick is personal and emotional, but the term is not. "Calling it universal health care, you've just essentially completely emotionally sterilized it," Westen said. Instead, he and others testing the phrase found that people responded strongly to the statement, "I believe in a family doctor for every family."

~

Westen pointed out that our human ancestors navigated their world through feelings. "They expected either positive feelings or they fled from things associated with negative feelings. We are no different. If you don't feel it, don't use it." Both movers and shakers and regular citizens respond to stories that evoke positive emotions, he added.

"We learned very quickly that decision makers respond first like people and second like decision makers. So the messages that speak to their values and that give them the gut level feeling that this is the right thing to do or wrong thing, they gravitate toward those," he said. "And then they come up with the rationalizations based on cortex decisions."

As for the vast differences between Democrats and Republicans, Westen challenged the idea of creating separate messages for the two audiences. "The best messages actually cut across progressive and conservative targets," he said.

He said traditional phrasing of social determinants language, the kind found in journal articles, consistently tested poorly. When messages are presented in "colloquial, kitchen-table, values-driven, emotionally compelling language, they're far more effective," he said. "That's the language that's going to stick with them." He added that including one "killer fact" emotionally strengthened a message, but that additional facts actually reduced the receptivity.

People can understand "the idea that where we live, learn, work, and play influences our health," Westen said. In fact, that is not a new concept: the 1986 Ottawa Charter for Health Promotion,[5] from the World Health Organization, uses the same language, asserting that where people "live, love, work, and play"[6] exerts a significant influence on health. To improve well-being, the charter advocates for good public policy, supportive communities, skill building, and education among residents to expand their options. That recommendation is virtually identical to the philosophy of the BHC campaign, which "challenges us to think about people's health beyond the doctor's office and beyond the good versus bad choices people make. In reality, our health happens where we live, learn, work and play."[7]

That simple message is a start, and Westen said that appealing to Americans' fundamental sense of fairness, blended with a theme of personal responsibility, makes it even more effective. For example, virtually all agree that "money can't buy happiness, and it shouldn't buy health," reflecting a value of fairness. A message that emphasizes personal responsibility for health also resonates with most political persuasions. Most are also willing to accept a caveat, agreeing that "all Americans should have equal *opportunity* to make the decisions that allow them to live a long healthy life, regardless of their level of education, income, or ethnicity." And people widely agreed that it's not fair if they don't have that opportunity, Westen said.

Forr, the Olson Zaltman researcher, added that Republicans applauded the notion of helping people help themselves, a philosophy that has been around for nine hundred years, starting with the Jewish philosopher Maimonides.

∿

The debate over how much responsibility an individual bears for her or his health is a very familiar one to S. Leonard Syme, PhD. He's a sociologist and emeritus professor with the School of Public Health at the University of California, Berkeley who is widely credited with building the foundation for the modern field of social determinants of health.[8] (Sir Michael Marmot, the lead investigator of the seminal Whitehall Studies on job rank and health among British civil servants, attended UC Berkeley to learn under Syme. Marmot earned his PhD in public health in 1975 at UC Berkeley and his master's there in 1972. Given their long relationship, Syme says he doesn't have to call Marmot "Sir.")

Syme agrees that personal responsibility is part of the equation, but he framed it this way: "Effective behavior change requires that we do our best as individuals, but that we work together with one another to create more healthful and supportive environments."[9]

When we talked in 2009, in his office packed with books and journals, Syme used safe water supplies as an example of the dividing line between personal responsibility and outside factors affecting health. "What if I told you your community had a contaminated water supply, and I asked you to boil your water, forever. You'd say, 'Fix up the water supply!'" He added, "Why can't I just ask everybody to look after themselves? Because we wouldn't permit it. We ask people to come together in many ways."

Water supplies are one thing, but what about aspects of health that are typically considered under our own control, such as obesity? "If ever there was a personal responsibility issue, that would be it, right?" Syme asked.

It turns out, Syme continued, that compared with high-income areas, obesity rates are much higher in low-income areas "where there are no supermarkets, where there's no fresh produce, where buying McDonald's is actually easier. And where exercise is not so easy, because if you go outside, you might be in danger. So clearly we live in a society where it's not just up to individuals, but there are social circumstances that affect our choices," Syme said.

I talked with Dr. Tony Iton, the senior vice president at the California Endowment who oversees the BHC campaign, about the role of personal responsibility in health. He believes that responsibility and community empowerment go hand in hand, allowing people to better control their conditions and destiny, he said. "The traditional American notion of a barn raising, where people come together and help somebody build a barn, is what community organizing really is," Iton said. "So we found that when you express it in that way, when you talk about people taking individual initiative to get their neighbors together to simply solve a problem, that has appeal across the partisan divide. And we think that's in fact what we're doing."

Epilogue

When the Building Healthy Communities campaign began in 2010, the plan was to sunset the $1 billion initiative at the end of 2020. In preparation, about midway through the ten-year endeavor, community organizations in the fourteen sites were asked to start seeking additional funding to maintain the effort, particularly the all-important collaboration among nonprofit organizations and local agencies. Several of the sites had identified some outside funding and said they were sure the relationships built up over the campaign would endure.

No one knew, of course, how realistic it was to expect the momentum to continue without the California Endowment's involvement. After all, the Endowment not only funds the staffing and supplies needed to run the local actions teams, but it also lends cachet to the work. It also serves as a neutral convener, bringing together various community organizations, many of which had never worked with any of the others. In talking with the local BHC leaders about plans post 2020, most expressed confidence that they'd somehow keep it going, but weren't clear on the blueprint.

Then, at a campaign convening in the spring of 2016, Robert Ross mentioned "BHC 2.0." He didn't elaborate, but the comment suggested that leadership was considering extending the campaign. A year later, during a March 2017 speech in San Diego, he expressed appreciation that the Endowment had the option to stick it out for longer than usual in communities. "So if it takes us twenty years to fix something, meaningfully, then it's just going to take twenty years," he said. "We have the time. Let's take the time to engage folks, hearing their vision for what is a healthy community, and how they can deploy their assets with agency and power." When we talked in June 2017, he explicitly mentioned "the next chapter of BHC" and said the board of directors—the ultimate decision makers—would be discussing next steps in the coming months. "My impression is that the board would not be interested in just dropping the curtain and closing things down on BHC," Ross said.

Iton, the senior vice president for the BHC campaign, confirmed that the campaign will continue past 2020. When I asked him what led to that decision, he said, "Well, so two things have happened. One is that there has been almost unanimous recognition on the board that BHC is working," he said. The Endowment counts 524 successes in changing policies and systems and new amenities in the fourteen sites, with three years still to go in the original ten-year plan.

The Endowment's tally includes 199 "wins" in changing public policy locally or statewide, including the striking example of reducing suspensions by 46 percent and expulsions by 42 percent across the state. There were 231 incidents of "systems change," or shifts in the way government agencies make decisions about their policies, programs, and budgets to respond better to the needs of historically disadvantaged neighborhoods. Finally, the first seven years of the BHC campaign brought about 94 "tangible benefits," such as new parks, health centers, community centers, or physical improvements (walking trails, sidewalks, park equipment, murals).

"The board said to us, 'So why would we stop this? Tell us why we would stop?'" Iton said. "And our response was, 'Well, we think there may be some things we want to do slightly differently, but we don't want to stop. We think that this is working.'"

In another development, Iton said, a few new members—including the former director of the Shasta County Health and Human Services Agency—joined the Endowment's board of directors. Shasta County is a rural northern California county that is near Del Norte County, a BHC site that is becoming a template for work in distressed, largely white rural regions. Iton also spearheaded a large research project that revealed a previously undetected rise in white mortality rates in California among middle-aged residents.[1]

To get the data, the Endowment partnered with Virginia Commonwealth University to analyze mortality rates in counties across California. The research initially focused on Kings, Tulare, Fresno, and Kern counties in California's agricultural Central Valley (with BHC sites in the Fresno and Kern counties).

The research found that although mortality rates among black, Hispanic, and Asian middle-aged adults statewide fell by 16 to 20 percent since 1995, the mortality rate for whites in California decreased by only 5 percent. Stunningly, however, the mortality rate for middle-aged whites in the four Central Valley counties actually *increased* by 11 percent in that time frame, reversing decades-long trends of mortality declines among all groups, aside from periods following the outbreak of the HIV/AIDS epidemic and the 1918 flu pandemic. The lead author of the report said that although the opioid crisis was one factor in the rising white mortality rate in California, it wasn't the only one.

"Household incomes have been stagnant and poverty rates have been climbing in these counties over a period of many years," said Dr. Steven Woolf, director of the Center on Society and Health at Virginia Commonwealth University. "Stress, anxiety and depression are taking their toll on this population. The economy is literally costing lives."[2]

Iton spoke about the data before a state senate health committee in January 2017, saying, "Underlying this crisis is chronic stress. People who feel that they have lost a shot at the American dream," he said. "And when people lose hope, they turn to tobacco, drugs, alcohol for relief. Or commit suicide in desperation. In fact, these causes of death are increasingly referred to as 'deaths of despair.'"

The California research followed a headline-grabbing 2015 study from Princeton University describing an unexpected increase in US mortality rates between 1999 and 2013 for middle-aged whites, whereas they declined nationally for other racial groups. No other rich country saw a similar reversal. The Princeton researchers concluded that suicides, drugs, and alcohol were behind the tragic trend among middle-aged whites, although the effect was largely confined to those with no more than a high school education. For them, death rates rose by 22 percent, whereas overall they fell for whites with a college education.[3,4]

As an aside, I commented to Iton that people living in these distressed rural counties are usually called "white working class," but the term *working class* is virtually never applied to those in distressed urban neighborhoods, even though the majority of them hold jobs, often more than one. "It's an interesting semantic point," Iton said. "I think that that [rural] population is also working poor. But there's stigma to calling white people 'poor,' where there's not stigma to calling black, or Latinos poor, because it's just done so often."

When he first began speaking about California's new white mortality, Iton used the term *working poor*, but, he said, "I got a lot of pushback, typically from white audiences. I backed off of that term. But when you look at where they are economically, they are pretty much in the same economic band as a lot of the people we're working with in Building Healthy Communities."

Iton said the "deaths of despair" in rural communities reflect the same distress behind lower life expectancies and more illness in inner-city neighborhoods. "It's this lack of hope, this lack of agency and a lack of a way forward, a visible way forward," Iton said. "It's an existential crisis. People have lost the sense of purpose in their lives, and they've completely lost their grasp on the American Dream. And *that's* making them sick." He added, "I saw the same thing in inner-city Baltimore," referring to his time in medical school at Johns Hopkins University.

He also noted that counties around the country with rising white mortality rates also tracked closely with those where Donald Trump won the majority vote in the 2016 US presidential election. "You see these deaths of despair and you can just map the Trump support map right on top of those," Iton said. "There have been real consequences to ignoring the shared suffering across this population."

Ross agreed. "The results of the Trump election and the civic, political, racial divide highlighted as a result of the election tell us that there's a fair amount of hopelessness and pain in low-income white communities as well, and we need to be attuned to that reality in our healthy communities work," he said. "So I expect us to be more intentional and assertive about bringing rural white poverty into the Building Healthy Communities tent."

Ross also expects to keep stretching the work of the foundation. He is mindful that school discipline wasn't initially on the Endowment staff's radar and wants to be on the lookout for other unrecognized social factors harming health that the foundation could tackle.

Ross said the BHC work will keep disrupting the "school-to-prison pipeline." The phrase describes how excessive school discipline and campus law enforcement policies, among other factors, expose a disproportionate number of young people of color—young males especially— to the juvenile justice and criminal justice systems, later snaring many of them into the prison system and thus severely damaging their future prospects and, by default, their health.

"I cannot use enough boldfaced, italicize, capitalized, underlined words to describe how angry and frustrated communities are about the prison pipeline and the relationship with police. It's thick," Ross said in a 2017 speech in San Diego

Gentrification poses the latest challenge to Ross because it's far outside the normal purview of health promotion work, but at a gut level it clearly relates. He's hesitated to take it on "because it wasn't at all a garden-variety health issue," he explained. "But there's so much civic and community energy, and anger and frustration, around the issue of gentrification, displacement, affordable housing. I told Tony [Iton], 'We're a health foundation. We don't do housing.'" But Ross said Iton and other Endowment leadership told him, "'We can't stop hearing about this.'" Ross just received a proposal outlining the issue.

"We still have to justify the deployment of our resources with a link towards our health mission. I would say that's probably the most ongoing, consistent tension that we manage at the foundation," Ross said. "And do we simply accept that if the community believes that the issue is central and important to their wellness, is that good enough? It's not a yes or no answer. But I would say the place-based aspect of our work, in the fourteen sites, has certainly introduced us to a broader definition of health."

Acknowledgments

I owe thanks to the many people who generously shared their time describing their thoughts, actions, and feelings about improving the health of communities and the people who live in them, all of which made this book possible.

Many come to mind, but chief among them is Dr. Robert Ross, president of the California Endowment. He never hesitated to make himself available for lengthy interviews during the five years it took to report and write this book, despite his always packed schedule. When we talked, he was candid, heartfelt, and expansive in his answers, which allowed me to get a far fuller picture of the story behind this ten-year campaign than I might have otherwise. He also quickly responded, through various staff members, to any request for information or materials. It made reporting on this multifaceted campaign in fourteen communities, from the northernmost to the southernmost reaches of the state, much easier. This book would not be the same without his supportive engagement.

Thanks go to Island Press for recognizing the powerful potential of this work in California and its applicability elsewhere. Special thanks go to Emily Turner, my editor at Island Press, for her superb editing and manuscript suggestions, which most assuredly improved this book, as well as for her suggestion of its title, which captures the fundamental purpose of the Building Healthy Communities campaign. In addition to her professionalism on every level, Emily was also a true pleasure to work with.

Another critical partner in this project was the Aspen Institute, which provided the research funding that made this book a reality; moreover, Sheri Brady and the institute's Forum for Community Solutions were ideal partners in this project, and Aspen's early work in this field provided critical background on community change work, as described in chapter 1.

Thanks also go to the many staff members in the BHC sites who showed me around their communities, openly shared their goals and frustrations, and—critically—introduced me to residents partnering with them to drive change. I am grateful for staff's efforts and time in all the communities I visited—Del Norte County, Richmond, Sacramento, Salinas, Coachella Valley, Fresno, South Los Angeles, Boyle Heights, and the City Heights neighborhood of San Diego—but I will single out a few for special thanks. That has to start with Melissa Darnell in Del Norte County and the adjacent tribal lands who took two days in August 2012, early in the book reporting process, to drive me for hours throughout the vast and beautiful region and introduce me to numerous remarkable residents and partners in the work. Thereafter, she shared quality information on new advances. Laura Olson and Geneva Wiki also generously shared their time, knowledge, and key introductions. Dr. Tony Iton, head of the BHC campaign, championed this book and supported my early access into the communities. In addition, this book ultimately arose from his decision while he ran the Alameda County Public Health Department to lend an epidemiologist to a reporting project I was involved in with the *Oakland Tribune*. That epidemiologist's work formed the backbone of a unique four-part series on health disparities the newspaper ran and ultimately led to my focus on health disparities and this book project. On that note, a thank-you goes out to Michelle Levander with the University of Southern California, who runs a health journalism fellowship program that inspired that newspaper project. In addition, Larry Adelman, codirector of California Newsreel, set the standard for telling compelling stories about health inequities and provided major inspiration for the newspaper project through his incredible four-hour series *Unnatural Causes*, broadcast by PBS in 2008.

Thanks also go to Diane Aranda and Roxanne Carrillo Garza in Richmond, who paved the way for valuable interviews. The welcome by Silvia Paz in Coachella Valley made my quick trip there highly productive, including arranging a fascinating tour and interview with Megan Beaman, an attorney and the lead for the Neighborhoods Action Team there. In Sacramento, Christine Tien opened doors for reporting on groundbreaking healthy food access work, and Castle Redmond aided in research on the school discipline reform campaign. Tamu Jones and Charles Fields introduced me to many South Los Angeles partners and residents while also sharing stories from the community as they drove me around the site, and Steve Eldred and Mark Tran in City Heights organized an excellent visit to their community. Thanks go to Sarah Reyes, who arranged phone interviews not only with Endowment staff, but also with the Fresno police chief. Daniel Zingale's invitation to a state team meeting yielded key insights into the endeavor, and Albert Maldonado's guidance while I visited the summer Sierra camp greatly expanded my understanding of the work with boys and young men of color.

I am especially grateful for the trust accorded me by the many residents and community partners I met with in these sites and whose stories bring this book to life. All the stories were valuable and contributed to a more complete picture of life in these communities. Thanks especially go to Gary Blatnick, Makenzy (Williams) Cervantes, Patrick Cleary, Chris and Lisa Howard, Thomas O'Rourke Sr., Terry Supahan, and the many young people I interviewed in Del Norte County and the tribal lands; Kimberly Aceves, DeVone Boggan, LaVon Carter, Bill Lindsay, Toody Maher, Rohnell Robinson, Sam Vaughn, and Tamisha Walker in Richmond; and Lisa Bettencourt, Davida Douglas, Shawn Harrison, Randy Stannard, and Chanowk and Judith Yisrael in Sacramento. In Salinas, Rinku Sen and Jerry Tello cultivated my understanding of the challenging world of racial equity training, while Ray Corpuz and Gary Petersen showed what enlightened city leadership looks like. In South Los Angeles, thanks go to Alberto Ayala, Teresa Blanco, and Tina Sandoval as well as the staff and youth activists at Community Coalition. Thanks also go to Robert Egger with L.A. Kitchen and Mott Smith with L.A. Prep whose pioneering work with food access in Los Angeles helped inform chapter 8. In City Heights, stories and background from Godwin Higa, Bridget Lambert, Leslie Renteria, and Terry Stanley brought out pivotal dimensions of the work there.

As for the experts contributing to this project, my deepest thanks go to S. Leonard Syme, PhD, the distinguished and honored University of California, Berkeley sociologist. He courageously laid the groundwork, starting in the 1950s, for the now-robust field of research into social determinants of health while overcoming entrenched views and skepticism. He generously gave his time to speak with me on several occasions about the field and enthusiastically embraced this book project. Thanks also go to Jason Corburn, PhD, at UC Berkeley for additional perspective on the work in Richmond and to James Forr with Olson Zaltman Associates, whose firm's powerful work in understanding deep metaphors defined chapter 10. In addition, many thanks go to the scientists at the Primate Center at the Wake Forest School of Medicine, who welcomed me for a visit and then patiently cooperated with fact-checking on their groundbreaking research. And I greatly appreciated Elissa Epel, PhD, and Robert Sapolsky, PhD, for taking the time to share their views on the health toll of chronic stress. My appreciation also goes to Dr. Steven Schroeder, a friend and the former president of the Robert Wood Johnson Foundation, for many stimulating talks on a topic he understands well.

I also give my thanks to my agent, Joelle Delbourgo, with whom I was fortunate to connect. She exemplifies just what one wishes for in an agent: high professional standards, deep knowledge of the book publishing field, and a love for the world of books and literature.

Finally, my greatest thanks go to Glenn E. Thompson, my husband and behind-the-scenes partner in this project. He supported me unequivocally in pursuing this work, and at critical junctures he offered invaluable advice and insights about both the book's content and the overall project, for which I am deeply grateful.

~

I'll end with a tribute to one young man whose life embodied the spirit of the work written about in this book. One Sunday in October 2017, I unexpectedly received a heartbroken email from Dr. Robert Ross. He inquired if it was possible to acknowledge a young man named Brandon Harrison who was on his President's Youth Council, a group of young people whose insights and experiences Ross prizes. The twenty-year-old man had overcome a turbulent past and was emerging as a powerful young leader. The California Endowment was in fact working with a nonprofit organization in his city to relocate him to Los Angeles because Brandon feared that old grievances in his hometown could come back to haunt him. His instincts proved tragically correct, as he was gunned down and killed in the early hours of that fateful Sunday. I hadn't met Brandon, but I know that he exemplifies the frustrating reality that not all young people escape the snare of unhealthy forces in their communities, despite their strenuous and heroic efforts to do so. So I asked Ross to write a tribute, and these are Ross's words:

> *Brandon Harrison's short but impactful life epitomized our journey and vision: A young African American male who transformed a history of violence, gangbanging, and juvenile hall into a spirit of leadership and activism for positive social change. We carry on our work in his memory and the memory of young people whose lives have similarly been prematurely extinguished.*

Notes

Chapter 1: How Neighborhoods Kill

1. Los Angeles County Department of Public Health, "Health Atlas for the City of Los Angeles," June 2013, http://healthyplan.la/the-health-atlas/.
2. Annie Park, Nancy Watson, and Lark Galloway-Gilliam, "South Los Angeles Health Equity Scorecard," Community Health Councils, Los Angeles, December 2008, 53, 58, http://lahealthaction.org/library/SouthLAScore card.pdf.
3. Christopher Ingraham, "14 Baltimore Neighborhoods Have Lower Life Expectancies than North Korea," *Washington Post*, April 30, 2015, https://www.washingtonpost.com/news/wonk/wp/2015/04/30/baltimores-poorest-residents-die-20-years-earlier-than-its-richest/.
4. Suzanne Bohan and Sandy Kleffman, "Three East Bay ZIP Codes, Life-and-Death Disparities," *Contra Costa Times*, December 2, 2009, http://www.eastbaytimes.com/2009/12/02/day-i-three-east-bay-zip-codes-life-and-death-disparities/.
5. L. Dwyer-Lindgren, A. Bertozzi-Villa, R. W. Stubbs, C. Morozoff, J. P. Mackenbach, F. J. van Lenthe, A. H. Mokdad, and C. J. L. Murray, "Inequalities in Life Expectancy among US Counties, 1980 to 2014 Temporal Trends and Key Drivers," *JAMA Internal Medicine* 177, no. 7 (2017): 1003–11. doi:10.1001/jamainternmed.2017.0918.
6. Maggie Fox, "Who Lives Longer? Study Finds Colorado Wins by 20 Years," *NBC News*, May 8, 2017, https://www.nbcnews.com/health/health-news/who-lives-longer-study-finds-colorado-wins-20-years-n756471.

7. Gina Kolata, "Death Rates Rising for Middle-Aged White Americans, Study Finds," *New York Times*, November 2, 2015, https://www.nytimes.com /2015/11/03/health/death-rates-rising-for-middle-aged-white-americans -study-finds.html.

8. "To Fight Crime, a Poor City Will Trade in Its Police," *New York Times*, September 28, 2012, http://www.nytimes.com/2012/09/29/nyregion/overrun -by-crime-camden-trades-in-its-police-force.html.

9. S. J. Olshansky, D. J. Passaro, R. C. Hershow, J. Layden, B. A. Carnes, J. Brody, L. Hayflick, R. N. Butler, D. B. Allison, and D. S. Ludwig, "A Potential Decline in Life Expectancy in the United States in the 21st Century," *New England Journal of Medicine* 352, no. 11 (March 17, 2005): 1138–45.

10. National Center for Health Statistics, "Health, United States, 2010: With Special Feature on Death and Dying," 2011, 134, https://www.cdc.gov/nchs /data/hus/hus10.pdf.

11. Centers for Disease Control and Prevention, "Ten Great Public Health Achievements—United States, 1900–1999," *Morbidity and Mortality Weekly Report* 48, no. 12 (April 2, 1999): 241–43, https://www.cdc.gov/mmwr /preview/mmwrhtml/00056796.htm.

12. P. Lee and D. Paxman, "Reinventing Public Health," *Annual Review of Public Health* 18 (1997): 16–17, http://www.annualreviews.org/doi/pdf/10 .1146/annurev.publhealth.18.1.1.

13. N. E. Adler and K. Newman, "Socioeconomic Disparities in Health: Pathways and Policies," *Health Affairs* 21, no. 2 (2002): 71, https://www.ncbi .nlm.nih.gov/pubmed/11900187.

14. Lee and Paxman, "Reinventing Public Health."

15. Mario Sevilla, "Oakland Sideshow Crowd Fire Guns, Throw Bottles at Police," KRON video, February 13, 2014, https://www.policeone.com/crime /articles/6861371-Video-Oakland-sideshow-crowd-fire-guns-throw -bottles-at-police/.

16. B. Egolf, J. Lasker, S. Wolf, and L. Potvin, "The Roseto Effect: A 50-Year Comparison of Mortality Rates," *American Journal of Public Health* 82, no. 8 (1992): 1089–92.

17. Sandy Kleffman and Suzanne Bohan, "Health Problems Persist When Options Are Limited," *Contra Costa Times*, December 7, 2009, http://

www.eastbaytimes.com/2009/12/03/day-ii-health-problems-persist-when
-options-are-limited/.

18. Adler and Newman, "Socioeconomic Disparities," 66.

19. "Largest Health Foundations: 2013," *Modern Healthcare*, March 13, 2013,
http://www.modernhealthcare.com/article/20130313/DATA/500029147.

20. Faith Mitchell, "A New Generation of Health Foundations," *Healthcare
Finance*, October 13, 2014, http://www.healthcarefinancenews.com/news
/new-generation-health-foundations.

21. Maureen Glabman, "Health Plan Foundations: How Well Are They Spending the Money?," *Managed Care*, August 2008, https://www.managedcare
mag.com/archives/2008/8/health-plan-foundations-how-well-are-they
-spending-money.

22. L. Schwarte, S. E. Samuels, J. Capitman, M. Ruwe, M. Boyle, and G. Flores,
"The Central California Regional Obesity Prevention Program: Changing
Nutrition and Physical Activity Environments in California's Heartland,"
American Journal of Public Health 100, no. 11 (2010): 2124–28. doi:10
.2105/AJPH.2010.203588.

23. Anne C. Kubisch, Patricia Auspos, Prudence Brown, and Tom Dewar, "Voices
from the Field III: Lessons and Challenges from Two Decades of Community Change Efforts" (Washington, DC: Aspen Institute, 2010), 10, 17.

Chapter 2: The Stress Effect

1. Christopher Ingraham, "14 Baltimore Neighborhoods Have Lower Life
Expectancies than North Korea," *Washington Post*, April 30, 2015, https:
//www.washingtonpost.com/news/wonk/wp/2015/04/30/baltimores
-poorest-residents-die-20-years-earlier-than-its-richest/.

2. David Brown, "Life Expectancy in the U.S. Varies Widely by Region and in
Some Places Is Decreasing," *Washington Post*, June 15, 2011, https://www
.washingtonpost.com/national/life-expectancy-in-the-us-varies-widely-by
-region-and-in-some-places-is-decreasing/2011/06/13/AGdHuZVH_story
.html?utm_term=.f920935f98d7.

3. Randy Villegas, "Study: Life Expectancy in Decline for Middle Aged Whites
in Central Valley," *South Kern Sol*, February 16, 2017, http://www.south
kernsol.org/2017/02/16/study-life-expectancy-in-decline-for-middle-aged
-whites-in-central-valley.

4. K. A. Phillips et al., "Why Primate Models Matter," *American Journal of Primatology* 76, no. 9 (2014): 801–27. doi:10.1002/ajp.22281. Epub April 10, 2014.

5. Carol A. Shively and Mark E. Wilson, eds., *Social Inequalities in Health in Nonhuman Primates: The Biology of the Gradient* (New York: Springer, 2016), Kindle Location 515.

6. R. Paxton, B. M. Basile, I. Adachi, W. A. Suzuki, M. E. Wilson, and R. R. Hampton, "Rhesus Monkeys (Macaca mulatta) Rapidly Learn to Select Dominant Individuals in Videos of Artificial Social Interactions between Unfamiliar Conspecifics," *Journal of Comparative Psychology* 124, no. 4 (2010): 395–401. doi:10.1037/a0019751.

7. Larry Adelman et al., *Unnatural Causes: Is Inequality Making Us Sick?* (San Francisco: California Newsreel, 2008).

8. Shively and Wilson, *Social Inequalities*, Kindle Location 2195.

9. M. G. Marmot, G. Rose, M. Shipley, and P. J. Hamilton, "Employment Grade and Coronary Heart Disease in British Civil Servants," *Journal of Epidemiology and Community Health* 32, no. 4 (1978): 244–49, https://www.ncbi.nlm.nih.gov/pmc/articles/PMC1060958.

10. M. G. Marmot et al. "Health Inequalities among British Civil Servants: The Whitehall II Study," *Lancet* 337, no. 8754 (1991): 1387–93. doi:10.1016/0140-6736(91)93068-K.

11. S. R. Kunz-Ebrect, C. Kirschbaum, M. Marmot, and A. Steptoe, "Differences in Cortisol Awakening Response on Work Days and Weekends in Women and Men from the Whitehall II Cohort," *Psychoneuroendocrinology* 29, no. 4 (2004): 516–28. doi:10.1016/S0306-4530(03)00072-6.

12. H. Kuper and M. Marmot, "Job Strain, Job Demands, Decision Latitude, and Risk of Coronary Heart Disease within the Whitehall II Study," *Journal of Epidemiology and Community Health* 57 (2003): 147–53.

13. W. B. Cannon, "The Interrelations of Emotions as Suggested by Recent Physiological Researches," *American Journal of Psychology* 25, no. 2 (1914): 256–82. doi:10.2307/1413414.

14. Robert M. Sapolsky, *Why Zebras Don't Get Ulcers: The Acclaimed Guide to Stress, Stress-Related Diseases, and Coping*, 3rd ed. (New York: Henry Holt, 2004), 38, 60.

15. Sapolsky, *Why Zebras Don't Get Ulcers*, 211.

16. B. Q. Hafen, K. J. Karren, K. J. Frandsen, and N. L. Smith, *Mind/Body Health: The Effects of Attitudes, Emotions, and Relationships* (Boston: Allyn and Bacon, 1996), 59.

17. Sapolsky, *Why Zebras Don't Get Ulcers*, 29.

18. Sapolsky, *Why Zebras Don't Get Ulcers*, 8.

19. "Dr. Hans Selye Dies in Montreal; Studied Effects of Stress on Body," *New York Times*, October 22, 1982, http://www.nytimes.com/1982/10/22 /obituaries/dr-hans-selye-dies-in-montreal-studied-effects-of-stress-on -body.html.

20. Istvan Berczi, "My Teacher, Hans Selye, and His Legacy: A Personal Re-membrance," accessed November 2, 2017, https://home.cc.umanitoba.ca /~berczii/hans-selye/my-teacher-hans-selye-and-his-legacy.html.

21. S. Szabo, Y. Tache, and A. Somogyi, "The Legacy of Hans Selye and the Origins of Stress Research: A Retrospective 75 Years after His Landmark Brief 'Letter' to the Editor of *Nature*," *Stress* 15, no. 5 (2012): 472–78. doi: 10.3109/10253890.2012.710919.

22. Sapolsky, *Why Zebras Don't Get Ulcers*, 43.

23. Sapolsky, *Why Zebras Don't Get Ulcers*, 42.

24. Sapolsky, *Why Zebras Don't Get Ulcers*, 154.

25. Hafen et al., *Mind/Body Health*, 63.

26. Hafen et al., *Mind/Body Health*, 71–72.

27. S. Cohen, D. Tyrrell, and A. P. Smith, "Psychological Stress and Sus-ceptibility to the Common Cold," *New England Journal of Medicine* 325 (1991): 606–12.

28. D. Janicki-Deverts, S. Cohen, R. B. Turner, and W. J. Doyle, "Basal Salivary Cortisol Secretion and Susceptibility to Upper Respiratory Infection," *Brain, Behavior, and Immunity* 53 (2016): 255–61. doi:10.1016/j.bbi.2016 .01.013.

29. E. Wargo, "Understanding the Have-Nots: The Role of Stress in about Everything," *APS Observer*, December 2007, 18–23.

30. Sapolsky, *Why Zebras Don't Get Ulcers*, 67.

31. Shively and Wilson, *Social Inequalities*, Kindle Location 5226.

32. Shively and Wilson, *Social Inequalities*, Kindle Location 5886.

33. M. Coelho, T. Oliveira, and R. Fernandes, "Biochemistry of Adipose Tissue: An Endocrine Organ," *Archives of Medical Science* 9, no. 2 (2013): 191–200. doi:10.5114/aoms.2013.33181.

34. E. Blackburn and E. Epel, *The Telomere Effect: A Revolutionary Approach to Living Younger, Healthier, Longer* (New York: Grand Central Publishing, 2017).

35. Telephone interview with Elissa Epel, PhD, February 20, 2017.

36. Ingraham, "14 Baltimore Neighborhoods."

37. Anthony Iton, "Change the Odds for Health," TEDxSan Francisco, October 6, 2016, https://www.youtube.com/watch?v=0H6yte4RXx0.

38. Email interview with Robert M. Sapolsky, PhD, February 28, 2017.

39. A. Wagstaff and E. van Doorslaer, "Income Inequality and Health: What Does the Literature Tell Us?," *Annual Review of Public Health* 21 (2000): 543–67.

40. Sapolsky, *Why Zebras Don't Get Ulcers*, 375–76.

Chapter 3: Keeping Kids in School

1. Fania E. Davis, "Interrupting the School to Prison Pipeline through Restorative Justice," *Huffington Post*, October 5, 2015, https://www.huffingtonpost.com/fania-e-davis/interrupting-the-school-t_b_8244864.html.

2. South Jersey Times Editorial Board, "Camden Schools Teach a Good In-Class Lesson," *South Jersey Times*, August 29, 2017, http://www.nj.com/opinion/index.ssf/2017/08/camden_schools_teach_a_good_in-class_lesson_editorial.html.

3. Michael Bott and Ty Chandler, "California's School Suspensions Show Racial Disparity," *USA Today*, February 20, 2015, https://www.usatoday.com/story/news/nation/2015/02/20/california-school-suspensions-racial-racism/23724843/.

4. Stephanie Francis Ward, "Schools Start to Rethink Zero Tolerance Policies," *American Bar Association Journal*, August 2014, http://www.abajournal.com/magazine/article/schools_start_to_rethink_zero_tolerance_policies.

5. Russell Skiba, Cecil R. Reynolds, Sandra Graham, Peter Sheras, Jane Close Conoley, and Enedina Garcia-Vazquez, "Are Zero Tolerance Policies Effective in the Schools? An Evidentiary Review and Recommendations," American Psychological Association Zero Tolerance Task Force, August 9, 2006, 13, http://www.apa.org/pubs/info/reports/zero-tolerance-report.pdf.

6. Sabrina Tavernise, "Life Spans Shrink for Least-Educated Whites in the U.S.," *New York Times*, September 20, 2012, http://www.nytimes.com/2012/09/21/us/life-expectancy-for-less-educated-whites-in-us-is-shrinking.html.

7. S. Egerter, P. Bravemen, T. Sadegh-Nobari, R. Grossman-Kahn, and M. Dekker, "Education and Health," Robert Wood Johnson Foundation Issue Brief No. 5, April 2011, https://www.rwjf.org/en/library/research /2011/05/education-matters-for-health.html.

8. Chris Chapman, Jennifer Laird, Nicole Ifill, and Angelina KewalRamani, "Trends in High School Dropout and Completion Rates in the United States: 1972–2009," National Center for Education Statistics, October 2011, 1, https://nces.ed.gov/pubs2012/2012006.pdf.

9. Clive Belfield and Henry Levin, "The Economic Losses from High School Dropouts in California," California Dropout Research Project Report No. 1, August 2007, https://all4ed.org/articles/the-economic-losses-from-high -school-dropouts-in-california-new-study-pegs-annual-loss-at-46-4 -billion/.

10. Elizabeth Becker, "As Ex-Theorist on Young 'Superpredators,' Bush Aide Has Regrets," *New York Times*, February 9, 2001, http://www.nytimes.com /2001/02/09/us/as-ex-theorist-on-young-superpredators-bush-aide-has -regrets.html.

11. Clyde Haberman, "When Youth Violence Spurred 'Superpredator' Fear," *New York Times*, April 6, 2014, https://www.nytimes.com/2014/04/07/us /politics/killing-on-bus-recalls-superpredator-threat-of-90s.html.

12. Civil Rights Project/Proyecto Derechos Civiles, "Opportunities Suspended: The Devastating Consequences of Zero Tolerance and School Discipline," Report from A National Summit on Zero Tolerance, June 15–16, 2000, Washington, DC, https://www.civilrightsproject.ucla.edu/research/k-12 -education/school-discipline/opportunities-suspended-the-devastating -consequences-of-zero-tolerance-and-school-discipline-policies.

13. Nirvi Shah, "Findings Stoke Concerns over 'Zero-Tolerance,'" *Education Week*, October 11, 2011, https://www.edweek.org/ew/articles/2011/10/12 /07discipline_ep-2.h31.html.

14. Jeffrey H. Lamont, "Out of School Suspension and Expulsion," *Pediatrics*, February 2013. doi:10.1542/peds.2012-3932.

15. Sam Dillon, "Study Finds High Rate of Imprisonment among Dropouts," *New York Times*, October 8, 2009, http://www.nytimes.com/2009/10/09 /education/09dropout.html?mcubz=3.

16. Civil Rights Project, "Opportunities Suspended," 4–6.

17. Kenneth J. Cooper, "Group Finds Racial Disparity in Schools' 'Zero Tolerance,'" *Washington Post*, June 15, 2000, https://www.washingtonpost.com/archive/politics/2000/06/15/group-finds-racial-disparity-in-schools-zero-tolerance/0ad585b4-c814-44a8-919e-09ad82ab0b9b.

18. T. Tobin, "Video Shows Police Handcuffing Five-Year-Old," *Tampa Bay Times*, April 22, 2005, http://www.sptimes.com/2005/04/22/Southpinellas/Video_shows_police_ha.shtml.

19. Tony Fabelo, Michael D. Thompson, Martha Plotkin, Dottie Carmichael, Miner P. Marchbanks III, and Eric A. Booth, "Breaking Schools' Rules: A Statewide Study of How School Discipline Relates to Students' Success and Juvenile Justice Involvement," Council of State Governments Justice Center, 2011, https://csgjusticecenter.org/youth/breaking-schools-rules-report.

20. Russell J. Skiba, Robert H. Horner, Choong-Geun Chung, M. Karega Rausch, Seth L. May, and Tary Tobin, "Race Is Not Neutral: A National Investigation of African American and Latino Disproportionality in School Discipline," *School Psychology Review* 40, no. 1 (2011): 87, http://goo.gl/mUK2NE.

21. Skiba et al., "Race Is Not Neutral," 87.

22. Skiba et al., "Race Is Not Neutral," 87.

23. Frances Vavrus and Kim Marie Cole, "'I Didn't Do Nothin': The Discursive Construction of School Suspension," *Urban Review* 34, no. 2 (June 2002): 87–111.

Chapter 4: Changing Schools' Rules

1. Robert Ross, "State Must Include Suspension Rates as Measure of School Success," *EdSource*, May 10, 2016, https://edsource.org/2016/state-must-include-suspension-rates-as-measure-of-school-success/564005.

2. Daniel J. Losen, Tia Martinez, and Jon Gillespie, "Suspended Education in California," University of California, Los Angeles, Center for Civil Rights Remedies, April 10, 2012, https://www.civilrightsproject.ucla.edu/resources/projects/center-for-civil-rights-remedies/school-to-prison-folder/summary-reports/suspended-education-in-california.

3. CADRE, Mental Health Advocacy Services, Inc., Public Counsel Law Center, "Redefining Dignity in Our Schools," June 2010, 7, http://www.publiccounsel.org/publications?id=0134.

4. CADRE, "Redefining Dignity," 10.

5. Tia Martinez, Arnold Chandler, and Nancy Latham, "Case Study: School Discipline Reform in California," California Endowment, August 1, 2013, 4–5, http://california.foundationcenter.org/reports/case-study-school-discipline-reform-in-california.

6. Martinez, Chandler, and Lathlam, "Case Study," 6.

7. "Students and Parents Push Back against School 'Pushout,' Barriers to Graduation," Children's Defense Fund–California press release, October 5, 2011, http://www.cdfca.org/newsroom/related-news/2012/students-and-parents-push.html.

8. Losen, Martinez, and Gillespie, "Suspended Education."

9. "Virtual Rally for School Discipline: Week of Action," California Endowment, posted October 6, 2011, https://www.youtube.com/watch?v=U6Llm_Iw9u4.

10. Centers for Disease Control and Prevention, "Health Risk Behaviors among Adolescents Who Do and Do Not Attend School—United States, 1992," *Morbidity and Mortality Weekly Report* 43, no. 8 (1994): 129–32.

11. Maria Hinojosa, "The Playground to the Big Yard, Deconstructing School to Prison Pipeline," *Latino USA*, March 2, 2016, http://latinousa.org/2016/03/02/the-playground-to-the-big-yard-deconstructing-school-to-prison-pipeline/.

12. "Teens and Cops Discuss How Education Can Be the Great Equalizer," Council for A Strong America, Washington, DC, September 2, 2014, https://www.strongnation.org/articles/47-teens-and-cops-discuss-how-education-can-be-the-great-equalizer.

13. Tony Fabelo, Michael D. Thompson, Martha Plotkin, Dottie Carmichael, Miner P. Marchbanks III, and Eric A. Booth, "Breaking Schools' Rules: A Statewide Study of How School Discipline Relates to Students' Success and Juvenile Justice Involvement," Council of State Governments Justice Center, 2011, https://csgjusticecenter.org/youth/breaking-schools-rules-report.

14. "Why Are California Schools Suspending More Students than They Graduate?," Fix School Discipline website, September 5, 2012, http://www.fixschooldiscipline.org/2012/09/05/why-are-california-schools-suspending-more-students-than-they-graduate/.

15. Losen et al., "Suspended Education in California."

16. "CA Enacts First-in-the-Nation Law to Eliminate Student Suspensions for Minor Misbehavior," ACLU, September 27, 2014, https://www.aclusocal

.org/en/press-releases/ca-enacts-first-nation-law-eliminate-student -suspensions-minor-misbehavior.

17. Tia Martinez, "Case Study," 16.

18. "Restorative Justice and Positive Behavior Intervention Support," *Fight Crime: Invest in Kids* (blog), April 25, 2017, https://www.strongnation.org /articles/411-restorative-justice-and-positive-behavior-intervention-support.

19. Evan Horowitz, "When will minorities be the majority?" *Boston Globe*, February 26, 2016, https://www.bostonglobe.com/news/politics/2016/02/26 /when-will-minorities-majority/9v5m1Jj8hdGcXvpXtbQT5I/story.html

20. "Statewide School Discipline Hearing: Introduction and Keynote Address with Russlyn Ali," California Endowment, Los Angeles, September 10, 2012, https://www.youtube.com/watch?v=QRlNCemnHBw.

21. Craig Clough, "Brown Signs Bill Limiting 'Willful Defiance' Suspensions, Expulsions," *LA School Report*, September 29, 2014, http://laschoolreport .com/brown-signs-bill-limiting-willful-defiance-suspensions-expulsion.

22. "State Schools Chief Tom Torlakson Announces Fifth Year in a Row of Declining Student Suspensions and Expulsions," California Department of Education, November 1, 2017, https://www.cde.ca.gov/nr/ne/yr17/yr17rel 80.asp.

23. Ross, "State Must Include Suspension Rates."

24. Lindsay Warner, Maggie Thompson, and Barrie Becker, "Classmates Not Cellmates," Fight Crime: Invest in Kids California, 2012, 3, http://fight crime.s3.amazonaws.com/wp-content/uploads/CA-School-Discipline -Report.pdf.

Chapter 5: A Safe Place to Play

1. M. Purciel-Hill, C. Tsui, J. Lucky, S. Simon-Ortiz, B. Staton, and J. Heller, "A Health Impact Assessment of a Skatepark in City Heights, San Diego," Human Impact Partners, Oakland, CA, July 2014, 11.

2. Michael Smolens, "Mid-City Has Growing Pains: Critic Particularly Pained That Development Lacks Planning," *San Diego Union*, April 22, 1984.

3. Purciel-Hill et al., "A Health Impact Assessment," 17.

4. "Where We Work," Environmental Health Coalition, 2011, http://www .environmentalhealth.org/index.php/en/where-we-work/local/city-heights.

5. "City Heights," California Endowment, accessed May 18, 2017, http:// www.calendow.org/places/city-heights/.

6. Smolens, "Mid-City Has Growing Pains."

7. City of San Diego, Housing and Community Development Services, "San Diego County: Area Median Income (AMI) and Income Limits," accessed May 17, 2017, http://www.sandiegocounty.gov/content/sdc/sdhcd/rental -assistance/income-limits-ami.html.

8. Purciel-Hill et al., "A Health Impact Assessment," 9.

9. Leonardo Castañeda, "San Diego County Numbers Show Lifespan Gap between Rich and Poor," inewsource, April 10, 2017, http://inewsource.org /2017/04/10/san-diego-life-expectancy/.

10. Media Arts Center San Diego's Teen Producers Project, "Skatepark: Necessity or Disturbance?," *City Heights Speaks*, September 21, 2012, https:// www.youtube.com/watch?v=PIZLeV9UWlE.

11. Alan Ward, "Case Study: City Heights Skate Park," California Endowment, October 2013, http://www.pewtrusts.org/en/research-and-analysis/analysis /hip/hip-case-study-city-heights-skate-park.

12. Ward, "Case Study," 16.

13. Anna Daniels, "Whose Park? City Heights Struggles to Define 'Our' Park," *San Diego Free Press*, November 24, 2014, http://sandiegofreepress.org/2014 /11/whose-park-city-heights-struggles-to-define-our-park.

14. Purciel-Hill et al., "A Health Impact Assessment."

15. "City Heights welcomes new 19,000-square-foot skate park," *ABC10*, January 17, 2008, https://www.10news.com/news/city-heights-welcomes -new-19000-square-foot-skate-park

16. "Tony Hawk Foundation Backs Public Skate Parks Coast to Coast," Tony Hawk Foundation, August 27, 2013, http://tonyhawkfoundation.org/tony -hawk-foundation-backs-public-skateparks-coast-to-coast.

17. "Building Healthy Communities: South Kern," *Newsletter*, October 2015, http://www.healthysouthkern.org/wp-content/uploads/2015/09/BHC -South-Kern-E-Newsletter-Vol.-16.pdf.

18. "Why Skateparks?," Tony Hawk Foundation, accessed October 9, 2017, https://tonyhawkfoundation.org/public-skateparks/.

19. "California Health Interview Survey of 14 Building Healthy Communities Sites," UCLA Center for Health Policy Research, 2015, http://healthpolicy .ucla.edu/chis/bhc/Pages/dashboard.aspx.

20. Bonnie Ratner and Connie Chan Robison, "The Changing of Fresno: A Profile of Collaboration, Community and Culture Coming Together to

Improve in Neighborhoods," Public Health Institute, Oakland, CA, May 2013, 15.

21. California Endowment, "California Youth Leaders Prioritize #Parks4All," *Health Happens Here*, Winter 2015–2016, http://www.calendow.org/wp -content/uploads/Newsletter_WINTER_2015_ENGLISH.pdf.

22. Tim Sheehan, "Nonprofit Upset That City Rejected Bus Ad Criticizing Park Disparity," *Fresno Bee*, May 28, 2015, http://www.fresnobee.com/news /local/article22569339.html.

23. George Hostetter, "Fresno's Future Is a Carved Up, Identity Politics Mess," *CVO*, October 19, 2016, http://www.cvobserver.com/fresno/fresno-future -carved-up-mess.

24. "Parks and Recreation in Underserved Areas: A Public Health Perspective," National Recreation and Parks Association, Ashburn, VA, accessed May 31, 2017, http://www.nrpa.org/uploadedFiles/nrpa.org/Publications_and _Research/Research/Papers/Parks-Rec-Underserved-Areas.pdf.

25. Bee Editorial Board, "Thumbs Up, Thumbs Down," *Fresno Bee*, May 29, 2015, http://www.fresnobee.com/opinion/editorials/article22660653.html.

26. "California Youth Leaders Prioritize #Parks4All."

27. Letisia Marquez, "Park Perks: Teenagers Who Live Close to a Park Are More Physically Active," UCLA Public Affairs, March 27, 2013, http://newsroom .ucla.edu/releases/park-perks-teenagers-who-live-244449.

28. Kelly Rayburn, "Oakland Ranked 4th Most Dangerous U.S. City, Richmond Ranked 9th," *Bay Area News Group*, November 19, 2007, http://www .mercurynews.com/2007/11/19/oakland-ranked-4th-most-dangerous-u-s -city-richmond-ranked-9th/.

29. "Iron Triangle: Walkable Neighborhood Plan," Fehr and Peers, Los Angeles, February 2015, 6–7, http://www.fehrandpeers.com/wp-content/uploads /2015/06/Overview-Strategy.pdf.

30. "Federal Poverty Guidelines," Families USA, February 2017, http://families usa.org/product/federal-poverty-guidelines.

31. Penny Wilson, *A Playwork Primer* (New York: Alliance for Childhood, 2010).

32 32. "Activist Plans European-Style Playground for American Inner-City," *Voice of America*, November 2, 2009, https://www.voanews.com/a/a-13 -2009-09-16-voa26-68758542/410504.html.

33. "2015 Statewide Comprehensive Outdoor Recreation Plan," California Department of Parks and Recreation, accessed May 25, 2017, http://www.parks forcalifornia.org/scorp.

34. Deborah Cohen, Roland Sturm, Bing Han, and Terry Marsh, *Quantifying the Contribution of Public Parks to Physical Activity and Health: Introducing SOPARC* (Santa Monica, CA: Rand Corporation, 2014), https://www.rand .org/pubs/research_reports/RR774.html.

35. "Who We Are," Pogo Park, Richmond, CA, accessed December 3, 2017, http://pogopark.org/#.

36. "Meeting the Park Needs of All Californians: 2015 Statewide Comprehensive Outdoor Recreation Plan," California Department of Parks and Recreation, https://www.parks.ca.gov/pages/1008/files/Calif_SCORP2015_Print Res.pdf.

Chapter 6: A Safe Place to Live

1. Kelly Rayburn, "Oakland Ranked 4th Most Dangerous U.S. City, Richmond Ranked 9th," *Bay Area News Group*, November 19, 2007, http://www .mercurynews.com/2007/11/19/oakland-ranked-4th-most-dangerous-u-s -city-richmond-ranked-9th/.

2. Megan Thompson, "California Program Offers Cash to Reduce Gun Crimes," *PBS News Hour*, May 7, 2016, http://www.pbs.org/newshour/bb /controversial-california-program-offers-cash-to-reduce-gun-crimes/.

3. Mark Follman, Julia Lurie, Jaeah Lee, and James West, "The True Cost of Gun Violence in America," *Mother Jones*, April 15, 2015, http://www.mother jones.com/politics/2015/04/true-cost-of-gun-violence-in-america/.

4. Jason Motlagh, "A Radical Approach to Gun Crime: Paying People Not to Kill Each Other," *The Guardian*, June 9, 2016, https://www.theguardian .com/us-news/2016/jun/09/richmond-california-ons-gun-crime.

5. "Community Safety: A Building Block for Community Health," Advancement Project and California Endowment, February 2015, https://www .preventioninstitute.org/publications/community-safety-a-building-block -for-community-health.

6. T. G. Veenema, "Children's Exposure to Community Violence," *Journal of Nursing Scholarship* 33, no. 2 (2001): 167–73.

7. A. J. Apter, L. A. Garcia, R. C. Boyd, X. Wang, D. K. Bogen, and T. Ten Have, "Exposure to Community Violence Is Associated with Asthma Hospitalizations and Emergency Department Visits," *Journal of Allergy and Clinical Immunology* 126, no. 3 (2010): 552–57. doi:10.1016/j.jaci.2010.07.014.

8. J. C. Lumeng, D. Appugliese, H. J. Cabral, R. H. Bradley, and B. Zuckerman, "Neighborhood Safety and Overweight Status in Children," *Archives of Pediatrics and Adolescent Medicine* 160, no. 1 (2006): 25–31.

9. S. L. Johnson, B. S. Solomon, W. C. Shields, E. M. McDonald, L. B. McKenzie, and A. C. Gielen, "Neighborhood Violence and Its Association with Mothers' Health: Assessing the Relative Importance of Perceived Safety and Exposure to Violence," *Journal of Urban Health* 86, no. 4 (2009): 538–50. doi:10.1007/s11524-009-9345-8. Epub April 3, 2009.

10. Joaquin Palomino and Kimberly Veklerov, "In Richmond, High Number of Homicides Go Unsolved," *San Francisco Chronicle*, April 7, 2017, http://www.sfchronicle.com/crime/article/In-Richmond-many-murders-go-unsolved-11055724.php.

11. A. M. Wolf, A. Del Prado Lippman, C. Glesmann, and E. Castro, "Process Evaluation for the Office of Neighborhood Safety," National Council on Crime and Delinquency, Oakland, CA, 2015, 5.

12. Sam Vaughn, "Ending Violence with an Inspiring Antidote," TED MED Talk, 2015, http://www.tedmed.com/talks/show?id=527628.

13. Richard Gonzales, "To Reduce Gun Violence, Potential Offenders Offered Support and Cash," *NPR*, March 28, 2016, https://www.npr.org/2016/03/28/472138377/to-reduce-gun-violence-potential-offenders-offered-support-and-cash/.

14. Wolf et al., "Process Evaluation," 17.

15. Wolf et al., "Process Evaluation," 20.

16. Wolf et al., "Process Evaluation," 14.

17. Lexi Pandell, "ONS Returns from South Africa with New Goals," *Richmond Confidential*, September 27, 2011, http://richmondconfidential.org/2011/09/27/ons-returns-from-south-africa-with-new-goals.

18. DeVone L. Boggan, "Saving Lives: Alternative Approaches to Reducing Urban Gun Violence," Advance Peace, Richmond, CA, April 2016, http://webcache.googleusercontent.com/search?q=cache:tyv8ogDG7AYJ:www.apainc.org/wp-content/uploads/2016_AdvancePeace.Strategies_March2016_DRAFT.ppt+&cd=1&hl=en&ct=clnk&gl=us.

19. Motlagh, "A Radical Approach to Gun Crime."

20. Motlagh, "A Radical Approach to Gun Crime."

21. Anna Challet, "A Richmond Mother and Son Navigate Life after Prison, Together," *Richmond Confidential,* June 1, 2013, http://richmondpulse.org /2013/06/01/a-richmond-mother-and-son-navigate-life-after-prison -together.

22. Robert Rogers, "East Bay Profile: Veteran of Richmond's Neighborhood Wars Changes Life," *Mercury News,* May 20, 2013, http://www.mercury news.com/2013/05/20/east-bay-profile-veteran-of-richmonds-neighbor hood-wars-changes-life/.

23. Sarah Tan and Alessandra Stanley, "Richmond: Head of City's Office of Neighborhood Safety Will Be Stepping Down," *East Bay Times,* February 16, 2016, http://www.eastbaytimes.com/2016/02/16/richmond-head-of -citys-office-of-neighborhood-safety-will-be-stepping-down/.

24. Anita Chabria and Ryan Lillis, "Sacramento Hopes Program Will Persuade 50 'Shooters' to Change Their Violent Ways," *Sacramento Bee,* December 1, 2017, http://www.sacbee.com/news/local/article187438548.html/; Tom Miller, "Stockton Hopes to Curb Gun, Gang Violence through Monetary Incentives," SFGate.com, January 10, 2018, http://www.sfgate.com/news /article/Stockton-hopes-to-curb-gun-gang-violence-through-12488072 .php.

25. Sujatha Baliga, Sia Henry, and Georgia Valentine, "Restorative Community Conferencing," Impact Justice and Community Works, Oakland, CA, Summer 2017, http://impactjustice.org/restorative-justice-project/.

26. "Restorative Community Conferencing Pilot Project: Status Report May 2014 through April 2017," National Conflict Resolution Center, San Diego, CA, May 1, 2017, http://www.ncrconline.com/sites/default/files/rcc _summary_report_may17.pdf.

27. Dana Littlefield, "Program Helps Keep Minors Out of Justice System," *San Diego Union Tribune,* August 20, 2015, http://www.sandiegouniontribune .com/sdut-program-helps-keep-minors-out-justice-system-2015aug20-story .html.

28. Gordon Bazemore and Mark Umbreit, "A Comparison of Four Restorative Conferencing Models," Juvenile Justice Bulletin, Department of Justice, Washington, DC, February 2001, http://www.ncjrs.gov/pdffiles1/ojjdp /184738.pdf.

29. "Restorative Community Conferencing (RCC)," California Conference for Equality and Justice, accessed June 15, 2017, http://www.cacej.org/restorative-community-conferencing-rcc/.

30. "Conferencing," Centre for Justice and Reconciliation, Washington, DC, accessed June 15, 2017, http://restorativejustice.org/restorative-justice/about-restorative-justice/tutorial-intro-to-restorative-justice/lesson-3-programs/conferencing.

31. Community Justice Conference—Fresno Superior Court, accessed June 15, 2017, http://www.courts.ca.gov/27588.htm.

32. "Scaling Restorative Community Conferencing through a Pay for Success Model: A Feasibility Assessment Report," National Council on Crime and Delinquency and Third Sector Capital Partners, Oakland, CA, March 2015, http://www.nccdglobal.org/sites/default/files/publication_pdf/rj-pfs-feasibility-report.pdf.

33. Lee Taylor, "Salinas' Acosta Plaza Shining a Light on Crime Problem," *Monterey County Herald*, October 16, 2015, http://www.montereyherald.com/article/NF/20151015/NEWS/151019850.

34. Robert Robledo, "Acosta Plaza in Salinas Coming Out of the Shadows," *Salinas Californian*, March 9, 2015, http://www.thecalifornian.com/story/news/2015/03/06/acosta-plaza-salinas-coming-shadows/24521833/.

35. Taylor, "Salinas' Acosta Plaza."

36. Ciclovia Salinas website, accessed November 7, 2017, https://cicloviasalinas.org.

37. Roberto Robledo, "Smiles, More Smiles in Salinas," *Salinas Californian*, October 6, 2016, http://www.thecalifornian.com/story/news/2016/10/06/smiles-smiles-salinas/91710466/.

38. Ciclovia Salinas website.

39. Amy Wu and Chelcey Adami, "Salinas Public Safety Center Projected to Open 2019," *Salinas Californian*, April 19, 2017, http://www.thecalifornian.com/story/news/2017/04/19/salinas-public-safety-center-projected-open-2019/100655084.

Chapter 7: Rural Activism

1. "Building Healthy Communities: Del Norte County Health Profile," University of California, Los Angeles Center for Health Policy Research, No-

vember 2011, 1, https://www.google.com/search?q=www.BHC_Fact_Sheet_Del+Norte_County.pdf&ie=utf-8&oe=utf-8&client=firefox-b-1-ab.

2. J. Van Arsdale, L. Peeters-Graehl, K. Patterson, J. Barry, and A. Bayer, "Rural Poverty and Its Health Impacts: A Look at Poverty in the Redwood Coast Region," California Center for Rural Policy, Humboldt State University, Arcata, CA, 2008.

3. Katherine Schoenfield, "Del Norte and Adjacent Tribal Lands: Selected Findings from the Community Health and Wellness Survey, Native American Residents," California Center for Rural Policy, Humboldt State University, Arcata, CA, April 2016.

4. "County Health Rankings and Roadmaps," Robert Wood Johnson Foundation, 2011, http://www.countyhealthrankings.org/app/california/2011/rankings/del-norte/county/outcomes/overall/snapshot.

5. "Life Expectancy by County and Sex (US), 1989–2009," Institute for Health Metrics and Evaluation, University of Washington, Seattle, WA, 2012.

6. J. Van Arsdale, T. Uyeki, C. Stewart, J. Barry, A. Leigh, G. Mahony, L. Hannig, J. Oliveros, L. Peeters-Graehl, and K. Patterson, "Community Health Indicators for Del Norte County, Version 1.2," California Center for Rural Policy, Humboldt State University, Arcata, CA, May 17, 2011.

7. Kelley Atherton, "Bad News on Youthful Obesity," *Del Norte Triplicate*, November 14, 2011, http://www.triplicate.com/csp/mediapool/sites/Triplicate/News/story.csp?cid=4373854&sid=923&fid=151.

8. Kevin Hartwick, "Coastal Voices: Kidtown in CC: A Community Asset," *Del Norte Triplicate*, June 1, 2015, http://www.triplicate.com/csp/mediapool/sites/Triplicate/Opinion/story.csp?cid=4396765&sid=926&fid=151.

9. "Fast Facts: Income of Young Adults," US Department of Education, National Center for Education Statistics, 2015, https://nces.ed.gov/fastfacts/display.asp?id=77.

10. Van Arsdale et al., "Community Health Indicators."

11. Sabrina Tavernise, "Life Spans Shrink for Least-Educated Whites in the U.S," *New York Times*, September 20, 2012, http://www.nytimes.com/2012/09/21/us/life-expectancy-for-less-educated-whites-in-us-is-shrinking.html.

12. J. Van Arsdale, A. Leigh, and J. Oliveros, "Del Norte County: A Look at Educational Achievement," California Center for Rural Policy, Humboldt State University, Arcata, CA, May 9, 2011.

13. Leila Fiester, "Early Warning Confirmed: A Research Update on Third-Grade Reading," Annie E. Casey Foundation, November 2013, http://www.aecf .org/resources/early-warning-confirmed.

14. Hedy N. Chang, "Present, Engaged, and Accounted For: The Critical Importance of Addressing Chronic Absence in the Early Grades," Annie E. Casey Foundation, September 2008, http://www.aecf.org/resources/present -engaged-and-accounted-for/.

15. Jessica Van Arsdale, "Del Norte County Unified School District: School Absence 2012–2013," California Center for Rural Policy, Humboldt State University, Arcata, CA, August 2013.

16. "Literacy Initiative, Del Norte and Adjacent Tribal Lands," Building Healthy Communities Del Norte and Adjacent Tribal Lands, Crescent City, CA, accessed September 26, 2017, https://spark.adobe.com/page/gU9F Qkrsrgo82/.

17. Julia B. Isaacs, "Starting School at a Disadvantage: The School Readiness of Poor Children," Brookings Institution, March 2012, https://www.brook ings.edu/wp-content/uploads/2016/06/0319_school_disadvantage_isaacs .pdf.

18. Leila Fiester, "Early Warning! Why Reading by the End of Third Grade Matters," Annie E. Casey Foundation, 2010, http://www.aecf.org/resources /early-warning-why-reading-by-the-end-of-third-grade-matters.

19. "Students Who Don't Read Well in Third Grade Are More Likely to Drop Out or Fail to Finish High School," Annie E. Casey Foundation, April 8, 2011, http://www.aecf.org/blog/poverty-puts-struggling-readers-in-double -jeopardy-minorities-most-at-risk/.

20. Jessica Cejnar, "Literacy Programs Showing Success," *Del Norte Triplicate*, May 9, 2017, http://www.triplicate.com/news/5291372-151/literacy -programs-showing-success.

21. "Literacy Initiative: Del Norte and Adjacent Tribal Lands."

22. Heidi Graham, "School District Kicks Off with Ready? Set! 'K,'" *Del Norte Triplicate*, July 17, 2016, http://www.triplicate.com/csp/mediapool /sites/Triplicate/News/story.csp?cid=4532123&sid=923&fid=151.

23. "Literacy Initiative."

24. Van Arsdale et al., "Community Health Indicators."

25. "Walmart Locks Up Their Hard Liquor in Crescent City," *KIEM-TV*, February 1, 2017, http://kiem-tv.com/video/walmart-locks-their-hard-liquor-crescent-city.

26. Jessica Cejnar, "Alcohol, Tobacco Sales May Be Limited," *Del Norte Triplicate*, April 24, 2014, http://www.triplicate.com/csp/mediapool/sites/Triplicate/News/story.csp?cid=4392976&sid=923&fid=151.

27. Joe Mozingo, "How a Remote California Tribe Set Out to Save Its River and Stop a Suicide Epidemic," *Los Angeles Times*, May 19, 2017, http://www.latimes.com/local/california/la-me-salmon-demise-yurok-suicides-20170519-htmlstory.html.

28. "Resighini Rancheria Tribe Sociocultural/Socioeconomics Effects Analysis Technical Report," *Reclamation: Managing Water in the West* (Denver, CO: US Department of the Interior, July 2012), 35, https://klamathrestoration.gov/sites/klamathrestoration.gov/files/2013%20Updates/Econ%20Studies%20/04.Resighini_28JUL12.pdf.

29. Mozingo, "How a Remote California Tribe Set Out to Save Its River."

30. Alexander Nazaryan, "California Slaughter: The State-Sanctioned Genocide of Native Americans," *Newsweek*, August 17, 2016, http://www.newsweek.com/2016/08/26/california-native-americans-genocide-490824.html.

31. "Resighini Rancheria Tribe Sociocultural/Socioeconomics Effects," 62.

32. Will Houston, "Council Recommends Full Closure of Klamath River Salmon Fishing," *Eureka Times-Standard*, April 11, 2017, http://www.times-standard.com/article/NJ/20170411/NEWS/170419968.

33. "Donor Yearbook 2013/2014," Humboldt Area Foundation, Bayside, CA, 2013–2014, 98, http://www.hafoundation.org/Portals/0/Uploads/Documents/Financials/Yearbook/HAF-2013-2014-Yearbook.pdf.

Chapter 8: Good Eats

1. Dana Griffin, "Oak Park Community Marches for Peace after Recent Homicides," KCRA 3, June 30, 2017, http://www.kcra.com/article/oak-park-community-marches-for-peace-after-recent-homicides/10248902.

2. Allison Joy, "Local Food Desert to Get Fresh Produce," *Sacramento Press*, May 23, 2013, https://sacramentopress.com/2013/05/23/local-food-desert -to-get-fresh-produce/.

3. Ecology Center, "10 Ways Urban Farms Benefit the Community," March 1, 2016, https://www.theecologycenter.org/resources/10-ways-urban-farms -benefit-the-community/.

4. "The Potential for Urban Agriculture in New York City," Urban Design Lab, Columbia University, New York, June 2014, http://urbandesignlab .columbia.edu/projects/food-and-the-urban-environment/the-potential -for-urban-agriculture-in-new-york-city/.

5. Lydia Oberholtzer, Carolyn Dimitri, and Andy Pressman, "Urban Agri- culture in the United States: Baseline Findings of a Nationwide Survey," Na- tional Center for Appropriate Technology, November 2016, https://attra .ncat.org/urban_ag.html.

6. Reis Thebault, "Urban Tilth Launches New Farm in North Richmond," *Richmond Confidential*, October 19, 2016, http://richmondconfidential .org/2016/10/19/urban-tilth-launches-new-farm-in-north-richmond/.

7. "Philadelphia's Healthy Corner Store Initiative, 2010–2012," Food Trust, 2012, 3, http://thefoodtrust.org/uploads/media_items/hcsi-y2report-final .original.pdf.

8. Angela Glore, "Gleaning Wisdom: Waste Not, Want Not," *Del Norte Triplicate*, July 15, 2014, http://www.triplicate.com/csp/mediapool/sites /Triplicate/News/story.csp?cid=4393726&sid=923&fid=151.

9. Jessica Cejnar, "Schools' Summer Food Program Honored," *Del Norte Triplicate*, December 10, 2016, http://www.triplicate.com/news/5291372 -151/literacy-programs-showing-success.

10. Angelo Eliades, "Why Food Forests?," Permaculture Research Institute, New South Wales, Australia, October 21, 2011, https://permaculturenews .org/2011/10/21/why-food-forests/.

11. Roxanne P. Shepelavy, "Ideas We Should Steal: Food Forests," *Philadelphia Citizen*, June 5, 2017, http://thephiladelphiacitizen.org/ideas-we-should -steal-urban-food-forest/.

12. Annie Park, Nancy Watson, and Lark Galloway-Gilliam, "South Los An- geles Health Equity Scorecard," Community Health Councils, Los Angeles, December 2008, 54, http://dhss.delaware.gov/dph/mh/files/southlascore card.pdf.

13. "A Case Study Examining the Development and Implementation of FreshWorks," Sarah Samuels Center for Public Health Research and Evaluation and InSight at Pacific Community Ventures, Oakland, CA, May 2016, https://www.pacificcommunityventures.org/2016/06/15/examining-the-development-and-implementation-of-california-freshworks/.

14. "About FreshWorks," California FreshWorks Fund, 2016, http://cafresh works.com/about/.

15. Subcommittee on Arsenic in Drinking Water, *Arsenic in Drinking Water* (Washington, DC: National Academy Press, 1999), https://www.nap.edu/read/6444/chapter/1.

16. "Agua4All–South Kern County," Rural Community Assistance Corporation, West Sacramento, CA, December 4, 2016, http://www.rcac.org/success-stories/agua4all-south-kern-county/.

17. "California Budget Includes Crucial Funds for Water in Schools," Rural Community Assistance Corporation, West Sacramento, CA, June 28, 2016, http://www.rcac.org/press-release/ca-budget-includes-crucial-funds-for-water-in-schools/.

18. Jean Merl, "Coachella Water District Agrees to Change Elections System," *Los Angeles Times*, November 12, 2013, http://articles.latimes.com/2013/nov/12/local/la-me-pc-coachella-elections-20131112.

19. Ian James, "Estrada: New CVWD Election System a 'Better Way,'" *Desert Sun*, November 11, 2014, http://www.desertsun.com/story/news/environment/2014/11/11/coachella-valley-water-district-election/18898387/.

20. Anna Rumer, "CVWD Pushes for Safe Water in Disadvantaged Communities," *Desert Sun*, February 17, 2017, http://www.desertsun.com/story/news/environment/2017/02/17/cvwd-pushes-safe-water-disadvantaged-communities/97904606/.

21. Jacques Leslie, "California's Water Crisis Is Dangerous, Just Like Flint's. Will the State Clean It Up Once and for All?," *Los Angeles Times*, May 4, 2017, http://www.latimes.com/opinion/op-ed/la-oe-leslie-californias-contaminated-water-20170504-story.html.

22. Jacey Fortin, "America's Tap Water: Too Much Contamination, Not Enough Reporting, Study Finds," *New York Times*, May 4, 2017, https://www.nytimes.com/2017/05/04/us/tapwater-drinking-water-study.html.

Chapter 9: Healing Trauma

1. Jane Stevens, "At Cherokee Point Elementary, Kids Don't Conform to School; School Conforms to Kids," *ACES Too High News*, July 22, 2013, https://acestoohigh.com/2013/07/22/at-cherokee-point-elementary-kids -dont-conform-to-school-school-conforms-to-kids/.

2. "What Is a Trauma-Informed School?," Treatment and Services Adaptation Center, accessed July 21, 2017, https://traumaawareschools.org/traumaIn Schools.

3. David Finkelhor, Heather Turner, Anne Shattuck, Sherry Hamby, and Kristen Kracke, "Children's Exposure to Violence, Crime, and Abuse: An Update," *National Survey of Children's Exposure to Violence* (Laurel, MD: US Department of Justice, Office of Justice Programs, September 2015), 5, www.ojjdp.gov/pubs/248547.pdf.

4. "Trauma-Informed Schools," Robert Wood Johnson Foundation County Health Rankings and Roadmaps, last updated October 19, 2016, http://www.countyhealthrankings.org/policies/trauma-informed-schools.

5. "Child Abuse and Neglect: Consequences," Centers for Disease Control and Prevention, last updated April 5, 2016, https://www.cdc.gov/violence prevention/childmaltreatment/consequences.html.

6. Jane Stevens, "7 Ways Childhood Adversity Changes a Child's Brain," *ACES Too High News*, September 8, 2016, https://acestoohigh.com/2016 /09/08/7-ways-childhood-adversity-changes-a-childs-brain.

7. Lindsey Tanner, "How Severe, Ongoing Stress Can Affect a Child's Brain," *AP News*, July 12, 2017, https://apnews.com/e3f679e07a0a4303ba092bd 92c407daf.

8. Jane Ellen Stevens, "Resilience Practices Overcome Students' ACEs in Trauma-Informed High School, Say the Data," *ACES Too High News*, May 31, 2015, https://acestoohigh.com/2015/05/31/resilience-practices -overcome-students-aces-in-trauma-informed-high-school-say-the-data.

9. "Trauma-Informed Schools."

10. Michael Alison Chandler, "Trauma Is a Hidden Cause of Academic Struggles for Many in D.C., Report Finds," *Washington Post*, June 24, 2015, https://www.washingtonpost.com/local/education/trauma-is-hidden-cause-of -academic-struggles-for-many-in-dc-report-finds/2015/06/24/c00a5356 -19b3-11e5-ab92-c75ae6ab94b5_story.html.

11. "Trauma-Informed Practices (TIP)," San Diego Unified School District website, accessed November 7, 2017, https://www.sandi.net/staff/secondary-schools-office/trauma-informed-practices-tip.

12. Nadra Nittle, "San Diego Unified Transitions toward a Trauma-Informed School District," *Chronicle of Social Change*, October 1, 2015, https://chronicleofsocialchange.org/featured/san-diego-school-drives-progress-toward-trauma-informed-school-district+&cd=1&hl=en&ct=clnk&gl=us.

13. "How Big of a Difference Is $31 Billion Making on Education?," *KXTV*, August 8, 2017, http://www.abc10.com/news/local/are-31-billion-making-a-difference-in-education/462978051.

14. John Fensterwald, "How Does California Rank in Per-Pupil Spending? It All Depends," *EdSource*, February 28, 2017, https://edsource.org/2017/how-does-california-rank-in-per-pupil-spending-it-all-depends/577405.

15. Jane Meredith Adams, "Suspensions and Expulsions Decline as Districts Adopt Alternatives, State Says," *EdSource*, January 13, 2016, https://edsource.org/2016/suspensions-and-expulsions-decline-as-districts-adopt-alternatives-state-says/93297.

16. "El Circulo, Circulo de Hombres. Men's Retreats," National Compadres Network, accessed November 7, 2017, http://www.nationalcompadresnetwork.org/our-history/.

17. Chelcey Adami, "DA Clears Salinas Police in Fourth 2014 Shooting Death," *Californian*, September 4, 2015, http://www.thecalifornian.com/story/news/crime/2015/09/04/da-clears-salinas-police-fourth-shooting-death/71735452/.

18. Jamilah Bradshaw Dieng, Jesús Valenzuela, and Tenoch Ortiz, "Building the We: Healing-Informed Governing for Racial Equity in Salinas," Race Forward, Oakland, CA, 2016, https://www.raceforward.org/research/reports/building-we-healing-informed-governing-racial-equity-salinas.

19. Ray Corpuz, "Governing for Racial Equity and Healing Week Reflections" (blog), December 18, 2014, http://www.calendow.org/governing-racial-equity-healing-week-reflections/.

Chapter 10: Red and Blue Visions of Health

1. "'Resist' Billboards Appear Around Sacramento," *CBS Sacramento*, May 29, 2017, http://sacramento.cbslocal.com/2017/05/29/resist-billboards-appear-around-sacramento.

2. Drew Westen, *The Political Brain: The Role of Emotion in Deciding the Fate of the Nation* (New York: Public Affairs, 2008).

3. "A New Way to Talk about Social Determinants of Health," webinar, Robert Wood Johnson Foundation, January 1, 2010, http://www.rwjf.org/en/search-results.html?u=&k=A+new+way+to+talk+about+social+determinants+of+health.

4. "A New Way to Talk about the Social Determinants of Health," webinar, Robert Wood Johnson Foundation and Grantmakers in Health, July 29, 2010, https://www.youtube.com/watch?v=xtQBRtTxpH0&feature=youtube.

5. "The Ottawa Charter for Health Promotion," World Health Organization, November 21, 1986, http://www.who.int/healthpromotion/conferences/previous/ottawa/en/index1.html.

6. Ilona Kickbusch, "Tribute to Aaron Antonovsky—What Creates Health?," Health Promotion International, March 1, 1996, https://academic.oup.com/heapro/article-pdf/11/1/5/1565297/11-1-5.pdf.

7. "Overview," California Endowment, accessed December 3, 2017, http://healthyrichmond.net/about/about-the-california-endowment/.

8. Irene H. Yen, "Historical Perspective: S. Leonard Syme's Influence on the Development of Social Epidemiology and Where We Go from There," *Epidemiologic Perspectives and Innovations*, May 25, 2005, https://www.ncbi.nlm.nih.gov/pmc/articles/PMC1175097/.

9. Daniel Callahan, *Promoting Healthy Behavior: How Much Freedom? Whose Responsibility?* (Washington, DC: Georgetown University Press, 2000).

Epilogue

1. "An Epidemic of White Death: A Canary in the Coal Mine?," California Endowment press release, January 19, 2017, http://www.calendow.org/press-release/epidemic-white-death-canary-coal-mine/.

2. Sarah Reyes, "An Epidemic of White Death: A Canary in the Coal Mine? An Alarming National Trend Wreaks Havoc in California's Central Valley," California Endowment press release, January 18, 2017, https://www.prnewswire.com/news-releases/an-epidemic-of-white-death-a-canary-in-the-coal-mine-300393045.html.

3. Anne Case and Angus Deaton, "Rising Morbidity and Mortality in Midlife among White Non-Hispanic Americans in the 21st Century," *Proceedings*

of the National Academy of Sciences USA 112, no. 49 (December 8, 2015): 15078–83. doi:10.1073/pnas.1518393112. Epub November 2, 2015.

4. Gina Kolata, "Death Rates Rising for Middle-Aged White Americans, Study Finds," *New York Times*, November 2, 2015, https://www.nytimes.com/2015/11/03/health/death-rates-rising-for-middle-aged-white-americans-study-finds.html.

Index

Island Press | Board of Directors

Pamela B. Murphy
(Chair)

Terry Gamble Boyer
(Vice-Chair)
Author

Deborah Wiley
(Secretary)
Chair
Wiley Foundation, Inc.

Tony Everett
(Treasurer)

Decker Anstrom
Board of Directors
Discovery Communications

Melissa Shackleton Dann
Managing Director
Endurance Consulting

Katie Dolan
Environmental Writer

Margot Ernst

Alison Greenberg
Executive Director
Georgetown Heritage

David Miller
President
Island Press

Georgia Nassikas
Artist

Alison Sant
Cofounder and Partner
Studio for Urban Projects

Ron Sims
Former Deputy Secretary
US Department of Housing
and Urban Development

Sandra E. Taylor
Chief Executive Officer
Sustainable Business
International LLC